Oliver Optic

Young America in England and Wales

A Story of Travel and Adventure

Oliver Optic

Young America in England and Wales
A Story of Travel and Adventure

ISBN/EAN: 9783744685795

Printed in Europe, USA, Canada, Australia, Japan

Cover: Foto ©Andreas Hilbeck / pixelio.de

More available books at **www.hansebooks.com**

McLeish in the Josephine. — Page 24.

RED CROSS;

OR,

YOUNG AMERICA IN ENGLAND AND WALES.

A Story of Travel and Adventure.

BY

OLIVER OPTIC.

BOSTON:
LEE AND SHEPARD.
1869.

Entered according to Act of Congress, in the year 1867, by

WILLIAM T. ADAMS,

In the Clerk's Office of the District Court of the District of Massachusetts.

ELECTROTYPED AT THE
Boston Stereotype Foundry,
No. 19 Spring Lane.

To My Young Friend

WILLIAM INGALLS MONROE,

This Volume

IS

AFFECTIONATELY DEDICATED.

YOUNG AMERICA ABROAD.

BY OLIVER OPTIC.

A Library of Travel and Adventure in Foreign Lands. First and Second Series; six volumes in each Series. 16mo. Illustrated.

First Series.

I. *OUTWARD BOUND;* or, Young America Afloat.
II. *SHAMROCK AND THISTLE;* or, Young America in Ireland and Scotland.
III. *RED CROSS;* or, Young America in England and Wales.
IV. *DIKES AND DITCHES;* or, Young America in Holland and Belgium.
V. *PALACE AND COTTAGE;* or, Young America in France and Switzerland.
VI. *DOWN THE RHINE;* or, Young America in Germany.

Second Series.

I. *UP THE BALTIC;* or, Young America in Denmark and Sweden.
II. *NORTHERN LANDS;* or, Young America in Prussia and Russia.
III. *VINE AND OLIVE;* or, Young America in Spain and Portugal.
IV. *SUNNY SHORES;* or, Young America in Italy and Austria.
V. *CROSS AND CRESCENT;* or, Young America in Greece and Turkey.
VI. *ISLES OF THE SEA;* or, Young America Homeward Bound.

PREFACE.

RED CROSS, the third of the "YOUNG AMERICA ABROAD" series, contains the history of the Academy Ship and her consort, while in the waters of England and Wales. The students visit London, Liverpool, Birmingham, Manchester, Bristol, Holyhead, Whitehaven, Milford Haven, Cardiff, Cowes, Hull, York, "Snowdonia," the Lake District, and other localities of interest. The descriptive portions of the work are derived from personal observation, and from the most reliable sources of information. England, so far as a knowledge of the country can be obtained from the printed page, is so familiar to the American juvenile reader, that minute descriptions have been avoided, because the whole volume would not afford space enough for the traveller to do justice even to his own ideas and impressions.

Though the boys and girls of our country are supposed to be familiar with the geography and history of Great Britain, these topics are very briefly touched upon, rather to refresh the memory than with the expectation of instructing the reader; and they occupy less space in this than in the preceding volume of the series.

If the book had been called "The Young Commander, or The Cruise of 'A Yankee Ship and a Yankee Crew,' the officers, boys, and the seamen too," perhaps it would have conveyed a better idea of the volume. The story of Paul Kendall, in command of the Josephine, of his trials and troubles as captain, and his experience with rebellious seamen, is related, yet the events which occurred on board of the Young America are not neglected. Though several evildoers appear in the narrative, the author is confident that their experience will prove far less attractive to the youthful reader than that of the honest, upright, and truthful students, even when they are reviled and laughed at by "our fellows."

While the author trusts that the story contained in RED CROSS will be received with the same favor as former books, which he has so often gratefully acknowledged, he is not without the hope that the young reader will be improved in mind and heart by its perusal.

HARRISON SQUARE, MASS.
November 29, 1867.

CONTENTS.

CHAPTER		PAGE
I.	On Board the Josephine.	11
II.	McLeish in the Brig.	27
III.	The Anchor Watch.	43
IV.	"All Hands, attend Lecture, ahoy!"	59
V.	A Glance at Liverpool.	76
VI.	Blue Lights on the Mersey.	93
VII.	Off the Calf of Man.	108
VIII.	Captain Kendall's Guests.	124
IX.	Grace Arbuckle.	140
X.	The Excursion to Chester.	156
XI.	The New Hand.	173
XII.	The Conspirators in the Brig.	189
XIII.	Captain Kendall's State-room.	206
XIV.	The Knights of the Red Cross.	225
XV.	A Tramp though Snowdonia.	243

CHAPTER		PAGE
XVI.	THE BANK OF ENGLAND NOTES.	259
XVII.	BRISTOL TO THE ISLE OF WIGHT.	275
XVIII.	AROUND THE ISLE OF WIGHT.	292
XIX.	UP THE THAMES.	308
XX.	LONDON. — FAREWELL TO ENGLAND.	324

RED CROSS.

(9)

RED CROSS;

OR,

YOUNG AMERICA IN ENGLAND AND WALES.

CHAPTER I.

ON BOARD THE JOSEPHINE.

"ALL the crew of the Josephine, on deck, ahoy!" shouted the boatswain of the Young America, on the first day of July, which was the beginning of a new term, while the Academy Ship lay in the Mersey, off Liverpool.

"The officers of the Josephine will prepare to go on board their ship," added Flag-officer Gordon.

The officers and crew of the consort brought up their private property, and stood on deck in readiness to take possession of their new floating home. They were in a state of high excitement, for the novelty of a new vessel filled their minds with brilliant expectations. They hardly thought now of the unvisited shores on both sides of the broad river, so overpowering was the interest created by their appointment to the trim little craft which rested like a swan on the waves, a short distance from the ship.

It was three months since the Young America had sailed from Brockway, and the students had, in a very hasty manner, "done" Ireland and Scotland. They had seen a great deal, and doubtless learned something of foreign sights and sounds. In a company of eighty-eight students, varying in age from fourteen to eighteen, there was an abundance of life and spirit, which, with the diversity of taste, temperament, and character among them, had laid the foundation for a variety of incident and adventure. Besides the minor events of interest which occurred every day, three of the students had run away from the ship; and this was thus far the most important item in the history of the cruise. But the deserters had returned, one of them voluntarily, and the other two by the persuasive efforts of a couple of detectives. At the commencement of the term, these latter, Wilton and Monroe, were confined in the brig, obdurate and unrepentant, while Pelham, whose pride, rather than his conscience, had prompted him to purge himself of the disgrace of being a runaway, had been pardoned in consideration of his noble conduct in saving the life of a child, and by extra effort had won the position of second master of the ship's consort. If he had not absented himself from his duties, he would probably have been a first or a second lieutenant of one of the vessels. He could be hardly said to have reformed, since it was disgrace, rather than error, that troubled him. But he meant to do well, and with a higher principle he would have been sure of success. He was a type of many a man in the community, who is kept in the path of rectitude because it is respectable, and because crime is disreputable, rather than a sin against God and man.

The ship's company were all sons of wealthy men, or of those who had the means to pay for the expensive course of tuition in the ship. Many of them were wild boys, brought up in ease and luxury, and unaccustomed to wholesome restraint before they joined the academy. But the discipline of the ship was strict, and it was surprising that there had been so little open mutiny and insubordination, though there were always many daring spirits ready to break through the routine of the ship, and engage in any wild adventure which the moment suggested. Mr. Lowington, the principal, had been careful to find sufficient scope, in a proper way, for the carrying off of their surplus enthusiasm. Reefing topsails in a gale of wind was a good outlet for the daring spirit. As the ship went from port to port, and new scenes were visited, the variety presented to the students had a tendency to repress mischievous inclinations, and render them contented with their lot, submissive to the regulations, and willing to perform the mental and physical labor assigned to them.

There were some exceptions to the general rule; some who were too utterly restless to be satisfied with anything; some who were continually plotting mischief, and watching for a chance to overstep the line of duty; some who could not be contented unless they were doing wrong. The ship had its communities of good and of bad boys; as well as the larger mass who were doubtful and indifferent, and could be led either way, as circumstances influenced them. The mutiny which had been projected on the voyage across the Atlantic would doubtless have numbered a majority in its ranks if the leaders had been skilful, and the affair better managed. The runaways, if they had dared to invite others to join them, could probably have taken half the crew with them, had the circumstances been favorable. Yet there were many young men of high principle and noble lives among them — more perhaps than could have been expected in a company of boys gathered as the students of the Young America had been.

While the ship was in the Clyde, Mr. Lowington had received as a pupil, at the urgent solicitation of his father, a Scotch boy, who had been several times expelled from school for misconduct. Arthur McLeish was a "hard boy" in the strongest sense of the term. He had been disciplined for insubordination and disobedience, and had spent a long time in the brig, from which he had been released on his promise to do his duty faithfully. But the evil spirit had not been driven out of him, and there was a mountain of trouble before him for the officers and himself.

The press of applications for admission to the Academy Ship before her departure for the United States had induced Mr. Lowington to procure another vessel; and the Josephine had been built to his order. She had just arrived at Liverpool, and the new students were expected in the next steamer. The vessel, on board the ship, was oftener called the "consort" than by any other name. She was to accommodate nine officers and twenty-four seamen at present, though she had berths for a crew of thirty-six, besides two instructors, a boatswain, carpenter, cook, and three stewards. The officers had been appointed by the merit roll, and one seaman in every three, as the names came on the list, was detailed for service in the Josephine. The crew were taken in this manner because there was a general desire among the students to be attached to the consort, and the principal, in this matter as in all others, was strictly impartial. The crew were not selected; they went by lot, as their names appeared on the list, and no one could complain.

This method sent many notoriously bad boys into the Josephine, including Sanborn, Grossbeck, Templeton, and McLeish, who had particularly distinguished themselves by their misconduct. Mr. Lowington was strongly tempted to interfere with the lot in the case of the Scotch boy, but as his offence had been against the principal personally, he was too magnanimous to do so. He was willing to let him take his chance, as the understanding was, that any student who did not behave well might be returned to the ship, and another sent to the consort in his place. Those of "our fellows," as certain evil-disposed boys had chosen to call themselves, who were detailed for duty in the Josephine, were glad to escape from the immediate supervision of the principal; for the Josephine was to be in actual command of her officers, the instructors on board having no authority outside of the academic department. The boatswain and the carpenter were the only adult seamen on board.

The two instructors who were to sail in the consort

were to arrive by steamer in charge of the new scholars. They were men of extensive and varied learning. One of them — Professor Hamblin — was quite celebrated as a scholar, and had spent his life as a professor in a college; but his health failing him, he had taken this position in order to obtain the benefit of sea air and foreign travel, without sacrificing the income he needed for his family. He was fifty years old, tall, and spare, with a thin face, and a head partially covered with reddish-gray hair. He was exceedingly formal and precise in everything he said and did. His associate, Professor Stoute, was short, fat, and forty, noted as a teacher, rather than a great scholar.

With this statement of the condition of affairs on board the ship, the reader is prepared to follow the students in their progress on ship and shore.

The officers and crew of the Josephine stood upon the deck of the Young America, waiting for the order to embark in the boats. Shoulder-straps and gold bands had been readjusted, so that all the officers of both vessels now appeared in their appropriate uniforms. Flag-officer Gordon wore six gold bands on his arms, and his shoulder-straps contained three anchors, which was one more than designated the two captains.

The first and second cutters conveyed the crew, and the captain's gig the officers, with Mr. Lowington and Dr. Winstock. A short pull brought them alongside the Josephine, but only those attached to her were permitted to go on board; whereat the crews of the gig and cutters grumbled like old sailors, for they were curious to see the new vessel.

"The officers and crew of the Josephine are not ready to receive company yet," Mr. Lowington replied to the requests for permission to go on board. "When they have put their ship in order, you shall have an opportunity to visit her."

"Isn't she a beauty?" exclaimed Captain Paul Kendall, as he stepped upon the deck of his craft.

"Magnificent!" replied George Terrill, his first lieutenant. "She is as nice as a new pin!"

"I feel just as though I should go up," said Paul, turning to his friend the doctor, and speaking in a confidential tone.

"Don't do it, captain," laughed Dr. Winstock. "Remember that you are the captain of the ship, and you don't go aloft."

"I shall not see much of you now, doctor."

"Not so much as before; but I am surgeon-general of the fleet, and it will be my duty to look after the sanitary condition of both vessels. I shall visit you often."

"I hope you will," replied Paul, as he glanced over the deck of the Josephine.

The plan of her construction was similar to that of the Young America, except that she had a camboose abaft the foremast, containing the cook's galley. The bulwarks were not more than three feet high, and the students could see over them, which was not the case in the ship. Except the skylights, the camboose, and the companion-ways, there was nothing to obstruct the deck. There were four sets of quarter davits at which hung two six-oar and two four-oar life-boats. Like the ship, her spars were light and adapted to the use for which she was intended.

Mr. Lowington sent the cutters to convey Captain Bean and the sailors who had come over in the Josephine to the shore. The boatswain and carpenter, cook and stewards, remained, and no one was now on board except the principal and the doctor, that was not attached to the consort.

"Now, young gentlemen, I will show you the vessel, and assign your berths," said Mr. Lowington to the officers. "The crew will remain on deck. Boatswain, close the fore hatch."

The principal descended the companion-way to the cabin of the schooner. The first apartment reached was large and richly furnished. There were no state-rooms on the sides, as in the Young America, and the berths were draped in front with heavy hangings or curtains. By this arrangement the space was economized, so as to afford a much larger cabin, though its occupants could not enjoy the luxury of private rooms. This cabin contained twelve berths, eight of which Mr. Lowington proceeded to assign to the lieutenants and masters, leaving four unoccupied.

"This is the captain's state-room," said the principal, opening a door in the forward part of the cabin, on the starboard side.

Paul entered this room, which contained but one berth, and all the appliances for utility and comfort found in the corresponding apartment in the ship. On the port side there was a similar room with two berths for the professors. Between them was a passage-way leading to the steerage, and two pantries, one for the cabin and the other for the steerage. In the Josephine officers and professors were to mess together. Passing into the steerage, they found an apartment similar to the main cabin. It was seven feet high, with three tiers of berths on each side, — thirty-six in all. It was in about the same style as the steerage of the ship.

Forward of this was the forecastle, divided fore and aft into two rooms, one for the boatswain, carpenter, and head steward, the other for the cook and under stewards. Below the berth-deck was the hold, about five feet deep, which contained the water-tanks, store-rooms, and cable tiers.

After the principal had shown the officers through the vessel, he conducted them back to the cabin.

"Captain Kendall," said he, "I shall now take my leave of you. The Josephine is in your charge, and from what I know of you, I am confident you will discharge your difficult duty acceptably to me and creditably to yourself."

"But, Mr. Lowington, you have given me no orders," replied Paul.

"Put your ship in order, give your officers and crew their stations, and make such regulations as you think proper. You and your officers will go on deck with me, and after I have spoken a word to your crew, I will leave you."

Captain Kendall was rather surprised to find himself so much his own master; but he followed the principal on deck. A quarter-master was ordered to run the ensign up to the peak, and the ship was declared to be in commission. Mr. Lowington spoke to the crew, putting them on their good behavior, and urging them to be prompt, obedient, and studious.

He and Dr. Winstock then went over the side into their boats, and returned to the ship.

Paul looked at his officers who stood around him on the quarter-deck, and more than ever before in his life he realized what it was to have a heavy responsibility resting upon him. He had expected the assistance of the principal and Mr. Fluxion — both of them familiar with all the details of the naval service — in establishing the discipline of the ship, in making out the station bills, and in arranging the watches and quarter watches. No such help was to be given; and as the young commander glanced at his crew, who were impatiently waiting for orders, he saw among them some of the most turbulent spirits of the ship, some whom he recognized as "our fellows," and especially he noticed the villanous face of Arthur McLeish.

Captain Kendall was equal to the position in which he found himself placed. If he had not been, he would not have been there. It was not possible for any young man in the institution to reach a high position without being a good seaman as well as a good scholar. More than this, he would not have been left alone to organize his crew, if he had not been deemed entirely competent by the principal.

"We have work to do," said he with energy, after he had glanced about him for a moment. "Mr. Terrill."

The first lieutenant stepped forward and touched his cap.

"You will pipe the crew below, and have them draw lots for berths. Mr. Robinson and Mr. Pelham will assist you," added the captain, as he walked aft.

In the matter of orders, he was disposed to do as he would be done by; for nothing is more annoying to a sensible inferior, fit for his position, than to be told how to do a thing, or to have his superior stand suspiciously near to observe its execution. Paul felt that he must have confidence in his officers in order to keep them worthy of confidence. He descended the companion-way, and took a further survey of the cabin. He might have been excused if he had been a little airy, for his position was vastly more responsible than that of the captain of the Young America, though he commanded a smaller force.

While he was in the cabin Pelham came down to prepare the papers for the lot. Presently the pipe of the boatswain was heard on deck, which assured Paul that Terrill was executing his order. He determined to keep out of the way till the crew had been berthed, and he went into his cabin, closing the door behind him. He was amazed and bewildered by his grand position. A boy of sixteen in command of a topsail schooner of one hundred and sixty tons, with thirty-three officers and seamen under him, to say nothing of half a dozen men! The two anchors on his shoulder-straps had a real meaning in his case.

But in spite of the glory of his rank and the greatness of his power, there was much in the circumstances that surrounded him to make him tremble. What if that brutal and turbulent McLeish should take it into his head to be obstinate and disobedient! Paul hoped he would not do anything of the kind; but if he did, he was determined to maintain the discipline of the ship. What if a dozen or more of the uneasy fellows in his crew should combine to resist their officers! While the young captain dreaded such an event, he was prepared to do what he fully believed to be his duty. He had enough to think of, and needed all the strength of character he possessed to sustain him in his difficult task.

When the boatswain piped the crew below, they found the third lieutenant stationed at the hatch to see that they went down in order; but the students were too much interested in the vessel to think of mischief thus early in their experience on board. They went below quietly, and Terrill stated the business of the hour, and explained how it was to be done.

"Mr. Terrill," said McLeish, touching his cap as he stepped up to the first lieutenant, "Rossfeldt is a particular friend of mine, and I would like a berth next to him, if you please."

Certainly the Scotch lad's manners had been marvellously improved since he came on board, for he spoke politely and observed all the required forms.

"It is the captain's order that the crew be berthed by lot, and of course no exceptions can be made," replied Terrill, mildly. "You will all draw a number, and you will all choose your berths in the order of the numbers drawn."

McLeish scowled a little, but he made no reply. Pelham presently appeared with the numbers on slips of paper. The first lieutenant observed some whispering among the crew, and he knew that it was "second nature" with some of them to endeavor to defeat the impartiality of the lot.

"Mr. Pelham, you will be seated at one of the

mess-tables, if you please, and the crew will pass in single file before you," said Terrill.

Pelham seated himself as directed, and Wheeler, the boatswain, was the first one to draw a number.

"Mr. Robinson, will you take a seat opposite Mr. Pelham, and write the name of each one on the paper he draws?" added Terrill.

"Confound him!" exclaimed McLeish, in a whisper; for he had already agreed with half a dozen of "our fellows" to exchange numbers with them, if his own did not come next to Rossfeldt's.

The third lieutenant wrote Wheeler's name against the number he had drawn, which rendered it impossible for the students to exchange the slips they drew, and certain little schemes were thus defeated. When each student had drawn a slip, No. 1 was called to the table, and when he had selected his berth, his name was entered on the ship's book, and the number of his berth was also his ship's number. Rossfeldt and McLeish were separated, in spite of their united efforts to get together.

"I'm no satisfied with this lot." said McLeish to the first lieutenant, when the berths were all assigned.

"It can't be helped if you are not," replied Terrill.

"What's the hairm of my being next to Rossfeldt?" demanded the new scholar.

"No harm that I am aware of; but you didn't happen to draw a berth next to him," answered the first lieutenant, moving towards the cabin.

"I'll no stand it!"

"Shut up!" interposed Rossfeldt, in a whisper.

"I'll not shut up. I'm not to be put down by these bits of nobs," said McLeish, angrily.

"You have said enough, and I shall report you to the captain," added Terrill.

"Will you, indeed?— will you?" continued the reprobate, placing himself between Terrill and the passage-way which led to the cabin. "I'll show you what a MacGregor is made of, and ye'll find ye canna insult him."

McLeish doubled up his fists, and it was evident that he intended to "pitch into" the first lieutenant. Terrill, though sixteen years of age, was quite slender in his frame; but his eye flashed when he saw the rebel in the attitude of defiance before him. The rest of the crew, even those who were the most inclined to turbulence, utterly disapproved of the stupid demonstration of McLeish, and, to avoid any suspicion of supporting him, remained near the berths they had just selected. Robinson and Pelham kept close to the first lieutenant, ready to assist him, physically or morally, as the occasion might require.

"Get out of my way!" said Terrill, sharply.

"I'll no get out of your way."

Quicker than a flash, Terrill sprang upon him, without any preliminary demonstration, and gave him a blow in the face which felled him to the deck, where he struck with a hard crack on the back of the head. McLeish, boiling over with passion, regained his feet, and rushed upon the first lieutenant with a fury which threatened to annihilate him. But Terrill was cool, and though he was hit two or three times, he succeeded in planting another heavy blow on the mouth of the rebel, which knocked in one of his front teeth, and threw him back against the bulkhead. The lieutenant sprang upon him, and, grasping him by the throat, bore him down, and put his knee upon his breast, so that he could not move.

"Come over here and halp me, ye cowards!" shouted the prostrate rebel, struggling to free himself from the grasp of his conqueror.

As this affray occurred near the captain's stateroom, his vision of glory was disturbed by the noise of the scuffle, and he hastened to the steerage to learn the cause of the disturbance. He found McLeish lying on the deck, held down by Terrill; and it was evident that the authority of the ship had been fully vindicated by her executive officer. Terrill choked the rebel till his breath came hard, and then he begged to be "let up." He was permitted to rise.

"If you speak another impudent word, I'll knock you down again," said Terrill, panting with the violence of his exertion.

McLeish, wiping the blood from his mouth, sneaked off to his berth.

"This way, McLeish," said the captain. "You have made a bad beginning, and your stay on board of the Josephine will be short," he added, as the rebel approached him.

"He didn't fight fair," replied McLeish, who seemed to be more astonished at his own defeat than at anything else, and claimed "a foul," as bullies usually do when overcome.

"Fight fair!" exclaimed Paul, in disgust. "You will hold yourself in readiness to return to the ship.

Mr. Terrill, was any other seaman concerned in this demonstration?"

"No other took any part in it," replied the first lieutenant. "McLeish was dissatisfied with his berth, and when I declined to change his place, he got mad, and when I threatened to report him to you, would not let me pass into the cabin. I knocked him down then."

"You did quite right," added the captain, decidedly, as he walked into the cabin, followed by the officers.

CHAPTER II.

MCLEISH IN THE BRIG.

THE officers of the Josephine were not a little annoyed by the event which had occurred in the steerage. They looked grave and thoughtful, fearing, perhaps, that this case of sharp discipline would produce an unfavorable impression upon the mind of the principal, and abridge the experiment of self-government which was in process of trial on board the schooner. Though a consultation had not been formally called for, all seemed to feel the need of comparing views and opinions.

The captain seated himself at the table, and the others followed his example. They all looked very sober, and even troubled. All but two of them had been cabin officers in the Young America, and nine better fellows could not have been selected from the students. The officers were as follows: —

PAUL KENDALL, *Captain.*

George W. Terrill,	*First Lieutenant.*
Henry Martyn,	*Second* "
Mark Robinson,	*Third* "
John Humphreys,	*Fourth* "

Andrew Groom,	*First Master.*
Augustus Pelham,	*Second* "
Amos Ritchie,	*Third* "
Reuben Lockwood,	*Fourth* "

"This is a bad beginning for all of us," said Captain Kendall.

"I think it is a good beginning," added Robinson.

"So do I," responded Pelham; "nothing could be better."

"I am sorry this trouble happened so soon," continued the captain. "I don't think Mr. Lowington will wish to have such an event occur very often."

"I couldn't help it, Captain Kendall," interposed Terrill. "I was obliged to do something, or let the fellow ride over me."

"You did perfectly right, Mr. Terrill. I entirely approve of your conduct, and am very much obliged to you for the firmness and decision with which you maintained your authority and the discipline of the ship. I should have done just what you did, if I had been in your place," added Paul, heartily.

"Nothing could be better than Mr. Terrill's behavior," said the third lieutenant. "He was master of the situation in the beginning, and held his ground to the last. I stood ready to help him, but he did not need any help."

"So did I," added Pelham. "I wanted to get my hand on the rascal, but the first lieutenant gave us no chance to do anything."

"It is better as it is," continued the captain. "Mr. Terrill has proved that he is not a child, and even Mc-

Leish will understand what he is made of. This is a very disagreeable affair, but it could not have been avoided. I do not like to call on Mr. Lowington so soon for assistance, but I suppose we must report McLeish's conduct to him."

"Not on my account," interposed the first lieutenant. "If he don't obey orders, I shall make him do so. I feel abundantly able to take care of him, so far as I am concerned."

Paul smiled as he glanced at the slender form and rather pale face of the first lieutenant.

"Have we a brig on board?" he asked.

"We have," replied Martyn, the second lieutenant: "there is a three-cornered room next to the forecastle, opposite the steerage closet."

"It will not do to let McLeish run at large after his bad conduct. Mr. Terrill, you will commit him to the brig, and we will settle the question of reporting him at another time. You may call Mr. Cleats, the boatswain, to assist you, if you choose."

"I do not need his help," replied Terrill. "If Mr. Pelham will go with me, it will be sufficient."

"Mr. Pelham will go with you," said the captain.

Terrill, as resolute as though his nerves had been made of iron, went into the steerage, attended by Pelham. The crew appeared to be busy in arranging their lockers and berths, and in exploring their new quarters. The first lieutenant proceeded to the part of the steerage indicated by Martyn as the locality of the "brig." There were two bulkheads between the steerage and the forecastle, one extending square across the between-decks of the vessel, and the other at right angles with the schooner's side, where it rounded in near the bow, thus saving a space of three feet next to the ceiling, which was not needed in the forecastle. The brig was simply a closet, with a door made of hard wood slats.

The first lieutenant took the key from the door, and assured himself that the place was in condition for the reception of the prisoner. It contained a stool, and there was space enough for a mattress on the deck within it.

"McLeish," called he, in decided tones.

"Here, sir," replied the rebel, who had cooled off since the affray, as he walked towards the first lieutenant.

"By the order of the captain, you will be committed to the brig."

"In there — is it?" asked McLeish, glancing into the brig.

"In there. Will you go in, or shall I put you in?" demanded the first lieutenant.

"It seems to me you have all come off here to this vessel for the purpose of insulting me," growled he.

"No words! Will you go in, or shall we put you in?"

McLeish was deliberating whether to obey or resist. He had derived no comfort from his shipmates in the steerage, after the officers went into the cabin. They had simply told him he was a fool to make a row with the officers for nothing; and some of them, seeing how easily he had been whipped by the first lieutenant, were disposed to pound him on their own hook for his folly, and for compromising them by his misconduct.

"If you want any help, Mr. Terrill, we are all ready to obey orders," said one of the crew, "for we don't approve of his conduct."

"I do not need any help," replied Terrill.

"You are hard on me, lieutenant," added McLeish, fretfully, as he stepped forward towards the door of his prison.

Instead of going in, as his movement indicated, he suddenly sprang upon the first lieutenant, intending to take him by surprise, and have his revenge; but Pelham seized him by the collar, and crowded him into the brig. The door was closed upon him, and locked. The rebel was safe now, and the officers returned to the cabin. Terrill reported to the captain the execution of his order.

"I think we had better get rid of that fellow as soon as possible," said Groom, the first master.

"We have him in the right place now," replied Pelham.

"Mr. Lowington gave me no orders in regard to reporting such cases to him," added Paul. "I don't like to call in any help in governing the crew, at least before the ship's company are organized."

"Do you feel obliged to report this case to the principal?" asked Terrill.

"I shall certainly inform Mr. Lowington what has happened, when I see him; but I was not ordered to give immediate notice of any trouble on board. I have concluded to say nothing about it at present, and we will proceed to organize. The principal told us, in his speech yesterday, that one of the objects of the Josephine was to afford the students an opportunity to cultivate the virtue of self-reliance; and if a turbulent seaman is not one of the paths to the attainment of confidence, I don't know what is. He expects the officers to govern the ship, and keep up strict discipline. We have done so thus far, and we will depend upon ourselves. Mr. Terrill, you will pipe to muster, if you please."

The first lieutenant went on deck, and presently the pipe of the boatswain was heard. All the officers went on deck, and took their stations. As all the seamen were well known, there was little difficulty in assigning to them their places aloft and on deck. The Josephine carried only a fore topsail, fore top-gallant sail, and a gaff topsail on the main mast, and only a few top men were needed. The lightest and smartest were stationed aloft, while the heavy, strong fellows were placed at the halyards, brails, and sheets. The petty officers had all been appointed on board of the ship, according to the merit roll. Though the schooner was provided with four boats, only two coxswains were selected; the choice of the other two being left until the vessel was fully manned.

At twelve o'clock the organization of the ship's company was completed, and all hands piped to dinner. The chief steward was very attentive to the young gentlemen in the cabin, and they enjoyed their first dinner on board; and, indeed, everything relating to their personal comfort was entirely satisfactory. In the steerage, the crew were not less delighted with their accommodations.

After dinner the crew were piped on deck again, and drilled in making and furling sail, and in all the evolutions of seamanship required in handling the schooner. The boats were lowered, and their crews required to become familiar with them; but they were all experienced rowers, and needed no special training. Before night Captain Kendall was satisfied that his ship's company were in condition to work the vessel, and nothing would have suited him better than an order to go to sea. A hard day's work had been done, both by the occupants of the cabin and the steerage, and all hands were tired enough to rest after the fatigue and excitement of the drill.

The officers spent a pleasant evening in the cabin, talking over the events of the day, discussing the merits of the Josephine, and anticipating the pleasure of sailing her.

"I think we ought to make a trial trip in her," said Terrill. "We don't know whether we can handle her or not."

"Probably we shall have a chance to test the Josephine's qualities before many days," added the captain.

"If Mr. Lowington wishes us to have confidence in ourselves, he must send us to sea," laughed Pelham.

"Do you think we could handle her yet?" asked Groom.

"Of course we can," replied Terrill. "Do you suppose Mr. Lowington would have given Captain Kendall the charge of her if he hadn't known he could handle her?"

"I think we need not discuss that question," said the captain. "I am pretty sure we shall be sent to sea soon."

"I hope so," added half a dozen of them.

"Do you apprehend any more trouble with the crew; Mr. Terrill?" asked Captain Kendall.

"I do not, as long as that McLeish is in the strait jacket. I don't think he has much influence with the crew; but we have some of the hardest fellows in the crowd on board, though I believe they are all well disposed at the present time. We may have some trouble with Rossfeldt, Lynch, Sanborn, Grossbeck, Templeton, and such fellows as they are, but it will not be until after the novelty of their situation has worn away."

"Those you mention are uneasy fellows, always trying to get into a scrape. Mr. Lowington advised me to keep an anchor watch while we are in port. Of course I shall do that; but I think we will do something more. There is nothing like keeping our eyes open. I intend, therefore, to have one officer on duty all night, in addition to the two seamen composing the anchor watch. He must pass through the steerage every half hour during his watch. We shall be pretty sure, then, that there is no mischief brewing among the crew."

The arrangements for this watch were made. The officers, except the captain, were to serve in turn, in the order of their rank, for two hours. The first lieutenant went to the steerage, and detailed the seamen who were to be the anchor watch. At eight o'clock the first watch was set. At ten all was quiet on board, all hands having turned in. Henry Martyn was on deck in charge of the vessel. At five bells everybody below appeared to be asleep, except McLeish, who stood at the grated door of his prison, looking out into the steerage. The watch officer had just been his rounds, and all was still again. He could hear the heavy breathing of some of the sleepers.

If there was a miserable and unhappy fellow on board, it was McLeish; not consciously rendered so by his own misconduct, but by the insults heaped upon a MacGregor. He was not yet able to see that he had done wrong, and he was only thirsting for revenge. He had carefully examined every part of the brig in order to find a weak place, if there was any. He had shaken the door, and tried his skill upon the lock with his knife. His prison appeared to be secure in every part, and everything was as hopeless as it could be. The culprit expected to be sent back to the Young America the next day.

He had exhausted his ingenuity in vain attempts to devise a method of getting out of his dungeon. He could neither break down the door nor pick the lock. He needed assistance from outside, with which he was satisfied that he could make his escape. The bars of the door were wide enough apart to permit him to thrust his arm through, and he had felt of the lock until he had hit upon a plan for opening his dungeon. The door swung out into the steerage, and was secured by a lock, screwed upon one of the slats. He had examined the screw heads with his fingers, and attempted to operate upon them with his knife. In this he failed; but a friend on the outside could let him out in five minutes.

In the middle berth, next to his prison, slept Lynch, whom the rebel knew to be one of "our fellows."

Above him was Baxter, one of the chaplain's "lambs," who was innocent enough to be a sound sleeper.

"Lynch!" said McLeish, in a whisper.

The occupant of the middle berth appeared also to be innocent, so far as his slumbers were concerned.

"I say, Lynch!" called he again, in a little louder tone; but it was not loud enough to rouse the heavy sleeper.

McLeish took from his pocket two or three big English pennies; and judging from the feeling of them in his pocket, they were heavy enough to crush the unconscious slumberer. Reaching through the bars of the door, he tossed one of the coins into the middle berth. It fell upon the bed-clothes, and did not disturb the tired seaman. He repeated the experiment; and this time the penny fell upon Lynch's face. It startled him, and waked him up. Doubtless he thought a rat was a fellow-occupant of the bunk with him, and he raised himself up in his bed, to find the intruder if he could.

"Lynch," whispered McLeish.

"Who's that?" demanded he.

"Whist! don't make a noise," added the prisoner.

"What do you want?" asked Lynch, in a whisper this time.

"Come to me — will you? Don't let any one hear you."

"What for?" inquired the cautious seaman.

"I want to see you."

Lynch carefully slipped out of his berth, and went to the door of the brig. He was hardly in the humor for a conspiracy with such a senseless rebel as

McLeish. He had acted so stupidly in the morning, that those who did not object to the principle of rebellion and insubordination, condemned his folly in making such a needless row.

"What do you want of me?" demanded Lynch, rather sourly, when he reached the door.

"I want to talk with you a bit."

"I don't care about talking with you to-night. I am sleepy, and I have to go on the anchor watch at eight bells," replied Lynch, with a long gape.

"Eight bals — when is that?" inquired the prisoner.

"Twelve o'clock."

"And who goes on with you?"

"Grossbeck."

"Excellent!" exclaimed the rebel.

"It may be, but I don't see it," growled Lynch. "What do you want of me? I'm not going to stand here all night, and perhaps get into a scrape for you."

"Just get into your bed again, if you hear that bal up stairs; for that's when the officer comes round to see that all is well."

"I shall not wait for the bell before I turn in, if you don't speak quick."

"I want to get out," said McLeish.

"I suppose you do; you were a fool to get in there, and I, for one, don't care how long you have to stay there," replied Lynch, in the most forbidding of tones.

"You are a good fallow, Lynch."

"I know that, but I'm not going to get into a scrape for a fellow that don't know enough to keep his fingers out of the fire," added the outsider, in an energetic whisper. "You will be sent back to the ship tomorrow; then all your fun will be spoiled, and I shall be glad of it."

"Don't be hard on me. I was only taking the nobs down a bit."

"I should think you were; but you better believe that nob of a first lieutenant took you down a bit. If you want anything of me, speak quick, for I'm going to turn in."

"I can whip the lieutenant any day in a fair fight."

"Why didn't you do it, then?"

"He didn't fight fair."

"Fight fair! You are a humbug! All night to you, till your muscle grows;" and Lynch moved towards his berth.

"Whist! Hold on a minute."

"I won't hold on any more, unless you tell me what you want."

"I'll no tall ye what *I* want first; I'll tall you what *you* want."

"Well, what do I want?" demanded Lynch, impatiently.

"You want to make a sovereign in about five minutes."

"That's so," answered the outsider, with refreshing promptness.

The insider could not have mentioned anything which Lynch wanted more than money, especially as the students were expecting a run on shore in a few days. Perhaps there was not a boy on board of either vessel who was more sorely distressed by the want of funds than he. Left to his own inclinations, he was a reckless, resolute fellow, disposed to gamble, to drink ale, and even liquors. No one needed the strict discipline and wholesome restraint of the ship more than he. If they did not reform, they at least kept him for the time in the path of decency. He wanted money now, and he always wanted it, for money was the key to the low pleasures he relished.

"I knew you wanted money," added McLeish.

"Have you any?"

"Sartainly I have — planty of it. But you'll no betray me."

"Of course I won't; I wouldn't blow on the meanest fellow on board. How much have you?"

"Never you mind how much I have. I haird the lads say my money would be taken from me, and I just put it where the nobs couldn't find it. Whist! there's the bal; turn in you, and come again when the nob has been through the place."

Lynch crawled carefully into his bed, and presently the second lieutenant went through the steerage. All was quiet as before, and he saw no reason to suspect the mischief which was brewing. As soon as he had gone on deck, the tenant of the middle berth, tempted by the prospect of making a sovereign, returned to the door.

"Now, speak quick, and tell me what you want," said he.

"I'll do that, if you'll bargain to do what I want for the sovereign."

"I won't till I know what I'm to do, you had better believe."

"You are to halp me out without danger to yourself."

"I'll do it; but not till you pay me the money, for I'm not so sure you have a sovereign about you," added the prudent Lynch.

"That's no fair. How do I know you'll let me out when you get my money. I'll give you ten shillings now, and ten more after I'm free: that's fair."

"Well, I agree to that."

McLeish retreated to the farther part of his cell, and presently reappeared with a half sovereign which he had taken from one of his stockings. He handed it to Lynch, who examined it very carefully to assure himself that it was pure coin. The weight and color satisfied him, and he intimated to the prisoner that the money was all right.

"Do you know where to find a screw-driver?" asked McLeish, nervously, as the prospect of carrying out his scheme improved.

"No, I don't; how do you expect me to find a screw-driver at this time of night?"

"Naver mind; a knife will just do as well. Here, take mine, and remove the four screws from the lock."

Lynch took the large jackknife handed to him, and went to work with it. The joiner's work was new, and the screws came out pretty easily. Within the five minutes allotted for the task, he had removed the lock and drawn the bolt out of the iron box into which it slid.

"My job is done," whispered the operator, holding the lock in his hand. "Now give me the other half sovereign, or I'll screw it on again."

"Don't be in such haste, mon," replied McLeish. "How am I to get away now?"

"I don't know; that's your lookout, not mine. I have done all I agreed to do. Hand over the stamps, or I'll put the lock on again," persisted the matter-of-fact occupant of the middle berth, starboard side.

"You're a good fellow, Lynch."

"So I am; pay up."

"I'll do it when I come out."

"Come out and do it then."

The prisoner retired to the dark part of his cell again to obtain the other half sovereign from the depths of his stocking. He produced it, came out of the brig, and handed it over to the outsider.

"That's all I want," said Lynch, as he took the coin and crawled back into his berth.

McLeish, who had taken the lock as a receipt for the last payment, inserted the bolt in the iron chamber, and restored the screws to their places, so that the door looked just as it had before it was tampered with. Hardly had he finished this job before seven bells struck, and the visit of the officer of the watch was again to be expected. The stroke of the bell almost paralyzed him, for he did not know which way to turn. To be discovered would defeat his plans. He heard the step of Lieutenant Martyn on the deck as he approached the fore hatch. The situation was desperate, and, without considering that there were twelve empty berths in the steerage, he sprang into Lynch's bunk, and crawled over next to the ceiling of the vessel.

"What are you doing?" growled his confederate.

"Hush! The officer is coming!" replied McLeish.

Both of them kept entirely still, and Martyn went

his rounds. There was not a sound to be heard save the breathing of the sleepers, and the lieutenant returned to the deck, assured that no mischief had been perpetrated during his watch.

"What did you get in here for, you fool?" snarled Lynch, as soon as the step of the officer was heard on the deck above them.

"I want to give you another sovereign for more halp," replied McLeish.

"Say on quick, then, for my watch on deck will be called in half an hour," answered Lynch.

CHAPTER III.

THE ANCHOR WATCH.

"YOU are a good fallow, Lynch," said McLeish, in the whisper to which all the conversation had necessarily been confined.

"Don't waste your time in telling me what I know as well as you do," protested Lynch. "Show me how you intend to get rid of the sovereign; that's all I want to hear."

"I'll tall you presently. Who will be the officer next in charge of the deck?"

"I don't know; the first and second lieutenants have been on; I suppose the third will come next — that's Robinson."

"We must muzzle him, and then lower a boat," continued the conspirator, evidently getting ahead of his story.

"Muzzle him?" added Lynch, inquiringly.

"Ay, sairtainly; muzzle him: there will be three of us, and we can do it just as easy as we can let him alone."

"I don't exactly understand the programme."

"In half an hour you and Grossbeck will go on deck — do ye mind? I will go with you. When the officer walks forward where we are, we'll just knock him down, and put a handkerchief in his mouth. Then we will lower away one of the boats, and pull for the shore. That's all easy enough — isn't it?"

"I think it is — just as easy as to put your head into a halter, or your fingers into the fire," replied Lynch.

"But you will go ashore, mon, and have a good time. Liverpool is a big place, and there's lots of fun there."

"We should be brought back in a few days, as Wilton was."

"That was because Wilton didn't know the country as I do. I'll take care of you."

"I don't know that Grossbeck will have anything to do with the scrape. The fellows are too well suited with their quarters here for the present."

"I will just give you and Grossbeck a sovereign apiece," said McLeish, punching his berth-mate in the side, to emphasize the liberality of his offer.

"How long would a sovereign apiece last us if we had to live at the hotels on shore? If I had twenty pounds, or so, as Wilton had, I would think of it; as it is, I believe I won't make another sovereign to-night," replied the cautious Lynch.

The Josephine had too many charms, even to a fellow like the occupant of the middle berth, to permit him to engage in such a hazardous enterprise as running away with only forty shillings in his pocket; for a second-class fare to London would use up more than half of his funds. The experience of Wilton and Monroe, as related by the principal to the students, was a lesson by which he was disposed to profit.

"You won't halp me?" said McLeish.

"I've helped you enough. I can't do any more."

"Hoot, mon! What am I to do? I might as well be in the brig as out of it, if you won't halp me to get ashore."

"I'll help you all I can; but I won't knock any lieutenants down, or do anything of that sort. I'm not going to spend a month in the brig for the sake of a day's fun on shore — not I."

"Then you desairt me?" said the culprit, moodily.

"Haven't I done all I agreed to do?" retorted Lynch.

"You have; but you knew very well it was no use for me to get out of the brig, if I couldn't leave the vessel."

"That wasn't any of my business."

"Well, mon, you'll just find it's your business. I'll tell the officers, when they find me in the morning, who let me out; and I'll have your good company in the brig when I go back," added McLeish, maliciously.

"Humph!" sneered Lynch; but after all, the announcement was a "poser" to him.

The reprobate would get him into a scrape, even before he had spent the money earned. He would not only be sent to the brig, but the sovereign would be taken from him. It is dangerous to enter into the counsels of rogues and villains, and Lynch found himself in a very unpleasant box. He knew his companion was mean enough to betray him, and his threats were not idle ones.

"I'm willing to do anything I can for you," said Lynch, uneasily.

"Then why don't you do it? If you don't halp me off, you shall spend to-morrow in the brig with me. We'll hang together, my good friend. You have taken my money, and you must do my work."

"Knocking an officer down is mutiny," said Lynch. "I don't want to do that; and I don't think there is any need of doing it. Leave the matter to me, and I will manage it."

"I'll just leave it to you, if you like."

"Keep still, now," said Lynch, who had whispered himself hoarse. "I want to think it over."

The culprit did keep still, and Lynch thought it over; but he was considering how he could untangle his relations with the prisoner, rather than devising a plan to get him away from the vessel. Before he had settled the matter in his own mind, eight bells struck.

"Keep still, McLeish. I shall be called in a minute," said he, in hurried tones. "When I rap twice three on the deck above your head, come up."

"Twice three," repeated McLeish.

"Yes; now keep down there out of sight."

Lieutenant Martyn came into the steerage, and after glancing at his watch list, under the lantern, he called Grossbeck and Lynch, and passed into the cabin to awaken his successor. Lynch and Grossbeck went on deck, and the two seamen whose watch had expired repaired to their berths. McLeish kept perfectly still in the bunk, waiting for the expected signal, though he knew it could not be given till the two who had just turned in had gone to sleep, and the circumstances on deck favored his going up.

There was a small top-gallant forecastle at the bow

of the schooner, on which the anchor watch were stationed, so that they could see everything that approached, in any direction. The officer of the watch "planked" the quarter-deck, or sat upon the seats on each side of the after skylight. The head steward had put a lunch on the cabin table, for something to eat was a great help in keeping awake. There was nothing for him to do except to make the round below, and to see that the watch forward were awake; and he amused himself in any manner that suited his fancy.

Lynch and Grossbeck seated themselves on the jib, stowed on the bowsprit, and made themselves as comfortable as possible. In a low tone Lynch told his watch-mate what had happened below, and that McLeish was in his berth, waiting for the signal to come on deck.

"In a word, Grossbeck, I'm in a bad fix," said Lynch, as he wound up his narrative. "The sneak will blow on me just as sure as he is discovered. He gave me these two half sovereigns; you take one of them, and we will call it square."

Grossbeck did not object to this arrangement; and without any compunction of conscience, he put the ten-shilling piece in his pocket, thinking of what it would purchase when the crew had liberty on shore.

"What shall we do with him?" asked Lynch, anxiously.

"That's the question," replied Grossbeck. "What shall we do with him?"

"Of course we can't lower one of the boats and

turn him adrift without the officer's seeing us," added Lynch. "I don't mean to get into any scrape."

"Nor I: this vessel suits me too well just now, and I don't want to leave her. I have it!" exclaimed Grossbeck, suddenly, as he glanced over the port bow of the schooner. "There is a plank stage hanging below the hawse-hole, where the carpenter was calking a seam. He has to paint it again in the morning, and he left his stage. We can turn him adrift on that. We can lower it into the water the next time the officer goes below."

"Do you think McLeish will go off with nothing but a plank under him?" asked Lynch.

"If he wants to go very bad, he will."

"The tide is going out, and it runs like sixty here. It would carry him out to sea."

"That's his business."

"I don't believe he'll do it. I wouldn't."

"Nor I either," added Grossbeck, candidly. "But if we give him the chance, it will show that we are ready to help him."

"That's so; but he would certainly be drowned if he went off on the plank."

"Never fear; he won't go."

"Well; what then?" asked Lynch. "What shall we do with him?"

"We must get him back into the brig, and lock him up again," laughed Grossbeck. "We must shake the dust off our feet, any how."

"There goes the lieutenant down into the cabin. We'll get McLeish on deck," added Lynch, jumping down from the top-gallant forecastle, and giving the signal with the heel of his shoe on the deck.

The prisoner lost no time in obeying the summons. He was directed to mount the forecastle, and was then assisted over the rail into the head, on the port side, where he could not be seen by the officer.

"We have arranged it all," said Grossbeck, "and you may go ashore as soon as you please."

"I knew you would be my friend," replied McLeish, gratefully.

"We have made it all right for you," added Grossbeck, in lively tones, as though he had no idea that his proposition would be declined.

"Well, where is the boat?" demanded McLeish.

"Boat! My dear fellow, we can't get a boat. The oars are all locked up in the captain's state-room; besides, the plugs are all pulled out of the bottoms, and the first lieutenant has them in his trowsers pocket. They wouldn't float a minute with a fellow in them."

Lynch thought his companion's statements were rather "steep;" but as the culprit did not question them, he did not feel obliged to contradict them.

"We would tip the officer over and gag him, as you suggested, and go ashore with you, if the boats were only in condition to carry us," continued Grossbeck. "You are a good fellow, McLeish, and we want to help you off."

"But how am I to go ashore without a boat?" asked McLeish.

"That's easy enough. You can swim — can't you?"

"Sairtainly I can; but you don't expect me to swim ashore — do you?"

"It's not more than half a mile," suggested Grossbeck.

5

"But I'll no do that."

"I didn't know but you would prefer to swim ashore."

"Sairtainly not."

"Then we can do something better for you! Hush! there comes the officer."

"One bell," said Mr. Robinson, coming as far as the foremast.

Lynch struck the bell, and the lieutenant went aft again, after he had visited the steerage.

"All right again," said Grossbeck.

"You were going to tall me how I was to get ashore," added McLeish.

"I was; and we have fixed that matter so that you can go ashore as nicely as you could in a boat. Do you see that plank stage under the hawse-hole?"

"I don't see it," replied the culprit, looking down into the darkness in the direction indicated.

"There's a plank there; get down on the bobstay, and you can see it."

McLeish changed his position so that he could discern the outline of the plank, which was about eight feet long and a foot wide.

"Surely you don't expact me to go to the shore on a bit of a plank like that!" exclaimed McLeish.

"Why not? My grandfather crossed the Atlantic Ocean on a plank no bigger than that."

"Hoot, mon! You are funning with me."

"No, I'm not. It's easy enough to go half a mile on a plank like that."

"Is there no danger?"

"Of course there is danger. There's always danger

when you are on the water. You don't expect to run away from your ship without getting into some danger — do you?"

"I'll no trust my life on a bit of a plank like that," said McLeish, decidedly.

"What can we do then?" asked Grossbeck, with apparent perplexity.

"You must get me a boat."

"Shall I go down into the cabin and ask the captain for the oars, and the first lieutenant for the plugs?"

"Surely not."

"We are ready to do all we can to help you, if you will only tell us what," pleaded Grossbeck. "If you will go on the plank, we will lower you down into the water the next time the officer goes below, which will be at two bells, if not before."

"I should sairtainly be drowned."

"Perhaps you would, but you must take that risk in running away."

"I'll no do it; I'm not ready to be drowned yet."

"See here," interposed Lynch; "this thing can be managed first rate by to-morrow or next day. We can get a shore boat to come alongside, when Grossbeck and I have our next watch. Leave the whole matter to us, McLeish, and we will fix it."

"That's the better way. When our next watch comes, we can have everything ready," added Grossbeck.

"But what am I to do?" inquired McLeish.

"You must go back to the brig, and stay there till there is a chance for us to put you ashore."

"I don't like that," growled the culprit.

"Well, if you will tell us what to do, we'll do it," said Lynch.

McLeish could not tell them what to do; and he finally consented to be locked up in his dungeon again, to await a more favorable opportunity to escape. It was a bitter necessity to him; and as his plan had failed, he insisted that Lynch should return the sovereign he had paid.

"Let's give it back to him," suggested Grossbeck, who was willing to shake off all connection with the transaction.

"I will, if he desires it," replied Lynch.

"Two bells," called the officer of the watch, as he came forward, and then descended to the steerage.

Robinson returned to the deck, and after a little while went down into the cabin. As soon as he disappeared, McLeish was sent below, when he removed the lock from the door, and went into the brig again. When the watch was relieved, an hour later, Lynch, who had procured a screw-driver from the carpenter's box, screwed it on again, and the culprit was once more a prisoner.

"You did not give me back my money," whispered the insider.

"No, but I will, if you say so," replied the other. "I did all I agreed to do for it, and if you made any blunder, it was not my fault."

"But here I am, and it's no right for me to pay twenty shillings for nothing," snarled McLeish.

"You bothered me and kept me awake half the night. I will give the money back to you, and you may stay in the brig till somebody besides me lets you out," answered Lynch. "I gave half a sovereign to Grossbeck; I will get that."

"Don't do it; keep the money, and halp me as you agreed to do," replied McLeish, alarmed at the terms on which the gold was to be returned. "Just keep it, and say no more about it."

Lynch was quite willing to do this; and leaving the prisoner to himself, he quietly turned in, to sleep as soundly as though he had been engaged in no plot. The night wore away without any further incident, and as no one except the conspirators had lost more than two hours' sleep, they were fresh and bright when all hands were called in the morning. The decks were washed down, and the usual ship's duty performed.

"Signal on board the ship, sir," said a quartermaster, reporting to the first lieutenant.

"Pass the word for the signal officer," replied Terrill.

Mr. Lockwood, the fourth master, was the signal officer, and he immediately appeared on the quarter-deck with the signal-book in his hand. Both the ship and her consort were provided with the numbers, a series of flags, each representing, by its combination and arrangement of colors, one of the Arabic figures or the zero. With these flags any number can be expressed. Vessels carry a printed signal-book, in which various nautical questions and answers are placed against the numbers. Other numbers are set against the names of ships, so that a vessel hoisting her number may thus communicate it to another vessel several miles distant.

On the evening before the officers of the Josephine left the ship, a private signal-book had been made, with questions, answers, and orders relating to the circumstances of the two vessels. The numbers commenced with one hundred, but the book had not been completed, only about twenty different messages being recorded. A copy of the code was written out for each vessel. Of course they could communicate on ordinary matters by means of the general signal-book.

"What's the number?" asked the signal officer.

"One hundred and five," replied the quarter-master.

Lockwood opened his book, and found this number.

"All hands attend lecture on board the ship," he read from the book, against the number.

The signal was hoisted on the Josephine to indicate that the message was seen and understood.

"We are to have Mr. Mapps's lecture on England, I suppose," said Captain Kendall.

"Does all hands include McLeish?" asked the first lieutenant.

"Certainly not; Wilton and Monroe will not leave the brig to attend, I presume."

At quarter before eight the boats' crews were called, and all hands embarked. The first lieutenant directed Cleats, the boatswain, to keep an eye on the brig, and see that the prisoner did not escape. In a few moments the ship's company were on the deck of the Young America. Their arrival created quite a sensation. Paul and his officers were warmly greeted by their late associates, and all the questions which the time would permit were asked and answered.

"How do you get along, Captain Kendall?" asked

the principal, with a kindly smile, as he took the hand of the young commander.

"Very well, I think, sir," replied Paul.

"I looked for McLeish, as your crew came over the side, but I did not see him," added Mr. Lowington.

"He did not come with us, sir; he is in the brig," answered Paul, doubtfully.

"In the brig!" exclaimed the fountain of authority.

"Yes, sir; he was committed by my order before he had been on board an hour."

"I did not expect he would give you any trouble so soon. What was the matter."

The first lieutenant was called to tell his story, and he gave all the particulars.

"I am sorry this has happened; but you have done well, all of you. You have kept up the discipline of your vessel, and I not only approve your action, but I thank you for it. Why didn't you send for me?"

"We needed no help, sir, and I had no orders to send for you," replied Paul.

"Very true; but didn't you want me?" added Mr. Lowington, with a smile.

"I should have been very glad to see you, as I always am, but I didn't like to acknowledge that we couldn't discipline our crew."

"You are aware that one of the numbers in your signal-book is, 'Trouble on board.' If you had hoisted this signal I should have visited you at once."

"There was trouble on board, but we did not need any assistance. If I had understood that you wished me to inform you immediately when any difficulty occurred, I should have sent for you, or hoisted the signal."

"The matter was left entirely to your own discretion. I do not purpose to interfere with the discipline of the Josephine, unless her captain requests me to do so, or unless I find, upon examination, that it is below our standard. I am entirely satisfied with what you have done. When you desire it, I will transfer any officer or seaman from the schooner to the ship, though not without a fair hearing, if the party complained of demands it."

"I thank you, Mr. Lowington, for the confidence you repose in me, and I will endeavor to merit it by being faithful to my duty," added Paul, blushing deeply.

"I suppose you wish to get rid of McLeish now — don't you?" said the principal, with a smile.

"No, sir; the first lieutenant does not ask for his removal, and I shall not, as long as he does not complain. I think we can manage him."

"Your experience with McLeish is just what every ship-master is occasionally obliged to pass through. The lowest and vilest men often get into the forecastle of a ship, and make trouble by their turbulence and disobedience. The lesson is one which every sea captain has to learn. He must be firm and decided, but at the same time he should treat his crew well. He should win their respect and confidence by kindness and consideration, as well as by prompt and energetic action in the time of trouble. You are learning this lesson now; and you will find that your cabin is not a bed of roses for you and your officers."

Mr. Lowington directed the captain of the ship to pipe the students to the steerage for the lecture.

"Captain Kendall, I have much to say to you, and I think you can afford to lose a portion of the professor's lecture," added the principal, as he led the way to a couple of seats near the wheel.

"I am tolerably well posted in the geography and history of England, though I suppose I should profit by Mr. Mapps's lecture," replied Paul, as he sat down at Mr. Lowington's side.

"I will not detain you long. We shall go on shore this afternoon; but I am tired of marshalling the whole ship's company in one body. We have sixty-nine seamen entitled to liberty. We have, including the chaplain, the surgeon, and myself, nine men to take charge of them, which will make seven or eight students to each. I purpose to let them visit the docks and other places of interest in small parties. Two or three would be better than seven or eight. I shall presume that the officers can take care of themselves; so can a portion of the seamen in the Josephine. How many of your crew can you trust without some one to watch them."

"Half of them, I think," replied Paul.

"Dr. Winstock and Mr. Mapps will take charge of such of your crew as need their supervision. You will arrange that."

"Wouldn't it be better to trust them all, sir?" asked Paul.

"Such students as Lynch and Sanborn?"

"If we put them on their good behavior, I think they will do well. I don't like to make any distinction among them."

The principal acknowledged that Paul was right, and he was permitted to use his own judgment in regard to liberty.

"One thing more, Captain Kendall," added Mr. Lowington. "I suppose you desire to try the sailing qualities of your vessel."

"Very much indeed, sir," replied Paul, with enthusiasm.

"You shall have the opportunity soon. To-morrow will be Sunday. Monday will be a holiday, when we shall celebrate the Fourth of July. On Tuesday you may start on your trial trip."

"Where shall we go?" asked Paul, delighted with the permission.

"Anywhere you please. I will give you three days for the trip. I have full confidence in you, Captain Kendall but you must be very discreet and very careful. Now we will go to the steerage, and hear what Mr. Mapps has to say."

CHAPTER IV.

"ALL HANDS, ATTEND LECTURE, AHOY!"

PAUL KENDALL was amazed at the confidence reposed in him by the principal. On Tuesday he was to go to sea in the Josephine, without any superior officer to control his movements. He had the privilege of going where he pleased, and was limited only as to time. But he was perfectly sure that he could take the schooner across the Atlantic Ocean, or even around the world. He went down into the steerage of the ship to hear the lecture with a feeling of elation he had not before experienced, and it was some time before he could get hold of the thread of the professor's discourse.

When the boatswain's call, "All hands, attend lecture, ahoy!" had sounded through the ship, the crews of the Young America and Josephine had mingled together, and taken their places as usual. A large outline map of Great Britain hung on the foremast, and the professor stood with the pointer in his hand ready to proceed. Most of the students were tolerably familiar with the geography and history of England, and it was not supposed that the instructor would tell them much that was new. The lecture was a kind of review, intended to refresh the memory of the students, and create or renew an interest in the country they were now visiting.

"Young gentlemen, what is the official designation of England, Scotland, Ireland and Wales?" the professor inquired.

"The United Kingdom of Great Britain and Ireland," replied the boys in concert.

"Now, what is meant by Great Britain?"

"The island which includes England, Wales, and Scotland."

"Very well; we will now confine our attention to England, reserving the distinctive features of Wales for a future lesson. What names have you ever heard applied to England?"

"Britannia."

"A Roman name," added Mr. Mapps. "What other?"

"Albion."

"Also a Roman name, and it doubtless came from the Latin word *albus*, meaning white, derived probably from the white, chalky cliffs of the county of Kent, whose shores are the portion of England lying nearest to France."

"John Bull," added a student.

"That is a name applied to the people of England, first used by Dean Swift. A satirical novel, called 'The History of John Bull,' by Arbuthnot, perpetuated the appellation. I think the popular idea of the English, as a people who believe in roast beef, is the most significant explanation of the term.

"From north to south, England has an extent of four hundred miles, and from east to west of two hundred and eighty miles. The perimeter is ten hundred and eighty-seven, but following all the indentations of the sea, the coast line would be about two thousand miles. The area of England is nearly fifty-one thousand square miles, or about the size of the States of Iowa or Alabama. Wales has about seven thousand four hundred square miles, which does not vary much from the State of Massachusetts, while England and Wales unitedly are about the size of the State of Georgia.

"The surface of the country is moderately uneven, nearly all of it being beautifully diversified by gentle elevations and by broad valleys and plains. The land is remarkably productive and fertile, and the system of agriculture is the best in the world. Of more than four and a half million acres in England, only six or seven thousand are unfit for cultivation, which could not be the case if the country were as rugged and uneven as Scotland, or portions of Ireland.

"Nearly all the mountainous region lies in the western part of the island. The Cheviot Hills, in part, divide England and Scotland," said Mr. Mapps, pointing them out on the map. "A continuation of them, running nearly south, is called the Pennine chain."

"Our maps don't say so," interposed Terrill, who always had an opinion of his own, and was always ready to back it up.

"What do your maps say?" asked the professor.

"The range you mention is called the Cumbrian Mountains."

"You are quite correct, Mr. Terrill," added Mr. Mapps. "Many of the school atlases have but one range, which is designated as the Cumbrian Mountains. This is not according to the best authorities. The continuation of the Cheviot Hills is now called the Pennine chain. They extend into Derbyshire, which is one of the middle counties of England, lying nearly due east of us. West of the Pennine chain, in Cumberland, Westmoreland, and Lancaster counties, is another range. These are the Cambrian Mountains. Among them, and in these three counties, are all the lakes of any note in England. Ullswater, nine miles long, and Windermere (the largest lake in England), ten and a half miles long, are noted for the beauty of the surrounding scenery. These sheets of water are about the size of Otsego and Saranac Lakes in New York. If you visit them, I dare say you will think they are very fine, but not at all equal to the recommendation of the English people.

"In Wales are the Cambrian Mountains. The Devonian range is in Devon and Cornwall, extending to Land's End, the south-western point of England. I have mentioned the principal mountains, though there are others which have attained the dignity of being named. There are no high mountains in Great Britain. Ben Nevis, in Scotland, is the highest, and Snowden, in Wales, three thousand five hundred and seventy-one feet high, is the loftiest peak south of the Cheviot Hills. Scawfell, Helvellyn, and Skiddaw, each about three thousand feet high, are in the Cumbrian range.

"As I have before stated, there are no large rivers in the United Kingdom, judged by the American standard. The Thames is the longest, and, as regards its navigation, the most important even in the world. The Severn is but five miles less in length than the Thames, having a course of two hundred and ten miles. The Trent comes next — one hundred and forty miles long. The Humber is the estuary of the Great Ouse and the Trent. The Mersey, in which our ship floats, is only sixty miles in length. Many of these rivers have broad mouths, which afford excellent harbors. We must not measure the importance of these rivers by their lengths, for on them are some of the greatest commercial cities in the world, which owe their prosperity to their navigable waters.

"If any other country in the world is richer in mineral products than England, none has more effectively and advantageously worked its mines, and profited by their wealth. Lead, coal, copper, zinc, tin, and iron are obtained in great quantities. England, to a greater extent than any other nation, is a manufacturing country. Its mines of iron have supplied the raw material for its artisans, and great cities, like Birmingham and Sheffield, have been built up by the manufacture of this metal alone.

"As a maritime and commercial power, England has been rivalled only by the United States.* To use the stale figure, the sails of its commerce whiten every sea. It long ranked as the greatest nation of the world, and its commerce has been the essential element of its greatness.

"The climate of England is moist and humid, but

---

* The tonnage of the United Kingdom, in 1862, was 4,394,400; of the United States, 5,112,165.

less rain falls in a year than in the United States. In one year thirty-two inches of rain fell in England; in Cambridge, Massachusetts, the rain-gauge indicated thirty-eight inches the same year. There is more cloudy, muggy weather here than in our country. In my last visit to Europe, I was in England sixteen days, on every one of which there was a fall of rain; but there was much pleasant weather, and some of the showers lasted but a few moments. In London, during some portions of the year, you may not see the sun for a week.

"I do not think it necessary, young gentlemen, to follow out in detail the history of England. It has been a progressive nation, and the story of freedom in our own land is but a continuation of the history of the struggle for liberty in this older country. Her people have often and stubbornly fought the battle against tyranny and oppression. They have done more than any other people to establish the right of the subject to himself and his earnings.

"Britain was invaded and conquered by the Romans. They held the country for about five centuries. It was afterwards invaded and ravaged by the savage Scots and Picts, against whom the Britons could not sustain themselves. In danger of being overwhelmed, they begged the Saxons, a warlike tribe in northern Germany, to help them. The Saxons did all they were asked to do, and more. They drove the northern barbarians back to their hills, and then, finding the country much superior to their own, they subdued and drove the Britons to the mountains and other retreats, and took possession of their lands. In this work the Saxons were leagued with the Jutes and the Angles, from the latter of whom England derived its name.

"A long and severe struggle followed between the Britons and the invaders, in which King Arthur is said to have defeated them in many engagements; but the Saxons finally prevailed. Seven kingdoms, called the Heptarchy, were established; but they were united into one monarchy by Egbert, under the name of England. The country was frequently invaded by the Danes and Northmen, and the kings for the next two hundred years had their hands full in repelling the incursions of their savage neighbors on the other side of the North Sea.

"Edward the Confessor, who died in 1065, bequeathed his crown to William Duke of Normandy, in France, which, according to monarchical rule, he had no right to do. Edgar Atheling was the true heir; but Harold, a descendant of King Sweyn, a Dane, who was also a descendant of Edward the Elder, was proclaimed King of England by the clergy and the nobility. William of Normandy, determined to establish his claim to the crown, invaded England with an immense army. Harold met him with his forces at Hastings, but was defeated and slain. The nation submitted, and the duke became king, under the title of William the Conqueror.

"The Saxon and the Norman families were united by the marriage of Henry I. to a descendant of one of the earlier kings. When he died, the crown belonged to his daughter Matilda, who had first married the Emperor of Germany, and then Geoffrey Plantagenet. Her son by her second husband became King Henry II., the first of the Plantagenet family, from which Queen Victoria is directly descended. The houses of Lancaster and York were branches of the Plantagenet family. Henry IV., the Duke of Lancaster, obtained the throne by displacing Richard II.

"The wars of the Roses broke out in 1455, in the reign of Henry VI., grandson of the first Lancaster. The symbol of the house of York was a white rose, of Lancaster, a red one. The former was descended from the third, and the latter from the fourth son of Edward III. The York branch had the right, and established it after some severe battles, and Edward IV. became King. He left two sons; but Richard, Duke of Gloucester, usurped the throne, and caused the rightful heir and his brother to be smothered in the Tower. The Earl of Richmond, belonging to the house of Lancaster, defeated Richard III. in the battle of Bosworth, and obtained the crown. In order to strengthen his claim, which was weak, he married the daughter of Edward IV., a Yorkist, thus uniting the two branches, which had so long been struggling for the throne. He was the first sovereign of the Tudor family. He was followed by his son, Henry VIII., who married so many wives, and left three children, all of whom became sovereigns of England. The son, Edward VI., succeeded to the throne at the age of ten, and died when he was sixteen. His successor was his sister Mary; and at her death, after a reign of only five years, Elizabeth ascended the throne. She was queen for forty-four years, and was the last of the Tudor line.

"Elizabeth was unmarried, and there was no direct successor to the crown. James IV. of Scotland had married the oldest daughter of Henry VII. of England, and their son was James V. of Scotland, the father of Mary Queen of Scots. James VI. of Scotland, son of Mary, and great-grandson of the daughter of Henry VII., was therefore the heir to the throne, and he succeeded Elizabeth, being the first of the Stuarts in England.

"His son, Charles I., followed him. During his reign, the struggle between the people and the despotic power of the Stuarts culminated, and the sovereign was beheaded. The people having wrested the authority from their rulers, the Commonwealth was established, and Cromwell became Protector. Monarchy was restored in the person of Charles II., who died after a reign of twenty-five years, and was succeeded by his brother, the Duke of York, who became James II. He was a Catholic, and endeavored to establish the Catholic religion in England. The effort cost him his crown, for he was compelled to abandon his throne, which was declared vacant. William, Prince of Orange, who had married James's oldest daughter, was invited to visit England, and landed with an army at Torbay. The principal nobles deserted the cause of the absent monarch, and flocked to the standard of his son-in-law. A convention decided that the king had abdicated his throne, and declared William III. and Mary the joint sovereigns of England. This event was the revolution of 1688.

"On the death of William — Mary having died seven years before — the crown descended to Anne,

Mary's sister, and the wife of Prince George of Denmark. She left no children. William III. had prevailed upon Parliament to establish the right of succession to the crown in favor of Sophia, wife of the Elector of Hanover, and granddaughter of James I. This was manifestly unjust, for there were no less than fifty-seven persons who had a better right than the Electress to the throne. Sophia died a short time before Anne, and her son, George I., succeeded to the crown. George II. was his son; George III. was the grandson of George II. George IV. was the son of George III., and was succeeded by his brother, under the title of William IV. At his death without children, Victoria came to the throne. She is the granddaughter of George III., and the niece of William.

"I have merely indicated the line of sovereigns who have sat upon the throne of England. Captain Kendall, I dare say you can box the compass, but it is a more difficult thing to repeat the names of the kings of England."

"I can do it from William the Conqueror," replied Paul.

"That is quite enough for any one to do," added the instructor, who saw that his pupils were getting tired of the subject, and found it necessary to change his tactics. "What was the first line of kings, Mr. Goodwin?"

"The Saxon."

"What next, Mr. Ward?"

"The Danes, who came in between the Saxons."

"What followed, Mr. Pelham?"

"The Norman."

"And then, Lynch?"

"The Stuart family."

"Not yet. Baxter?"

"Plantagenet family."

"Right; it had two branches. Which came into power first, Mr. Lavender?"

"Lancaster."

"Then, Caldwell?"

"York."

"Who was the last king of the house of York, Mr. Josselyn?"

"Richard III."

"How did he lose his crown, Mr. Robinson?"

"Killed in the battle of Bosworth."

"What house came then, Hyde?"

"Tudor."

"Who was the first king, Baker?"

"Henry VII."

"Why do we have no further mention of York and Lancaster, Lamb?"

"The two houses were united by the marriage of the king with the daughter of Edward IV."

"Who was the last of the Tudors, Mr. Ellis?"

"Elizabeth."

"What house then, Brown?"

"Stuart."

"Last of that line, Boyden?"

"Anne."

"What then, Johnson?"

"Hanover."

"Why so called, Captain Haven?"

"Parliament, at the desire of William III., entailed

the succession upon Sophia, wife of the Elector of Hanover. George I., her son, was the Elector of Hanover when called to the throne. It is sometimes called the house of Brunswick, because the Elector was also Duke of Brunswick."

"To what house does Victoria belong, Mr. Martyn?"

"Hanover, or Brunswick."

"These different houses of course are all connected by blood," added the professor. "Now, young gentlemen, what is the government of England?"

"Limited monarchy," shouted twenty of them.

"Who will be the next king?"

"Albert Edward, now Prince of Wales."

"He will reign as Edward VII. If he should die before his mother, who would succeed her?"

"His Royal Highness Alfred-Ernest-Albert," replied an officer who had been studying an English almanac, in which the names of the royal family were given in full.

"No, sir!" interposed Terrill. "Albert Victor, the baby."

"You mean the son of the Prince of Wales," said the professor.

"Yes, sir; the son comes before the daughters, and the daughters before the brothers of the prince."

"You said the government of England was a limited monarchy. Who limits it? What is it limited by?" asked Mr. Mapps.

"Limited by the people, who have, for hundreds of years, been taking away from the king some of his powers," replied Terrill. "They compelled the sovereign to give them their rights."

"Limited by what?"

"By the constitution," answered several.

"We have the constitution of the United States in our library. Is the British constitution there?"

"I never saw it," said a student, after a long silence.

"Then probably it is not there," laughed Mr. Mapps. "The British constitution is not a written document, like that of the United States. It is very much like the common law, which consists of certain well-established principles, rather than a written code. In a court of justice it is sometimes difficult to determine exactly what the law is. The legal gentlemen cite the decisions made by judges which have a bearing on the case. The British constitution is scattered through the history of the country, recorded in the legal decisions of the high courts, or existing in the established customs of the realm. For example, Charles I. claimed the right to tax his subjects to procure ships for his service, whenever he should think proper to do so. The people resisted the imposition, John Hampden foremost, and though not immediately successful, this and other arbitrary acts of the king finally cost him his life, and the principle was established that the sovereign could not tax the people without their consent. If Queen Victoria wants money of the people, Parliament, consisting of their representatives, must vote it. Who elect members of Parliament?"

"The people."

"All of them?"

"Everybody can't vote, as in the United States."

"The privilege of voting has been frequently extended, and the basis of representation equalized; but it does not even yet come up to the American idea of universal suffrage. In England there have always been at least two political parties — the Tories or conservatives, who represent old ideas, favor existing forms, and the privileges of the crown and the nobility; and the Whig, Liberal, or Radical party, which has favored progress, enlarged suffrage, and generally the rights of the people as distinguished from the nobility. Sometimes one of these parties, and sometimes the other, is in power; that is, it has a majority in the House of Commons, whose members are elected by the people. The sovereign is not supposed to belong to either party. If the party in power should be defeated on an important measure in Parliament, the cabinet, whose members carry on the government in the name of the king, and who are his advisers, are generally compelled to resign their offices. The king then calls in some powerful and influential statesman of the opposite party, and requests him to form a new government. Of course all these things are 'cut and dried' beforehand, and the premier, or prime minister, hands in a new list of ' Her Majesty's Chief Officers of State,' and they are duly installed in their positions. Fifteen of these officers are her majesty's advisers, and form the cabinet. The premier is First Lord of the Treasury, and the other principal officers are the Lord High Chancellor, who is 'keeper of the king's conscience,' and nominally at the head of the Judiciary; of the Chancellor of the Exchequer, who has charge of the finances of the country; the Lord President of the Council, the Lord Privy Seal, five Secretaries of State, and others.

"The dominant party is now in power, having a majority in the House of Commons, and being represented by the government. The cabinet officers are required to hold seats in one of the houses of Parliament, and the party is in condition to carry forward its measures, until the ministers are overwhelmed by a bad defeat, when they will be compelled to retire.

"The three estates of the realm are the lords spiritual, the lords temporal, and the commons, the first two forming the House of Lords. The lords spiritual are the archbishops of Canterbury and York, twenty-four English and four Irish bishops. It is now generally understood, I think, that the bishops hold their position in the Lords as territorial barons, rather than as ecclesiastics. Besides being a legislative body, the House of Lords is the highest court of justice in the realm, to which an appeal is had from other courts in certain cases; that is, it may sit as a court, or as a law-making power.

"The lords temporal are dukes, marquises, earls, viscounts, and barons, their rank being in the order mentioned. They are privileged persons, being entitled by birth or patent to a seat in the House of Lords, and to a trial by their peers, or persons of noble birth, if charged with treason or felony, and are exempt from arrest in civil cases."

"What is a lord?" asked one of the students. "You mentioned only dukes, marquises, earls, viscounts, and barons."

"Lord is a title applied to an earl, and to certain other persons by courtesy. For example, the eldest son of the Duke of Northumberland takes his second title, Earl Percy, or Lord Percy; the earl's son is a viscount; and the sons of a viscount are called 'Honorable.' The duke's younger sons are 'Lords' by courtesy, but they may have no legal right to the title."

"What is a baronet?" asked another student. "Is it the same as a baron?"

"No; a baron is a peer of the lowest grade in the House of Lords, while a baronet is a commoner, and has the lowest hereditary rank. A knight is an honorary distinction conferred by the sovereign. Knights and baronets are addressed as 'Sir.' Certain judges are called barons in virtue of their office.

"One word more, about the church of England, and I shall have finished. The church and state go together, the former being incorporated with the latter, and the sovereign being the head of both. The kingdom is divided, for church purposes, into two provinces, Canterbury and York, each of which is presided over by an archbishop, who has the general supervision of all the dioceses with it. A diocese is composed of all the churches in the care of a bishop, and the bishop's church is a cathedral, to which there are also attached a dean and chapter, by whom the bishop is nominally elected. The dean is a kind of assistant to the head of the diocese. Each of the two archbishops has a cathedral, and performs the duties of a bishop. The Archbishop of Canterbury is Primate of all England, and crowns the sovereign in virtue of his office. His revenues, derived mostly from lands, amount to fifteen thousand pounds a year. The Archbishop of York has ten thousand. The Bishop of

London also has ten thousand pounds a year, which is double the salary of the President of the United States. All the other bishops have from four to eight thousand pounds a year, while some of the clergymen have but fifty pounds, though the average is about two hundred and eighty pounds. The right to appoint the parish clergyman, called a benefice or 'living,' often rests with the nobility, who give them to their friends.

"I will not detain you longer, young gentlemen, though there are many other topics which need attention."

The professor retired, and the students were dismissed.

CHAPTER V.

A GLANCE AT LIVERPOOL.

WHEN the lecture was finished, Mr. Lowington invited Paul to his state-room for a further conference on business affairs.

"Captain Kendall," said he, "one matter has been overlooked in the appointment of your officers. You have no purser."

"I did not suppose I needed any," replied the young commander.

"When you give your crew liberty, they will want a little money, and it will not always be convenient to pipe them on board the ship to supply this need. I cannot now appoint a purser for you without deranging all the offices. You will therefore require your third and fourth masters to keep your accounts and pay the allowances. This must be done under your personal supervision, and you will approve each order before it is paid, precisely as I have done."

"But am I to keep the money on board the Josephine?" asked Paul.

"Certainly; a vessel should never be without the means of paying her way. When you go on your cruise, your steward must buy fresh provisions, if you go into port; you must pay the pilots, and you might need repairs. In your state-room, under your berth, doubtless you found an iron chest, like a safe. Here is the key of it."

Paul took the key, and felt that his responsibilities were increasing.

"I shall give you one hundred and fifty pounds, one hundred in gold, and the rest in small silver, suitable for paying the allowances. Dr. Winstock and Mr. Mapps will go on board with you, and you can make your arrangements immediately for the parties who are to go on shore."

"How much shall I pay the students for this afternoon?" asked Paul, after he had received the money.

"Two shillings each," replied Mr. Lowington.

They went on deck, and the officers and crew of the Josephine returned to the vessel, accompanied by Mr. Mapps and Dr. Winstock. The boats were made fast to the swinging boom, as the ship's company were so soon to go on shore in them. Paul and the surgeon had freely discussed the liberty question, and though the doctor had some grave doubts, the young captain decided to try the experiment of giving the students entire freedom on shore. He believed that the surest road to a boy's confidence is to trust him until he has proved himself unworthy to be trusted. All hands were piped to muster, and Paul explained the programme for the afternoon. He begged of them to behave like gentlemen, to refrain from drinking ale or any other strong beverages, and to be at the landing-place precisely at six o'clock.

The students were astonished at the degree of freedom granted, and when Captain Kendall finished his speech, three hearty cheers were given. Paul then announced that two shillings would be paid to each student, and they were required to march through the cabin and present their orders. As soon as they were dismissed, they went to the steerage, wrote their orders, and by this time the third and fourth masters were prepared to pay them. Captain Kendall sat at one table, and, with becoming gravity and dignity, affixed his initials to each paper as it was presented to him. The acting pursers paid the order, indorsed it on the receipt which Mr. Lowington had given to each boy, handed in with the order. The business proceeded as regularly as on board the ship, and the students passed up the companion-way to the deck, as soon as they received their allowance.

Strange as it may seem, there was no grumbling at the smallness of the amount. The boys all appeared to be in excellent humor, and to appreciate the privileges which had been granted to them. It was understood that, so far as liberty was concerned, they were faring better than their companions on board of the ship. The Josephine was intended for an experiment in self-government, and if any of her crew could not take care of themselves, could not be trusted, they were to go back to the Young America, where the strict supervision to which they had been accustomed was still retained, and where the boys were not to be permitted to go ashore without some one to take charge of them.

"I don't exactly understand this business," said Lynch to his friend Grossbeck, as they walked forward.

"What don't you understand?" asked the other.

"We are to go on shore, as the nobs themselves do, with no one to watch us."

"That's so; but I shouldn't wonder if it was a trap."

"A trap!" exclaimed Lynch.

"Don't you suppose Lowington wants to get all the chaplain's lambs into this vessel?" inquired Grossbeck.

"If he did, why didn't he send them on board?"

"Because it wouldn't look fair; but I can tell you this: if a fellow drinks a little beer, or overstays his time, you will find he will get his walking ticket."

"Then we had better keep our eyes wide open. The fellows say the captain has no orders from the principal, but does everything just as he pleases."

"I don't know anything about that, but I do know we are having plenty of liberty here, and, for one, I don't want to be sent back to the ship."

"I'm rather sorry we made that half sovereign apiece last night."

"Why?"

"I'm afraid it will come out. I'm going to leave mine on board — hide it somewhere."

"What for?"

"Then I shall not be tempted to spend it, and get into a scrape," replied the prudent Lynch, who was going to be good for the loaves and fishes, rather than because it was right to be good.

Grossbeck concluded to be equally cautious. They went below; they concealed the gold in the sole of one of their sea boots, which had begun to rip open.

"What about McLeish?" asked Lynch, after they had disposed of their ill-gotten gain.

"Nothing at all," replied Grossbeck. "Let him stay where he is."

"He will blow on us if we don't do something for him."

"What can we do?" asked Grossbeck.

"If we could contrive some way to get him off, it would be a good thing for all hands, and get us out of the scrape."

"I don't see any way to get him off."

"We can take him out of the brig any time we like. When will our anchor watch come round again."

Grossbeck made a calculation, and found their turn would come on Monday morning, from two till four.

"Then we can bargain with some shore boat to come alongside and take him off at three o'clock, say," added Lynch.

"But the officer will not let a boat come alongside."

"We can manage it somehow."

"Who will pay the boatman?"

"McLeish, of course."

"I don't know about it."

"I tell you we must get rid of McLeish, for our own sake. He will blow on us — tell the captain that we let him out, and took his money. I tell you we are in a bad scrape. McLeish is a mean pup, and he would betray his best friend."

"I'll leave it to you, Lynch; it is your affair, not mine; but I will help."

Lynch went below, and wrote on a piece of paper the question, "Will you pay one pound to the boatman that takes you off?" McLeish was standing at the grated door of the brig, and the writer slyly handed the paper to him. In a moment it was returned with an affirmative answer written upon it. The boatswain's pipe to dinner prevented him from saying anything more to Grossbeck. Having done a little wrong in meddling with the prisoner, he felt compelled to do more in order to save himself from the consequence; a frequent experience with the evil-doer, which ought to convince the tempted that the first step in error is the most dangerous one.

After dinner, the boats were manned, and with Gage the carpenter, and Cleats the boatswain, who were to act as boat-keepers, the ship's company embarked. The Mersey, between Liverpool and Birkenhead, is about a mile in width, and being open to the sea, the water is frequently quite rough. The ship and her consort were moored above Birkenhead, where they were partially sheltered. There are no wharves along the river, as in New York or Boston, and all ships taking in or discharging cargo go into the docks. The highest tides in the Mersey rise thirty-three feet, and the lowest twenty, so that, if the shores of the river were less exposed to the violence of the sea, it would not be practicable for vessels to lie at wharves.

The boats pulled for the George's Landing Stage, which is the starting-place for no less than seven ferries running to Birkenhead. The stage is a floating structure, like an American ferry-drop, rising and falling with the tide. It is, in fact, an immense box, made water-tight, and resting level on the water. It is reached by a kind of bridge, the descent of which at low tide is quite steep. This and two other stages like it, are the only convenient landing-places in front of the city.

Most of the ocean steamers plying between England and the United States have Liverpool for their eastern terminus. While in port these ships lie in the docks; but when ready to sail they are anchored in the river, and the passengers are taken off to them in tugs from the George's Landing Stage. On their arrival also, they moor in the stream, and their passengers are landed by the same means. Though the docks are the pride of Liverpool, New York is certainly more convenient for the landing of passengers.

The Josephine's boats, after a rough pull of a mile and a half, reached the Landing Stage, where they were soon joined by those of the Young America. The crew of the latter had been divided into parties, and each was in charge of one of the faculty; but the officers were permitted to go where they pleased, without any supervision. The boats were carefully secured between the Landing Stage and the shore, and left in charge of the adult forward officers. In a few moments the students had scattered in every direction.

Captain Kendall and the doctor walked off together, as by mutual consent, for they were much attached to each other, and were in company whenever their respective duties permitted. Paul, for the time, laid aside his cares and responsibilities. He was a keen observer, and was anxious to obtain information. The surgeon had been a great traveller, and was competent to explain the wonders of most of the European cities.

"Well, Paul, where are you going?" asked the doctor.

"I don't know, sir. I want to see the city," replied the captain.

"There is not much to see except the docks, and these are on both sides of us. Here is George's Dock in front of us."

"It doesn't seem to be anything but a wharf," added Paul, who had heard so much of the Liverpool docks that he had expected to see something wonderful.

"It is not a wharf. You perceive that it is surrounded by warehouses, and the tide does not rise and fall within the enclosure. A dock is an immense excavation or walled space, with gates, like those opening to the locks of a canal, through which ships are admitted. The gates are opened, of course, only at high tide. Those gates, you see, swing into the dock, and all of them are constructed on the same principle. Now, Paul, you are a philosopher: can you tell me why they never swing the gates outward?" asked Dr. Winstock, laughing.

"That's a plain case, I think," answered the student. "If they swung outward, the pressure of the water would open them when the tide goes down on the outside."

"Just so; and as soon as the water in the river goes down, the pressure of that in the dock keeps the gates shut."

"But a vessel can leave the port only at high tide."

"She can come out of the dock only at high tide."

"Do the coast steamers which run to Dublin, Cork, Belfast, and Bristol go into these docks?"

"Not into the closed ones. There are two kinds of docks, wet and dry, the latter being used only for repairing ships. And there are two kinds of wet docks, those with gates and those without, the latter being generally called basins. Half a mile below here is Clarence Basin, often called a dock, from which most of the coast steamers arrive and depart," said the doctor, as they crossed the bridge over the opening of the dock.

"Hallo!" exclaimed Paul. "This looks natural."

"What?"

"Why, here is a horse railroad."

"Yes, and that, I think, is the only one you will find in the United Kingdom. It runs along the docks, but is not permitted to extend up into the streets."

"These benighted Britishers are a hundred years behind the times. Of course they know what horse railroads are, for here is one."

"They are prejudiced against them. A tram-way, as they call it, was laid down in London, but it was deemed so great an innovation that it was removed. If you please, we will take a cab and ride down to the Canada and Huskisson Docks, which are the largest in the city. The latter has just been completed. Here is a Hansom!"

"A what?" asked Paul.

"A Hansom cab; I forgot that you had never been here. These vehicles are very convenient, and cheap, judged by our American standard of prices."

The doctor beckoned to the driver of the Hansom, which is peculiarly an English institution. The body of the vehicle is something like an American two-wheeled chaise, the bottom of which rests within about a foot of the pavement, so that the passenger takes but a single step to get into it. The driver is perched in a little seat attached to the back part of the top, the reins passing from the horse over the covering. A couple of wooden doors, curved to accommodate the legs of the occupants, close over him like a boot, and a glass partition can be shut to meet it, so as to protect them from the weather. We have seen one of these vehicles in New York.

Paul followed the doctor into the Hansom, which is named after its inventor, and when it started he was disturbed by an unpleasant apprehension that the thing would tip up, and throw the horse over his head; but no such calamity occurred, and after a drive of two miles, the passengers were landed on the bridge between the Canada and Huskisson Docks. The familiar steamers of the Cunard line, which Paul had seen in Boston and New York, were lying here.

"This is the Huskisson Dock," said Dr. Winstock, pointing to the left of the bridge. "It was built to accommodate these large ocean steamers. It has a water area of fourteen acres, and about two thirds of a mile of quay on its sides. Its widest entrance is eighty feet. No fires are allowed on board of any vessels in the docks, and ships are obliged to board their men on shore while they are in port. This is to prevent the danger of a fire among the ships and warehouses."

The aggregate area of the wet docks of Liverpool is one hundred and seventy-four acres, surrounded by fourteen miles of quays. Nearly all these docks open from basins, in which the tide rises and falls as in the river.

Liverpool is of modern growth and importance, for two hundred years ago only fifteen ships belonged to the port. It was once largely engaged in the African slave trade, and one hundred years ago more than half this trade was carried on by Liverpool merchants. It has now an immense trade in cotton and cotton goods, the great bulk of the raw material being received at this port, from which also the greater portion of the manufactured goods are exported to all parts of the world. Nearly one third of its tonnage is employed in the trade with the United States.

"Now, Paul, if you have seen enough of the docks, we will ride up into the city," continued the doctor, after they had walked by the fort, whose frowning batteries command the river, to the gates of the Canada Dock.

"I would like to get an idea of the city," replied Paul.

"Drive through Great Howard Street to the Exchange," added the surgeon, as he seated himself in the Hansom.

"Do you know the streets, doctor?" asked Paul.

"Certainly; I have spent two or three weeks in Liverpool at different times while waiting for steamers."

"I shouldn't think you could remember them, you have been to so many places."

"You have been to a dozen different cities in Europe; don't you remember the names of the streets?"

"But you have been to a hundred or more."

"That makes no difference; the mind has its picture of each one distinctly drawn. This street runs parallel with the river. Next beyond it is Vauxhall

Road, and beyond that Scotland Road. In the centre of the city the streets run in all directions, and it would bother a Philadelphian, accustomed to straight streets, and a square plan, to find his way. Most of the streets diverge from the square on which are situated the Lime Street railway station, where you may take the train for London, St. George's Hall, St. John's Church, and the Washington Hotel, where I always stay when here, because I like its name, as well as because it is a good house. From this point Renshaw Street runs to the north-east; Whitechapel and Paradise Streets to the east; Dale Street to the south: Scotland Road to the west, and London Road to the north. It is not easy to find your way about Liverpool."

"It looks like the meanest part of New York or Boston here."

"You are in a dirty part of the city now. Liverpool is more like an American city than any other European town I know of—like Boston in the irregularity of its streets. There, it is said, the streets follow the paths made by Mr. Blackstone's cows; and Liverpool may have been laid out on the same plan."

The Hansom soon left its passengers at the Exchange, and the vehicle was dismissed, the travellers preferring to walk for a time. They passed through the building, which is very much like similar edifices, though it is on a very extensive plan, forming three sides of a square around the Town Hall. The open space between the two buildings contains a statue of Nelson, and it is occupied by those busy men who throng Wall and State Streets in the busy hour of the day. The Town Hall is a handsome building surmounted by a dome, on which rests a statue of Britannia.

"Why don't they call this the City Hall, as we do in America?" asked Paul, as they entered the building.

"It is not the custom, I suppose; but the term city has not always been used in England as in our country. It was applied to a place in which the bishop's cathedral was located, and from which the diocese derived its name. Chester was a city, because it was the residence of the bishop; while Liverpool was not a city, because it had no bishop. In theory, the distinction holds good to the present time, I suppose; if so, this is a town hall, and not a city hall."

"It's a queer town hall," added Paul, as they ascended the broad staircase adorned with pictures. "It looks more like a dwelling-house than a place where the public business is transacted."

"You will find it is intended for other purposes than mere business affairs," added the doctor, as he engaged an attendant to show the rooms.

They were conducted through a saloon, two drawing-rooms, two ball-rooms, a banqueting-room, and a refectory, all of them fitted up and furnished in the most elegant and costly manner.

"I think the Lord Mayor has a good time here," said Paul when the attendant had been dismissed.

"He holds receptions, gives dinners, and has an occasional ball in these rooms. He is obliged to do these things to maintain the dignity of his position, and to do credit to the hospitality of the city. But, Paul, you must not call him Lord Mayor. He is simply a mayor, and is addressed as his 'worship,'" replied Dr. Winstock.

"I thought the mayors of all the large cities were lords. The mayor of Dublin was certainly called Lord Mayor."

"That is very true. The chief municipal officer of London and Dublin are Lord Mayors by special royal grant, but the mayors of York and Edinburgh also have this prefix. No other city is entitled to this distinction. There are a great many little things to learn," continued the doctor, as they walked through Castle Street to the Custom House.

"I know there are. One cannot pass through the streets without being perplexed with something he does not understand. There's a sign, 'Wine and Spirit Vault.'"

"That's merely a rum-shop. The keeper is licensed to sell liquor, and he makes a great spread. In London and other cities there are immense wine and ale vaults, containing millions of pounds' worth of beer or spirits. These men ape the large establishments, and call their cellars 'vaults.' Very likely some of them are entitled to the name."

"Just now I saw the sign, 'J. Grubbie, Hatter to H. R. H. the Prince of Wales.' I have seen a dozen such signs in Dublin, Edinburgh, and Glasgow."

"That is another weakness for high-sounding names. It is possible J. Grubbie made a hat for H. R. H.; but it is more probably that J. G. had some friend, who had another friend, whose intimate friend was a valet, of H. R. H.; and when H. R. H. was in particularly good humor, he was asked to write a line for J. Grubbie, hatter; but in that case, Grubbie would probably put on his sign, 'By special Appointment, Hatter to H. R. H.' If the Prince of Wales happens to want a pair of boots while in Liverpool, the lucky tradesman who has the good fortune to sell him a pair, immediately has a new sign, and announces to the public that he is bootmaker to H. R. H. Of course it is all a humbug, and when I wish to purchase anything, I avoid these signs, which are as thick as snow-flakes at Christmas in all the principal cities in the kingdom. Here is the Custom House. It is a magnificent building, both in size and in its architectural proportions."

A glance at the exterior was enough to satisfy Paul, and they walked up to St. George's Hall, passing St. John's Church, an ancient structure, the slope of the hill by the side of it being a cemetery in which there is a multitude of antiquated tombstones, and slabs lying flat on the ground. St. George's Hall is the finest public building in Liverpool. Its architecture is Corinthian, with columns forty-five feet high. It contains two large rooms used for the Assizes Court, and a great hall, one hundred and sixty-one feet long by seventy-five in width, and the same in height, in which concerts and public meetings are held. It cost nearly two hundred thousand pounds.

A ride in the omnibus to the Necropolis, a noted cemetery, and the Zoölogical Gardens, which are justly celebrated, completed the excursion for the day, and before six o'clock Paul reached the Landing Stage, having seen all he cared to see of Liverpool, though to one who had not all Europe before him, there was enough of sight-seeing to keep him busy for a week.

"You have an idea of the place, Paul — that's all," said Dr. Winstock, as they walked down the bridge to the Stage. "It is a very enterprising and liberal city, abounding in charitable and reformatory institutions. On the whole, it is the liveliest city in the United Kingdom.

"That's because it is so much in contact with the United States," laughed Paul, as he took from his pocket the "Mercury" which he had bought in the street. "What queer expressions they use here! 'Left-off clothing,' instead of old clothes, or second-hand clothes."

"Our expressions are as odd to them as theirs are to us," replied the doctor.

"To be sold 'by private treaty,'" added Paul, glancing at the advertisements, "instead of private sale. 'Wanted, — a lady to teach *good* music.' Of course they wouldn't want her to teach bad music; 'a shopkeeper, doing a ready-money trade,' instead of a cash business. 'To publicans' — those are men that keep ale-vaults. 'Wanted, — a servant of all work; wages £10' — less than a dollar a week. 'A certificated school-teacher, aged 31, declining school keeping, wants a situation as clerk.' 'Wanted — a situation to look after a horse and carriage.' Hope he'll find them when he has found the situation."

"Paul, there are a couple of your hopefuls on the other side of the Stage," said the doctor. "I was afraid they would give you trouble, but they are on time."

The young commander looked, and saw Lynch and Grossbeck; but he did not know that they had just made a bargain with a boatman to go off to the Josephine at three o'clock on Monday morning. Within a few minutes of the appointed time, the boats of both vessels left the Stage.

CHAPTER VI.

BLUE LIGHTS ON THE MERSEY.

SO far as Captain Kendall could judge after his ship's company were all on board, not one of them had abused his liberty. All of them had been at the Landing Stage within a few moments of the appointed time; and though there was no " smelling committee" appointed to investigate the matter, the fumes of beer or other interdicted beverages were not noticed even in the presence of those who were known to have no conscientious scruples in regard to the use of intoxicating drinks. The experiment appeared to be entirely satisfactory. Paul and the doctor had seen some of the crew in various parts of the city, but they were conducting themselves with perfect propriety.

Dr. Winstock and Mr. Mapps accepted an invitation to tea on board the Josephine, and were afterwards sent on board of the ship in the captain's gig. The anchor watch was kept during the night, and the next day, being Sunday, all hands, when the signal appeared on the ship, attended divine service on board of her.

On Monday morning, Lynch and Grossbeck had the anchor watch according to their calculations; but the first master was officer of the deck, instead of the third lieutenant, the turns of the officers not corresponding with those of the crew. The conspirators were sorry for this change, as they knew the habits of Mr. Robinson, and had yet to learn those of Mr. Groom. If he should be disposed to visit the forecastle often, or not care to take his lunch, it would be difficult, if not impossible, to get McLeish out of the vessel.

Grossbeck had deposited the carpenter's screw-driver in a place where it would be available for use, and before his watch was called, had released the prisoner and restored the lock to the door. Everything therefore was in a forward state of preparation for the carrying out of their plan. McLeish was in Lynch's berth when the watch was called.

"Do you suppose your boatman will come?" asked Grossbeck, when they had seated themselves on the heel of the bowsprit.

"Of course he will. It isn't every night that he gets a chance to make a sovereign, which is about the wages of a whole week to one of those fellows. He will be here, you may depend upon it," replied Lynch, confidently.

"I wish we were well out of the scrape. I'm afraid we shall be caught."

"I know there is danger, but I think it is safer for us to get him out of the vessel than to let him stay."

"Suppose we should be caught?"

"Then we must make the best of it, and go back to the ship when we are sent," replied Lynch.

"I don't like that idea. Saturday afternoon we went ashore without any one to watch us. All the fellows in the ship, except the officers, have a professor to take care of them. I don't want to leave the Josephine."

"Nor I; but we must take our chance now," added Lynch. "If I had known as much as I know now, I wouldn't have had anything to do with McLeish. If we don't get him off he will ruin us. We must run for luck now."

The first master paced the quarter-deck, walked forward to the waist occasionally, and finally went below, probably to take his lunch. The signal was given for McLeish to come on deck, and he immediately made his appearance. Before Groom returned, he had been stowed away in the head, ready to embark in the boat as soon as it came alongside. The night was dark enough to favor the enterprise, and the officer of the deck, though vigilant enough for all practical purposes, did not appear to trouble himself with affairs forward of the foremast. At five bells he made his round through the steerage.

It is sometimes the case that those who make the least fuss and parade about doing their duty, perform it the most thoroughly; and those who appear to have the least knowledge of what is "going on," have the most. Groom was a very quiet and unpretending officer, but he understood his duty thoroughly, and performed it faithfully. Instead of walking round the steerage, in the semi-darkness of the place, as most of the officers did, he took the lantern from the hook near the fore-hatch, and glanced into every berth to assure himself that its occupant was there.

When he came to the brig, he held the lantern up to the grated door, and looked in. He did not see the prisoner, for the simple reason that he was not there. He placed himself in such a position that he could observe the berth-sack on the floor, where McLeish ought to have been asleep; but he was not on his bed. Groom was astonished rather than alarmed, and he went to the captain's state-room, where the key was always kept, to obtain it."

"What's the matter, Mr. Groom?" asked Paul, as the master entered his room.

"I don't know that anything is the matter," replied the officer of the watch, "but I would like the key of the brig. I have looked in through the door, and I don't see anything of McLeish."

"Has he got out?" asked the captain, starting up in his bed.

"I don't know that he has: I want to ascertain."

Paul gave him the key, and anxiously awaited his report. Groom returned to the brig, unlocked it, and went in. The prison was certainly empty; but he had found the door locked, and no opening by which he could have escaped was visible. He returned to the captain's state-room, and informed Paul of the result of his investigation.

"Escaped — has he?" demanded Paul, filled with anxiety at this unfortunate circumstance.

"He certainly is not in the brig," replied Groom. "Whether he has left the schooner or not, I don't know."

"He was safe at eight o'clock, when the steward put his berth-sack in the brig," added the perplexed captain. "How did he get out?"

"That is more than I can tell. The door was

locked all right, and there is no hole or opening by which he could have crawled out," answered Groom.

"And the key has not been out of my room since the steward returned it to me. Call Martyn, Robinson, and Humphreys."

The three officers who had been in charge of the deck since eight o'clock were called to the captain's state-room, and questioned. They knew nothing of the prisoner, and each of them was sure that no boat had left the schooner during his watch.

"Who are in the watch now?" asked Paul.

"Lynch and Grossbeck," replied the first master.

"If McLeish has left the vessel, we can do nothing till morning. Keep a sharp lookout, Mr. Groom, and if anything occurs, call me," said Paul, as he dismissed all the officers.

But the captain did not go to sleep again that night. He was anxious and disturbed. He did not believe that McLeish had left the Josephine, and he did not wish to muster all hands at that hour; but he intended, in the morning, to make a thorough search in every part of the vessel, for he had come to the conclusion that the prisoner was secreted in some convenient place, where he could leave during the day. The officer of the watch returned to the deck. He had been absent about twenty minutes, and the time for the appearance of the boat was near at hand.

Groom paced the deck athwartships. He heard the dip of a pair of sculls ahead. He appeared to take no notice of the circumstance, but in his own mind he connected it with the escape of McLeish. As soon as he had satisfied himself that the boat was approaching the schooner, he went below and informed the captain.

"A boat appears to be coming to the schooner, but I don't know that it is," he added to his report, in explanation.

"Return to the deck, Mr. Groom: let things take their course; and remember that it is quite as important to ascertain who helped McLeish, as it is to prevent the prisoner's escape."

When Groom had gone on deck, Paul called the first lieutenant, who was directed quietly to wake the crew of the first cutter, and have them ready for immediate service, all of which was done before six bells struck. The officer of the deck, without seeming to notice anything, kept his eyes and his ears wide open.

By this time, Lynch and Grossbeck were congratulating themselves upon the success of their enterprise. The officer of the watch was very accommodating in spending so much of his time below, for on the topgallant forecastle they obtained no hint of what was taking place in the cabin and steerage. They saw the boat, which had pulled to a position ahead of the Josephine, and was now drifting with the tide towards her.

"Now, McLeish, you are all right," said Lynch, as he discovered the boat in the gloom of the night.

"Ay, that I am," replied the culprit, jubilantly. "If ye hear any one inquiring for me in the morning, give them my regards, and say I'll see them in the autumn."

"Don't make a fool of yourself, when you get into

the boat. Lie down in the bottom, and keep still," added Grossbeck.

"I'll just shout for joy, when I'm clear of the vessel."

"If you do, you will certainly be brought back," said Lynch.

"No fear of that if I once get into the boat."

"Hush! here comes the officer," whispered Grossbeck, as Groom walked forward.

"What boat is that?" asked the officer, halting on the forecastle.

"I don't know, sir," replied Grossbeck.

"Boat ahoy!" shouted Lynch, who had instructed the boatman what to say when he hailed him, as he intended to do if his approach was observed by the officer of the watch.

"On board the schooner," replied the boatman.

"What do you want?" demanded Lynch.

"Did you happen to see a boat adrift any time within the night?" asked the man.

"We have not."

"Our long-boat broke adrift, and I'm looking for her. I didn't know but you might have picked her up."

"We haven't seen her," answered Lynch.

All this seemed so natural, that Groom, though on the lookout for something wrong, did not suspect anything. The boatman had run under the bowsprit of the Josephine, and was holding on at the bobstay. He then explained that he belonged to a ship lying above, and was keeping anchor watch. He had missed the boat, and was looking it up. Groom was satisfied, and walked aft again.

"Now drop down into the boat, McLeish, and keep still," whispered Lynch.

"Wait a minute," interposed the boatman. "If you happen to have the sovereign about you, I'll take that first."

McLeish had transferred the balance of his funds from his stockings to his pocket. He produced the money, and handed it to the cautious boatman.

"Don't make a noise," said Lynch, and the culprit clumsily descended to the boat.

"It's little I care for the noise now," replied McLeish.

"But you will get us into a scrape," protested Grossbeck, in an energetic whisper.

"If I do, I just paid you for it; and it was mean of you to take a sovereign for halping a fallow in distrass."

"Lie down, McLeish!" called Lynch, as loud as he dared to speak.

"I'll no lie down," replied the mulish deserter. "Push off, boatman; I'm out of their clutches now: but I'd like to get my hand on the windpipe of that Terrill."

The boatman pushed off, and, taking his cue from his passenger, used no further precautions to conceal his movements. Before he could bring his oars to bear, the tide had set his boat away from the bow of the schooner, and it was drifting alongside of her. Groom heard the voices in her, and rushed to the railing. He saw that it contained two persons now.

"Boat ahoy!" he shouted.

"Shut your mouth, you sixpenny nob!" replied

McLeish, in tones so loud that Lynch and Grossbeck were appalled and terrified at the exposure.

Groom did not wait to hear any more, but rushing to the companion-way, he called for help.

"All the first cutter's crew on deck!" said Terrill, hastening to the steerage, where those who had been called were in readiness for the summons.

In an instant they tumbled up the hatch, and grasped the fall-ropes of their boat. Terrill appeared at the same time. It was now the turn of the conspirators on the forecastle to be astonished.

"Where's the boat, Mr. Groom?" demanded the first lieutenant.

"She went off towards Birkenhead," replied the officer of the watch.

"First cutter ready, sir!" reported the coxswain of the boat to the first lieutenant.

Terrill leaped into the stern-sheets of the cutter; the orders to shove off and let fall were rapidly given; the crew bent to their oars, and the boat disappeared in the gloom from the view of those on deck.

Captain Kendall came on deck before the departure of the first cutter, and immediately ordered Martyn to call all hands. In a brief period, every officer and seaman was on deck.

"Clear away the gig!" shouted the second lieutenant, by the captain's order.

Pelham was sent away in this boat, with directions to pull towards Birkenhead.

"Clear away the second and third cutters!" continued the captain. "Mr. Robinson, detail a crew for each boat."

It was not likely, after all these preparations for a pursuit, that McLeish would succeed in reaching the shore.

"It's all up with us!" said Lynch, in desponding tones, when Groom hailed his brother officers in the cabin.

"Perhaps not: they won't know we helped him off," replied Grossbeck.

"They can't help knowing it. Didn't McLeish get into the boat under our very noses? There are the first cutters. They must have been all ready. There's the captain! He hasn't had time to turn out since the alarm was given. I tell you some one has snuffed this business; and let us fall into the trap," added Lynch, desperately. "What shall we do?"

"What can we do? Of course we shall be reported to Lowington, and sent on board the ship."

"O, it's all up with us!" sighed Lynch. "Brig for a week or two, and all our privileges stopped! It makes me mad to think of it. McLeish is the biggest blockhead I ever heard of. It would have been all right if he had not been such an amazingly stupid fool!"

The chapfallen conspirators observed the preparations that were made for the capture of McLeish. The boatman could not have gone fifty yards before the first cutter was off; and if Terrill did not miss the boat in the darkness, the culprit was sure to be taken. The gig was the second sent off, and the second and third cutters lowered, and hauled up to the accommodation ladder, ready for use if needed.

"Can I do anything, sir?" asked Cleats, the boatswain, as he touched his cap to the captain.

"Nothing at present," replied Paul; "I only fear the gig and cutter will miss the boat, it is so dark."

"We can give them plenty of light, sir. We have some blue lights below," added Cleats.

"Bring them up and fire them at once," said Paul, delighted with the idea.

The boatswain brought up his blue fire, and placing the roll on a plank upon the rail, lighted it. The vessel and the river for a circuit of half a mile around her were brilliantly illuminated. It was three o'clock on the morning of the Fourth of July, and on board of an American vessel, manned by boys, the demonstration was not inappropriate.

The bright light revealed the position of all the boats, but the gig and cutter had both been steering wide of the chase until the blue fire disclosed it to them. The first cutter was the nearest, and a few strokes of the well-trained oarsmen brought her alongside the boatman's craft.

"Pull, man! Why don't you pull?" cried McLeish, when he saw the night turned into day, and the Josephine's cutter rapidly overhauling him.

"It's no use to pull," replied the boatman. "That boat can go two yards to my one."

"Then give me back my sovereign," retorted McLeish, angrily.

"When I do, tell your grandmother of it," answered the boatman in surly tones. "You are an idiot! If you had kept your mouth shut, as the lads told you, we had gone off clean."

"Pull, man! The boat is almost upon us!" exclaimed McLeish.

"I'm not going to break my back for an idiot," replied the man, who had the sovereign in his pocket, and did not care a straw what became of his passenger.

"I'll no be taken back," said McLeish, desperately, as he seized the boat-hook.

"Don't break that boat-hook," added the boatman, as the first cutter ranged up on the bow of his craft.

"Stand by me, man," pleaded the runaway, appalled by his situation. "Put me on the shore, and I'll give you another sovereign."

"I don't think I can," said the boatman, whose cupidity was excited by this liberal offer.

"McLeish, I'll trouble you to step into this boat," said Terrill.

"I'll not do it," replied the rebel, flatly, as he brandished the boat-hook over his head, and made sundry insane flourishes. "If you want me, come and take me."

"That I shall do," added Terrill, spunkily. "Pass the boat-hook aft," said he to the crew of the cutter.

At this moment Pelham in the gig dashed up to the battle-ground, and, unwilling to be behind the first lieutenant, he leaped forward to the bow of his boat, and then into that in which McLeish was just closing with Terrill. Seizing the culprit by the collar, he forced him down into the bottom of the boat. The rebel was effectually suppressed. The two officers tumbled him into the cutter, and both boats pulled for the schooner.

The blue fire had been kept burning till the gig and cutter returned to the Josephine. The recaptured prisoner, sullen and angry, was ordered on deck. He was too mad to obey the order, and a couple of officers dragged him on board. He was taken down to the brig again, and the door locked upon him once more.

"You may just put me in there if you please, but I'll no stay there," growled the prisoner, as the brig was opened for his reception.

"How did you get out?" asked Captain Kendall, probably not with the expectation that the question would be answered.

"It's just none of your business how I got out; but I'll be out again," replied McLeish.

"Lock him up," added Paul, who had decided not to investigate the matter till morning.

"I'll just burn your old hulk! I'll show you what it is to insult a MacGregor."

"Stop a moment," interposed Captain Kendall; "search his pockets."

"I'll kill the first one of you that comes near," said McLeish, retreating to the farthest corner of his cell, and thrusting his hand into his pocket for his knife.

Pelham, always prompt and decided in his action, rushed upon the culprit, who had taken the knife from his pocket, before he had time to open it. He wrested the weapon from him, and threw him down upon the berth-sack, where he held him until the first lieutenant had "fished all his pockets." There were no matches taken from him, but two sovereigns and two half sovereigns were found upon him. The knife and the money were taken, and everything else returned to him.

"You're a set of robbers!" exclaimed McLeish, when the officers let him up. "If I ever get ashore within the United Kingdom, I'll have you arrested for stealing my money."

"Lock him up," said the captain.

"You can just lock me up, but I'll get out in spite of you," howled the prisoner, crying like a baby, in the madness of his passion.

"Where is Mr. Gage?" asked Paul.

"Here, sir," replied the carpenter.

"Can you tell in what manner the door of the brig was opened?"

Gage examined the lock.

"I think these screws must have been removed, and the lock taken off," he replied. "It could not have been done by the fellow in the brig. He had some help on the outside."

"Very well; we will inquire into that in the morning. Can you make the door any more secure?"

"I can put on a heavy hasp and staple, and lock it with a padlock, such as we use for the bread-room in the hold. I have a spare one."

"Can you put it on without screws?" asked the captain.

"Yes — drive the staples in, and clinch them on the other side."

"You will do it at once, if you please," added Paul.

"I shall have to open the door."

"I'll take care of the prisoner," volunteered Cleats.

The carpenter went for the hasp and staples, and the job was commenced at once. As the captain turned to go on deck, the fourth master rushed down below, and informed him that the third cutter was missing. Paul was congratulating himself upon the success of the measures he had taken to capture the runaway, when this new misfortune was reported to him.

"What does this mean?" he asked of Terrill, when he reached the deck.

"More runaways, I am afraid," replied the first lieutenant.

"Pipe to muster," added the captain, sick at heart, as he thought of the danger which menaced the experiment with which he had been intrusted.

"All hands on deck, ahoy!" shouted the boatswain, after he had wound the shrill call.

"Mr. Ritchie, you will call the roll," said Paul, disconsolately.

The names of the officers were called, and then of the crew.

"Grossbeck!"

No answer.

"Grossbeck!"

Still no answer.

"I can tell who the other is," said Groom, the officer of the deck. "It is Lynch."

So it proved when the name was called. The two absentees had composed the anchor-watch at the time the boatman had come under the bows of the schooner, and it was plain that by their connivance McLeish had been assisted out of the brig, and then into the boat.

CHAPTER VII.

OFF THE CALF OF MAN.

IT was evident that Lynch and Grossbeck had left the schooner, not because they desired to get away, but in order to avoid the consequences of their misconduct in releasing the prisoner, and helping him to escape from the vessel. It was shown by the testimony of others that they were not dissatisfied with their position on board, but, on the contrary, had often expressed their appreciation of their good fortune in obtaining a berth on board of the Josephine.

Paul was in great trouble; but he ordered all the boats to be lowered again, detailed officers to go in them, and then went down into his state-room. Remembering what the other runaways had done before they left the ship, he opened his strong box to satisfy himself that it had not been robbed. Not a shilling had been taken from it, and he breathed easier. Locking the safe, he put the key in his pocket, and returned to the deck. It was now about daylight. Martyn was sent off in the gig, and Pelham in the first cutter, to search for the runaways.

The captain stepped into the stern-sheets of the second cutter, and ordered the coxswain to pull for the Young America, for he felt it to be his duty to report immediately the events which had occurred during the night. He found no one on deck but Mr. Bitts, the carpenter, for the anchor watch in port was always kept by the adult forward officers.

"Captain Kendall!" exclaimed the carpenter, when he saw who his early visitor was.

"I wish to see Mr. Lowington," said Paul.

"I think he is awake, sir, for I reported to him a while ago that you were burning blue lights on board the Josephine."

"What did he say?"

"He only laughed, and said you had begun early to celebrate the Fourth of July."

"We were not exactly celebrating the Fourth," replied Paul, rather gloomily, as he went below and entered the professors' cabin.

He knocked at the door of the principal's stateroom, and gave his name when asked for it. After waiting a few moments, Mr. Lowington invited him to come in.

"I hope nothing unpleasant has happened, Captain Kendall," said the principal, taking the hand of the young commander.

"I am sorry to say something very unfortunate has occurred," replied Paul, very much depressed in spirits.

"Don't be so sad about it, for whatever has happened, I am sure you have done your duty."

"Thank you for that, sir. I have lost two of my crew."

"Lost them!" exclaimed Mr. Lowington, alarmed by the equivocal phrase.

"I mean that they have run away, sir."

The principal was relieved. He feared they had been drowned.

"Who were they?"

"Lynch and Grossbeck."

"I should hardly expect anything better from such students. Did they get any of your money?"

"No, sir; that is all safe, and I have the key of the box in my pocket."

"You were celebrating the Fourth rather early in the morning — were you not?"

"No, sir."

"The carpenter reported that you were burning blue lights."

"That was for another purpose. Lynch and Grossbeck took the screws out of the lock on the brig, and let McLeish out. They must have engaged a boat to take him from the schooner when they were on shore Saturday; indeed, I saw Lynch talking with a boatman on the George's Landing Stage. The officer of the watch happened to discover that he was not in the brig. The prisoner got off, but we captured him again. We burned the blue fire so that the boats could find him."

"So you captured him again," added the principal, with a smile.

"Yes, sir, we did;" and Paul detailed all the circumstances of the departure and recovery of McLeish, and the desertion of Lynch and Grossbeck.

"That was very well done indeed, Captain Kendall. I thank you and your officers for the skill and promptness you have displayed. I am sorry you have lost the two seamen," said the principal.

"I feel very bad about it, sir; and I feel that I am to blame for it," added Paul.

"Am I to blame for losing three of the ship's company at Cork?" asked the principal, with a pleasant smile, which made Paul feel much better.

"I was so busy looking out for McLeish, that I did not think of those who had assisted him."

"I do not blame you, for you have been faithful, and that is enough. We all make mistakes, but if we mean right, we need not reproach ourselves. What have you done?"

"I have sent two boats to look for the runaways."

"Very well; I will send four more."

Mr. Lowington went to the after-cabin, and called the captain of the ship. In a short time the boatswain's call for all hands rang through the vessel, and the four boats were sent off to look for the runaways. Captain Kendall returned to the Josephine, relieved of some portion of his anxiety. Hardly had he stepped upon the deck before the gig was reported as approaching the schooner with the missing cutter in tow.

"Where did you find the boat?" asked the captain, as Pelham came up the side.

"I found it going up the river with the tide. But I saw nothing of Lynch and Grossbeck," replied the officer of the boat.

"Can they have fallen overboard?" said Paul, with emotion.

"Certainly not," answered Pelham, decidedly. "The boat was dry inside, and the oars lay on the thwarts in ship-shape order."

"And you have no idea what has become of the deserters?"

"I have an idea, but of course I don't know any thing about it," added Pelham.

"What is your idea?"

"Just before I found the boat, I saw an English brig standing down the river with a fair wind. In my opinion the deserters are on board of that vessel."

"Did you get the brig's name?"

"It was the Prince Alfred. She appeared to be in ballast."

Half an hour later, the first cutter returned, and Martyn reported that he had hailed a boatman, near the south-end Landing Stage, who informed him that he had seen two boys go on board of a brig, and turn their boat adrift. He had pulled for the boat in order to pick it up, but it had been secured by a six-oar cutter before he could reach it.

It was plain enough that the runaways had taken passage in the brig, and Paul went in the gig to the Young America to report the facts. The signal for the return of her boats was immediately hoisted, when the information had been communicated. Nothing more could be done, and Mr. Lowington said a great many kind words to comfort the young commander of the consort. The celebration of the day had already been commenced on board the ship, which was gayly dressed with flags, and Paul went on board the Josephine to put her in trim also.

After breakfast all hands were "piped to mischief," or, rather, to fun; and while the festivities of the occasion were still in progress, Paul was sent for by Mr. Lowington.

"Captain Kendall," said the principal, when the young commander had reported to him, "the boat has just come off with the mail. The steamer arrived at Queenstown yesterday afternoon, and will reach Liverpool before night. Our recruits are on board of her, and to-morrow your professors will join your vessel. There is a letter-bag made up for your ship's company. Mr. Fluxion went ashore in the boat, and upon inquiring at the custom-house, found that the brig Prince Alfred cleared in ballast for Belfast, to load for Quebec. If you and your crew are willing to dispense with the rest of the fun of the day, I propose that you follow the brig to Belfast, and reclaim your runaways."

Paul's heart leaped with delight at the prospect of taking the Josephine out upon the blue water, and he cordially agreed to the proposition.

"In order to keep your quarter watches full, — for you are short-handed now, — I shall draft seven more seamen into your vessel; for I find that instead of thirty students, about forty will arrive by the steamer. This will give you a crew of twenty-eight. Perhaps, before we leave Liverpool, I shall increase your crew to thirty-six, your full complement."

The ship's crew were piped to muster, and seven below the rank of petty officers were drawn by lot, and sent on board the Josephine. They were happy fellows, for it was fully understood in the Young America that the schooner's crew had extra privileges. Paul returned to his vessel with his crew.

Something was said by the principal about relieving the schooner of McLeish's presence; but it was finally decided that, as Wilton and Monroe still occupied the brig of the Young America, the reprobate should remain where he was; though Paul was reminded that it was his adult boatswain's duty to handle offenders, rather than his officers, even while it was conceded that the officers should enforce obedience.

"Mr. Terrill, you will get the schooner under way immediately," said Captain Kendall, as he stepped on the deck of the Josephine.

"Under way!" repeated the first lieutenant, in utter astonishment.

This was an unofficer-like reply, and Paul, without noticing it, went down to his state-room. But Terrill felt the reproof, and immediately gave the orders to hoist up the boats, and strip the vessel of the gay flags which adorned her. While he was doing so, Paul opened the mail-bag brought off by his gig, and found three letters for himself — two from home, and one from Belfast. He read the one from his mother first, and as the family were all well, he opened that from Ireland. He felt "queer," he knew not why, as he did so. The first three pages, after acknowledging the pleasure which the writer had derived from reading his letter from Greenock, contained an account of an archery match in the Botanical Gardens. On the fourth page, she informed him that she should start for London with her parents in the course of a week.

Paul was very fond of Grace Arbuckle; and since he had made her acquaintance in Belfast, he had thought a great deal more about her than he was willing to acknowledge even to himself. She was the prettiest and pleasantest young lady he had ever seen, and he prized her friendship very highly. He could not tell exactly how it was, but it afforded him very great pleasure to write to her, and a still greater pleasure to receive a letter from her. There was nothing sentimental in the correspondence, nothing "tender;" it was friendship — that was all — as they understood it.

He read this letter twice. The Josephine was bound for Belfast, and was getting ready for her departure at that moment. His bosom bounded with emotion as he thought of seeing Grace; of standing in her presence with the two anchors on his shoulder-straps, and the five gold bands on his sleeves. What a delight it would be to show her through the vessel! What a joy to stand upon the quarter-deck at her side, when she knew that he was the commander of the beautiful craft! As he was captain, he could give her a complimentary excursion. If she never before believed he was a great man, she would be convinced of the fact now.

Before he had read the third letter, which was from a former schoolmate, his rhapsody was disturbed by the call of the boatswain for all hands. Not a soul on board except himself knew that the Josephine was going to sea, for, in imitation of the principal of the Academy Ship, he determined to keep his own counsel, at least until the officers manifested some curiosity. The captain went on deck, and found the officers and crew at their stations. The first lieutenant had given the seven new seamen their places, and twenty-eight hands were now ready for duty.

The mainsail was hoisted, the foresail set, the stops on the jib and flying jib removed, and the anchor hove short.

"Anchor apeak, sir," reported the second lieutenant to Terrill.

"Wait a little while, Mr. Terrill," the captain interposed; for the pilot which Mr. Lowington had promised to send off, had not yet come on board.

Presently his canoe appeared, and he stepped on board. He was a burly, big man, over six feet high, and weighing "ten stone," as he said himself. He looked pleasant, and glanced about him, apparently amused at the juvenile aspect of everything on board.

"Where's the captain?" asked he, with a broad grin on his face, as he stepped up to Terrill, who received him at the gangway.

"There he is, sir," replied the first lieutenant, pointing to Paul.

"That!" exclaimed the pilot. "But I mean the captain of the vessel."

"I am the captain," said Paul, with becoming dignity.

"You!"

The pilot measured him from head to foot with his eye, and then burst into a violent fit of laughter.

"Is this the Josephine?" he asked, when he could speak again.

"This is the Josephine," answered Captain Kendall.

"But this can't be the vessel I'm to take to sea."

"Yes, it is, sir. Excuse me, but we are waiting your movements," added Paul, with spirit.

"My eyes!" ejaculated the pilot. "There are nothing but boys on board."

"The officers and crew are at their stations," added Paul. "If you are ready to unmoor ship, please to say so."

"I'm all ready, captain — my eyes! Am I to take this schooner to sea with these boys?"

"Certainly you are. Mr. Terrill, you will proceed to unmoor ship," said the captain.

"Man the capstan bars, ship and swifter them! Heave round!" shouted Terrill.

"Bless me! he talks salt enough," said the pilot, laughing till his fat sides jarred like a barrel of jelly.

"Anchor aweigh, sir," reported the boatswain on the forecastle; and the word was passed through the line of officers till it came to the first lieutenant.

"Man the jib and flying-jib halyards," added Terrill.

"Anchor's at the bow, sir," called the boatswain.

"Hoist away on the jib halyards! Avast heaving! Pawl the capstan! Stopper the cable! Cat and fish the anchor!" continued the first lieutenant.

These orders were obeyed as they were given, rapidly and in perfect order.

"Hoist away on the flying-jib halyards. Starboard the helm, quarter-master!" Terrill proceeded.

"The vessel is in your charge, Mr. Pilot," said the captain.

"My eyes!" replied the pilot, taking a long breath. "I knew that America was a fast country, but I didn't know they sent their babies to sea in command of vessels."

"I think you will find we can handle her," added Paul.

"I see you can; and I never saw anything better done in all my life, not even on board one of Her Majesty's men-of-war. Port a little, quarter-master! Steady!"

"Will you have more sail on her?" asked the captain.

"Ay; give her the fore-topsail and fore-topgallant-sail."

Captain Kendall ordered the first lieutenant to set these sails.

"Aloft, sail-loosers!" shouted the executive officer; and those whose stations were on the topsail and topgallant yards sprang into the rigging. "Lay out!" and they followed the foot-ropes out. "Loose!" "Let fall!" "Man your sheets and halyards!" "Sheet home and hoist away!"

"Capital!" exclaimed the delighted pilot.

"Man the fore-braces!" continued the first lieutenant, when the sails were set, and it was necessary to trim them. "Let go the weather braces, haul on the lee braces!"

The wind was about south-west, which gave it to the Josephine about on the beam.

"My eyes! I declare the lads are as handy as though they had been rocked in the cradle of the deep," said the pilot, who had hardly ceased to laugh since he came on board.

The breeze was fresh, and the schooner heeled over

and went into it as though she meant business. Officers and crew were delighted with her performance, and the pilot did not cease to express his wonder that "a parcel of lads" should be sent to sea in charge of such a fine vessel.

The approaches of the Mersey are full of rocks, shoals, and sand-bars. The channels are very intricate, and the navigation dangerous. The schooner passed out of Queen's Channel, and the pilot's duties were finished off the Bell Beacon, twelve miles from her berth in the river.

"Keep her N. W. ¾ N., quarter-master," said the first master, who, with his associates in the sailing department, had been consulting the chart.

The captain, when questioned, had been obliged to inform the first master what course to steer. He had simply told him to head the vessel for the Calf of Man, which is the south-western point of the Isle of Man. A lunch had been prepared for the pilot in the cabin, and as soon as the course had been laid, he was invited below to partake of it. He was treated with "distinguished consideration," and to the last he continued to express his astonishment that a company of boys should be sent to sea in such a fine vessel, and his admiration of the ease and skill with which she was handled. As the pilot boat to which he belonged appeared, the topsails of the Josephine were backed, and she lay to long enough for the pilot to embark.

"A pleasant voyage to you, Captain Kendall," said he, as he stepped into his canoe.

"Thank you," replied the young commander.

"My eyes!" exclaimed the burly pilot, in an under-tone. "A boy captain and a boy crew!"

The Josephine filled away again on her course. The officers and seamen of the port watch were piped to dinner. Half an hour later the starboard watch dined. The afternoon was spent in arranging the watches and quarter watches, and in drilling the crew; but the wind held fair and fresh, and there was not much real work to do. The schooner had taken her departure from Bell Beacon, off the entrance to the Queen's Channel, at one o'clock. For several hours she logged from eleven and a half to twelve and a half knots, and at this rate she would make the Calf by six o'clock. There were plenty of vessels on the same tack, and the Josephine went by scores of them. This was the kind of life which pleased the students on board, and all of them were in a state of satisfaction bordering upon rapture.

Paul planked the weather side of the quarter deck full of dignity, but also full of rejoicing. Everything was superlatively splendid. Among the officers and the crew, there had been many speculations as to the destination of the schooner; but so excellent was their nautical training, that no one asked the only person on board who knew.

"If this breeze holds, we shall make our port in the night," said the captain to Terrill, who, as the officer of the deck, shared the weather side with him.

"I think we shall," replied the first lieutenant, rather dryly; for he had not the least idea what that port might be.

"We are bound for Belfast," added Paul, appreciating the joke.

"We have been there," said Terrill.

"We are going there again. I expect to find our deserters there."

"Lynch and Grossbeck?"

"Yes;" and the captain obligingly explained the circumstances which had caused the sudden departure of the Josephine from Liverpool.

"You will keep a sharp lookout for an English brig in ballast," added Paul, "and instruct your officers to do so."

Captain Kendall went down into the cabin, and in a few moments every officer on board knew where the schooner was bound, and the object of her voyage. At four o'clock the port watch had the deck; and, as the studies were suspended until the arrival of the recruits, Paul decided to keep full watch on deck all the time. At the end of the first dog watch — from four till six — the starboard watch had the deck again for the second dog watch — from six to eight.

At five o'clock land on the starboard bow was sighted. It was the Isle of Man. In an hour and a half more the light-house on the Calf bore north, and Groom, the senior master on duty, gave out the course, N. $\frac{1}{2}$ W. The sheets of the fore and mainsail were let out, a pull given on the weather braces, and the bow of the Josephine headed according to the directions.

"An English brig in ballast, dead ahead!" reported Pelham, who, being off duty, had gone forward to look out for the vessel which the Josephine was expected to overhaul before morning.

The Josephine was making two knots to her one, —

for, being light ballasted, the brig could not carry sail, — and in half an hour came up with her.

Pelham was positive she was the vessel he had seen early in the morning. Everybody on board was excited, though Captain Kendall, in deference to his dignity, continued to look calm.

"Run up to the windward of her, and hail her," said Paul to the first lieutenant.

"Brig ahoy!" shouted Terrill, as the Josephine ran up on her weather beam, and took half the wind out of her sails.

"On board the schooner," replied a hoarse voice from the Prince Alfred, for her name had been read on the stern.

"We want two young men you took on board at Liverpool," yelled the first lieutenant through his trumpet.

"No young men aboard," replied the captain of the Prince Alfred.

But at this moment both Lynch and Grossbeck leaped upon the brig's rail, and proved the lie.

"Down from there, you young whelps!" cried the master, angrily; and he was seen to hit Lynch with a rope's end.

"Throw her up into the wind!" said Paul, as the Josephine was running by the brig.

"Help! Help!" shouted Lynch, not five minutes after the order had been given to put the helm down.

The officers and crew rushed to the lee side, and discovered Lynch in the water clinging to a spar, and Grossbeck swimming lustily towards him. The Prince

Off the Calf of Man. — Page 122.

Alfred was backing her main-topsail for the purpose of heaving to.

"Down with the helm!" shouted Captain Kendall, without waiting to give his orders through the first lieutenant. "Man the first cutter! Pelham, take charge of her!"

The first cutters sprang into their boat at the davits at Pelham's order; the falls were manned, and in a moment she was in the water. The falls were cast off, and the boat was carried by a wave to the leeward of the ship.

"Oars! let fall!" cried the coxswain with thrilling earnestness; and the cutter, mounting the waves, dashed off towards the deserters, both of whom were now clinging to the spar.

There was a scene of confusion on board the brig, and above the moaning of the wind in her rigging and the dash of the sea could be heard the savage oaths of her captain, as he hurried the crew in lowering the jolly-boat. They were behind time; the discipline of the students had done its perfect work, and by the time the brig's boat was in the water, the cutter had picked up the half-drowned deserters. They were taken to the schooner, and when the boat had been hoisted up, she filled away on her course again, amid the yells and the curses of the master of the brig, who was obliged to wait till the spar from which the runaways had been taken was secured.

CHAPTER VIII.

CAPTAIN KENDALL'S GUESTS.

LYNCH and Grossbeck were sent below to put on dry clothing. Both of them, independently of their dripping and draggled appearance, looked crestfallen and sheepish. It was clear enough to the officers of the Josephine that the experience of the runaways on board the Prince Alfred had been anything but pleasant; for had it been even tolerable, they would not have voluntarily exhibited themselves. The blow of the rope's end which the captain had given Lynch, indicated the character of the treatment they had received, and the further evidence that they had jumped overboard in order to escape, was conclusive, if the rest was not.

As soon as the runaways had made themselves comfortable in dry clothes, and eaten their supper, they reported to the first lieutenant on deck, as they had been ordered. They were handed over to the captain for examination.

"I am very sorry I ran away, Captain Kendall," Lynch began; "but I am ready to face the music, and take the consequences."

"So am I," added Grossbeck.

"We had no more idea of running away than you had, sir, till the trouble with McLeish began."

"Why did you run away then?" asked the captain, sternly.

"We were in a scrape, and we thought that was the best way to get out of it. We were wrong, sir; and both of us are sorry enough for what we have done."

"You helped McLeish out of the brig — did you?"

"I did, sir," replied Lynch. "Grossbeck had nothing to do with the affair till I had let him out."

"The first time," added Grossbeck; "for I let him out myself the second time."

"Then you let him out twice?"

"Yes, sir;" and Lynch related the facts that occurred on Friday night.

"What induced you to let him out?" asked Paul.

"It is rather natural for a fellow to help another when he is in trouble. He gave me a sovereign, also. Here is half of it; I gave the rest to Grossbeck," answered Lynch, delivering up his share to the captain; and his example was followed by Grossbeck.

Paul listened to the rest of their story, each relieving the other as his information was better, until they came to their own departure.

"We didn't want to leave the vessel," said Lynch; "we liked her, and we liked you — "

"None of that," interposed Paul. "No compliments; I don't feel the need of them from you."

"I only meant to say that we were well suited with our position on board. You trusted the fellows on Saturday as they had never been trusted before.

11*

Grossbeck and I had the half-sovereign each, and left it on board for fear we should spend it for beer, or something of that sort."

"Didn't you drink any beer on Saturday?" asked Paul, curiously.

"Not a drop, sir! You trusted us that time, and it was honor bright with me; and I know it was with Grossbeck, for neither of us tasted a drop of anything, or went into any bad places. We were pleased with things on board, and we didn't want to leave."

"But we couldn't help it," said Grossbeck, taking up the narrative, "when McLeish was caught. We were exposed then, and expected to go into the brig with him; so we went below and got our money; and while everybody was watching the boats on the starboard side, we dropped into the third cutter on the port side, cast off the painter, and let the tide take us up the river. As soon as the blue fire went out, we pulled till we came to that brig. She was just tripping her anchor. We hailed her, and asked the captain where he was bound. He said Belfast and Quebec, and told us he was short-handed. We took a rope he threw us, and climbed up into the main chains. He asked if we wanted to ship, and said he would give us men's wages. We didn't ship; we only told him we would see about it when he got to Belfast. Then he told us we were runaways from the Yankee school-ship, and if we didn't ship, he would hand us over to her captain."

"I didn't like that, for one," said Lynch, "and we jumped over the rail, letting the boat go adrift; for we were afraid you would see it and discover us as we passed the Josephine. Just as soon as the captain saw the boat adrift, I thought he had suddenly gone crazy; and such an awful blessing as he gave us! for he wanted to keep the boat. But his anchor was at the bow, and he was in danger of drifting upon another vessel that lay astern of him; so he had to fill away. Just afterwards we saw the first cutter pull by the brig, and we kept shady. We went to work with the crew, who were the worst set of men I ever saw, and helped them set the top-gallant-sails; but they had to take them in again, the vessel was so crank when she got the breeze.

"The captain and the mate treated the men like hogs, and I never heard so much swearing in my life as when we catted and fished the anchor. At breakfast we could not eat a mouthful; the salt junk smelled bad, and the tea tasted like herb drink, without any sugar and milk."

"It made me sick," put in Grossbeck. "Neither of us ate anything. At dinner it was worse. We tried to eat some ship-bread, but it was full of maggots."

"We were disgusted, and sorry enough that we had jumped out of the frying-pan into the fire," continued Lynch. "The captain brought up the shipping-papers, and told us to sign them. We refused to do so, for we had no idea of going to Quebec in that style. He swore and raved like a madman — just as you heard him when you picked us up. He said we might sign, or he would give us to the police as deserters from our ship; but we still refused to do so. He told us we needn't think to get away when the brig arrived at Belfast, for he would lock us up. He made us work all day like dogs in the hold, laying a platform on the ballast for the cargo. We hadn't eaten a mouthful all day, and we didn't feel like working; but the brute of a mate kicked us about as though we didn't cost anything. We didn't sleep much last night, but we were put on the first watch. I never felt so bad in my life."

"Nor I," added Grossbeck. "When we saw the Josephine, we were ready to shout for joy. The captain sent us into the forecastle, which was in a house on deck, when you hailed the brig. We heard the lie he told, and we ran out and jumped upon the rail so you could see us. Then he hit Lynch, and drove us back to the forecastle. There was a short spare spar hanging over the side between the chains. I told Lynch what we must do, and while the captain was watching you, I took a hatchet and cut the slings, letting the spar fall into the water, and we followed it. The brig ran ahead, and we swam for the spar. Lynch went over first, and reached the spar before I did. I would rather have been drowned than stay in the brig. The first cutter picked us up, and we were glad enough to get on board the Josephine again."

"Then you don't like going to sea in an English brig?" said Captain Kendall, with a smile.

"No, sir; no, sir," replied both, shaking their heads significantly.

"What did you expect to do with yourselves when you ran away?"

"We didn't know."

"Suppose you had got away from the brig in Belfast, — what could you have done, after your ten shillings were gone?"

"I don't know," answered Lynch, blankly.

"I hope you have found out that the best and safest way for you is to keep within the line of your duty."

"I think we have, sir," replied the penitent Grossbeck.

"I have," added Lynch, decidedly. "I solemnly promise you that I will behave like a man from this time."

"I hope you will; but do you expect to escape the punishment of your offence?"

"No, sir; I don't ask that," said Lynch. "Whatever the punishment may be, it will not be so bad as staying a single hour on board of that brig, — I'm sure of that."

"Of course you expect to be sent on board of the ship," added the captain.

"We cannot complain. It is all our own fault."

"As you are worn out with hard work, you may go below and turn in," replied Paul, whose pity was making sad inroads upon the stern dignity required of a commander on such an occasion.

The culprits touched their caps, and retired. They had expected to spend the night in the brig with McLeish; but they concluded that their punishment was only deferred. Paul could not find it in his heart to punish them after what they had suffered, for he was satisfied that their frank confession was not a sham. They had voluntarily, and at no little risk and pains, returned to the schooner. He had himself seen a specimen of the brutality of the captain of the brig

—enough to make the story of the runaways quite real to him. The worst thing he had any idea of doing was sending them back to the ship, when the Josephine returned to Liverpool.

At eight o'clock, the port watch went on duty, with Lieutenant Martyn as officer of the deck. The run from the Calf of Man to Little Copeland Light was about fifty miles; but when the sun set, at about eight o'clock, it was almost a dead calm. As the darkness gathered, however, the breeze freshened a little from the westward, and the schooner logged from four to six knots during the night. At eight bells, when the morning watch was called, the Josephine, with a pilot aboard, was off Belfast Lough, with the Copeland Light on her weather bow. When the sun rose the wind freshened, and before six she came to anchor off the custom-house.

"I don't exactly see what we have come to Belfast for," said Pelham. "We got the deserters last night."

"Don't you know?" asked Robinson, slyly.

"I'm sure I don't, unless it is to finish up the trial trip."

"I suppose that is the reason why the cruise was extended, but not the reason why we came to Belfast. Miss Grace Arbuckle lives here."

"Exactly so!" laughed Pelham. "They say the captain is really sweet in that quarter."

"I should be if I were in his place. Grace is as pretty a girl as ever smiled on a sailor," added Henry Martyn.

"And Captain Kendall is worthy of the prettiest girl that ever smiled on any fellow," said Terrill.

"The captain is sixteen — isn't he?" continued Pelham.

"Yes, in years; but he is twenty-five in knowledge and skill," replied Terrill.

"That's so; and he's old enough to make love to Grace Arbuckle, if he chose to do so."

"I think that's all nonsense!" exclaimed Humphreys, who was the oldest student on board. "Captain Kendall has no more idea of being in love with that girl, or any other, than I have."

"I don't know about that," added Pelham.

"I suppose you don't," laughed Martyn. "When you get in captain of the Josephine, you will want to run her up into Loch Lomond, when you make your trial trip."

Pelham was not above blushing, and he changed the subject; for he did not care to have Miss Maggie McLaurin discussed by his companions. He had his own private opinion about her, and it was not likely to be changed by any remarks that might be made. We must do these young gentlemen the justice to say that not an improper word was spoken in their conversation, and that their thought and speech were entirely respectful. To such, the company of young ladies like Grace Arbuckle, Maggie McLaurin, and others was in the highest degree elevating and ennobling. Cautious and prudent as Mr. Lowington was in the care of the boys, he encouraged among his pupils a respectful intimacy with well-bred young ladies on all proper occasions. Probably he did not expect any "entangling alliances" to grow out of this intimacy, though if such were the case, the result would not be unnatural.

After breakfast, the ship's company were piped to muster, and the captain informed them that liberty would be given to all hands, except Lynch and Grossbeck, until two in the afternoon, for the schooner would sail for Liverpool on the ebb tide at three. He again reminded them of what was expected of young gentlemen, and enjoined them to be punctual in their return.

The boats were hoisted out, and the officers and crew landed at the nearest quay. Of course all of them hastened to visit the families whose acquaintance they had made during their former stay at the port. Paul proceeded without delay to the residence of Mr. Arbuckle, on the Antrim Road. The servant who came to the door told him the family were engaged, and could not be seen; Mr. and Mrs. Arbuckle and Miss Grace were going to Dublin that afternoon. Paul insisted that his name should be sent in to Mr. Arbuckle; and it need hardly be said he was cordially welcomed. Mr. Arbuckle was surprised to see him, and immediately sent for his wife and daughter.

"Why, Mr. Kendall! I'm delighted to see you!" exclaimed Grace, as, with childish impetuosity, she rushed into the room and extended her hand to the young officer.

"I assure you this is the greatest pleasure I have had since we parted last," replied the gallant captain; and both of them blushed, for both were true to nature.

"How strange that you are here!" added Grace. "Is your ship in the harbor?"

"Not the ship; but the Josephine is at anchor off the custom-house."

"The Josephine! What a love of a boat she must be, according to your letter!"

"She is a beauty; and she logged twelve and a half knots yesterday afternoon."

"Logged!" repeated Grace, puzzled by the word.

"Sailed it, I mean. You must certainly see her," added Paul.

"I am very sorry," interposed Mr. Arbuckle, "but I fear we have no time. We leave for Liverpool to-day, by the way of Dublin."

"For Liverpool!" exclaimed Paul.

"On our way to London," added the gentleman.

"We sail for Liverpool this afternoon," continued Paul, musing and hesitating; for he was not exactly prepared to speak what was trembling for utterance on his tongue.

"Indeed! You make a short stay in Belfast this time," said Mr. Arbuckle.

"We only came out to try the Josephine."

"Why, Mr. Kendall, you have two anchors on your shoulders now!" exclaimed Grace.

"Yes," answered Paul, blushing again.

"And five gold bands on your sleeves! I remember their meaning. You are the captain of the ship."

"Not of the ship. I am the commander of the Josephine."

"Ah, Captain Kendall," said Mr. Arbuckle, smiling and bowing, "I congratulate you on your advancement."

"Thank you, sir," replied Paul. "As you are going to Liverpool, sir, might I——"

Paul broke down. He was too modest to utter the thought in his mind.

"What were you going to say, Mr. Kendall?" asked Grace.

"*Captain* Kendall," said her father, correcting her.

"Captain Kendall; excuse me," laughed Grace.

"I was about to say that you were going to Liverpool;" and Paul came to a dead halt again.

"You did say that, Mr. — Captain Kendall," added Grace, seeming to enjoy his embarassment.

"As you are going to Liverpool — as the Josephine is going to Liverpool — as we are all going to Liverpool —" stammered Paul, "may I not ask the pleasure of your company on board our vessel," he added, desperately; and when he had extended the invitation he tremblingly waited the reply.

"O papa!" cried Grace, "that would be elegant! Do let us go with Mr. Kendall — with Captain Kendall, I mean."

"I am very much obliged to you for your kind invitation, captain, and it would afford me very great pleasure to accept it; but I do not know what Mrs. Arbuckle will think of it. She is not fond of the sea, and is inclined to be sick," replied Mr. Arbuckle.

"Do go, mamma!" pleaded Grace.

"I can give you as good accommodations as you will find in the steamer, madam," added Paul.

The matter was considered for some time, and finally, to the great delight of Grace, and wholly to please her, the invitation was accepted. Paul promised to send the gig to Queen's Bridge at half past two. The lady and gentleman then begged to be excused, as they were busy in making the preparations for their departure, and Grace was left to entertain the visitor. He declined an invitation to lunch, and remained only an hour, during which time he told the history of the Josephine, and related his experience, as a traveller, in Liverpool.

Paul left the house more than delighted, and hastened on board the Josephine, for he was happier on board of her than in any other place, that which he had just left alone excepted. He informed the head steward that two ladies and a gentleman would take passage in the schooner for Liverpool, and directed him to put the professors' state-room in order, and to procure such provisions from the city as the proper entertainment of the guests required.

Again the officers and crew of the Josephine demonstrated that it was safe to trust them, for they not only returned at the time appointed, but also in good condition. Not one of them appeared to have indulged in the use of beer, or other improper beverages. The first master was immediately sent up to Queen's Bridge to bring off the passengers. Paul regretted that naval etiquette and the dignity of his position did not permit him to go himself. The pilot was on board, the foresail and mainsail were set, and the anchor hove up to a short stay.

Before three o'clock the gig was alongside. The "ladies' gangway," as the boys rather facetiously called it, because a genuine sailor needed no such help to board his ship, was rigged. It was a complete set of stairs, with a landing at the top and bottom, so that a person could go on deck as easily as he could enter a house. The first and second lieutenants went to the lower landing, and assisted the ladies out of the boat, while Captain Kendall stood at the upper one to receive them.

"What a splendid ship!" cried Grace, with childish delight, when Paul took her hand to assist her to the deck.

"She isn't a ship; she's a schooner," laughed Paul; "but she's more beautiful than any ship that ever floated could be."

"And you are the captain of her!" exclaimed Grace, as she retreated a step, and looked at him from head to foot.

"I am the captain of her, and I am as proud as a peacock."

"Well, I should think you would be."

"Get under way, Mr. Terrill, if you please," said Paul to the first lieutenant.

"Who is Mr. Terrill?"

"He is the executive officer, the one who gives all the orders in detail."

"That's what Mr. Haven used to be."

"Yes; and he is captain of the Young America now."

"Pray, where is Captain Gordon — that pink of a nice young man?" asked Grace.

"He has gone up higher. He is the commander of both vessels now. We call him Flag-officer Gordon."

Mr. and Mrs. Arbuckle had been duly welcomed before. Their luggage was taken below, and they were conducted to their state-room. The mother and daughter were to occupy the professors' room, and the father one of the spare berths. The passengers remained below but a few moments. They wished to see the process of getting under way. Paul gave them seats on the quarter-deck, and the officers and crew all " put the best foot forward " on this interesting occasion. The first lieutenant spoke up loud and smart, the officers followed his example, and the seamen seemed to be made of electrified wires.

Only one thing disturbed Paul; the wind was due west, which was fair for the voyage, but it was blowing half a gale, and he feared there would be too much of it for his guests. It was more favorable for a quick passage than for a comfortable one, though the pilot said it had not blown long enough to kick up a heavy sea in the Channel. When the tide turned he thought they would have to take it. The guests applauded the skilful handling of the vessel, as she stood down the lough. Paul then conducted them to every part of the vessel.

"What is that poor fellow shut up in the cage for?" asked Grace, in a whisper, as she saw McLeish through the bars of the brig.

"That poor fellow is shut up for mutiny, disobedience, and an attempt to run away," laughed Paul. "You must not pity him, for he does not deserve your sympathy."

"How long has he been in there?"

"This is the fifth day of his confinement."

"Poor fellow! Does he stay in that place all the time?"

"Night and day."

"Do let him out?" pleaded Grace.

"Let him out! Why, he threatened to burn the vessel."

"I dare say he didn't mean anything by it. He was angry."

"But we must keep up the discipline of the vessel, or we can't do anything."

"It is awful to keep a human being shut up in such a cage as that," added Grace, with something like a shudder.

"You must not interfere with the discipline of the ship, Grace," interposed her father.

The fair girl was disposed to be a little wilful, as fair girls will sometimes be, and she continued to beg that the "poor creature" might be released from the cage.

"Really, Miss Arbuckle, it is hard to resist your appeal," replied Paul.

"But I don't wish you to resist it," she added.

"I am sorry to do so, but I must."

"You will not refuse me, Captain Kendall."

Paul enlarged and explained, but Grace insisted upon begging the favor. He wanted to please her; it was exceedingly disagreeable for him to refuse, and, we must add, exceedingly improper for her to persist, though it was all from pure pity and human kindness. It seemed like a duty for her to plead, and it was just as much a duty for him to decline. Her father and mother were not in hearing while she pleaded her suit, or they would have checked her; and poor Paul was placed just where thousands of others have been placed — tempted by a fair one to flinch from a difficult duty. But he did not flinch; he resisted even Grace's eloquent appeal.

"Won't you let me see him and talk with him, Captain Kendall?" asked she, when her other effort had failed.

"See him! Do you wish to go into the brig with him?" asked Paul.

"Yes, I will go into the cage, if you will let me talk with him. I only want to persuade him to be good."

"You shall see him, if you wish it very much; but dinner is ready now;" and the gallant young commander escorted his guests to the cabin.

CHAPTER IX.

GRACE ARBUCKLE.

THE head steward had "spread himself" on the dinner. Lynch had given him a hint, and he prepared for an extraordinary occasion. The captain himself was astonished at the elaborate display of dishes, but he contrived to look dignified, and to regard the whole thing as a matter of course — and it was a matter of courses, for the caterer had seven of them.

The soup, fish, and roast and boiled, passed off well; but about the time the fourth course was brought on, the Josephine reached Little Copeland Light, and the sea, though not very heavy, began to interfere with the dignity of the dishes, if not of the guests, and they danced about the table in a very improper manner. The other three courses were served rather hurriedly, much to the disgust of the steward. The party at the table consisted of the officers of the starboard watch, the captain, and the guests.

It is doubtful whether Mrs. Arbuckle appreciated the steward's display of dishes, not many of which she tasted, and she was glad of an opportunity to return to the deck, and inhale the fresh air. Probably she would have preferred a much plainer repast, threatened as she was with the pangs of seasickness. As it would not be fair to cheat the officers of the port watch out of such a dinner, they were relieved from duty on deck, and the steward was permitted to go through with his programme again, and this time to the unanimous satisfaction of his party.

The pilot was discharged off the light, and the Josephine was again in charge of her officers. She was rushing through the water at a rapid rate, under jib, foresail, and mainsail. Paul, though in no haste to land his agreeable guests, wanted to make a quick passage, and he ordered the gaff-topsail and flying-jib to be set. As she still made good weather of it, and did not seem to be crowded, the foretop-sail and then the foretop-gallant-sail were shaken out. It was desirable to learn the vessel's capacity for carrying sail. The experiment was entirely satisfactory to the nautical young gentlemen on board, more so than it was to the passengers, whose nerves were a little disturbed by the exciting movements of the vessel. Under such a press of canvas in half a gale of wind, the Josephine heeled over considerably, and the spray dashed wildly about her sharp bow.

She behaved magnificently, however, and seemed to fly over the waves. Mr. Arbuckle had some doubts, for he was no sailor. Such a hissing, dashing, and roaring he had never heard before, and he did not feel quite safe. He saw Cleats, the boatswain, an old man-of-war's-man, standing in the waist, and he finally edged up to him, as if by accident.

"We go very fast," said he to the old salt.

"Yes, sir; the last time they heaved the log she was

making thirteen knots," replied the boatswain, politely.

"She tips badly," added Mr. Arbuckle.

"Tips! Why, sir, she walks along like a lady on Broadway. She's got her bearings, and she's as steady as a judge on the bench. See how she tosses her head, sir! Just like a lady in a ball-room, sir! She don't put her nose into it, like a pig does into his grub; she lifts herself over it, sir. I've been in a good many vessels, sir, but I never was in one that took a sea so easily."

"Don't you think it is very bad weather?" asked the nervous passenger, as he glanced at the white caps to windward.

"Bad weather? This is beautiful weather, sir. A smashing breeze, and everything lively and comfortable. I crossed the Atlantic in this vessel, and we ran through two piping blows, regular muzzlers. We lay to under a close-reefed foresail for six hours; but the vessel didn't wink nor blink under it, and never took a sea aboard in the whole of it — hardly a bucket of water at any time."

"But she was in charge of men then," suggested Mr. Arbuckle.

"Men! Well, sir, she's got a better crew on board of her now than she ever had before. Why, bless you, sir, that boy captain is fit to command a frigate. I never saw a man-of-war handled any better than this vessel is."

"Don't you think they are putting on too much sail?"

"Just right, sir. I hope you are not afraid, sir?"

"Not for myself," replied the guest. "My wife and daughter are on board."

"Well, sir, I must say I think they are safer here than they are on shore," added Cleats, hitching up his trousers. "For my part, I never feel quite safe when I'm on the land. I never go into the streets without being afraid I shall get run over; and as for those rail cars, I never get into one without shaking in my shoes. A man isn't safe ashore, sir —" and the boatswain shook his head. "But aboard a good vessel, well manned — well, sir, a man isn't so safe anywhere else as he is there."

"Then you do not think there is any danger?" asked Mr. Arbuckle.

"Not a bit, sir!" protested Cleats, with emphasis. "You and the ladies were never so safe in your lives, as you are at this moment, sir."

"I thank you for this assurance."

"Well, sir, I've only spoken the truth, according to a sailor's creed; and I don't see how anything can happen to you, unless you take the trouble to jump overboard. Do you see that steamer ahead, sir?"

"I see her."

"Well, sir, we've been overhauling her ever since the topsails were shaken out. She can read the name on the stern of this vessel before eight bells."

"She can't sail faster than a steamer — can she?" asked the guest.

"In a calm, she can't; and it depends a little on how fast the steamer sails, but not much. With this breeze we can beat almost any of these English steamers."

Mr. Arbuckle was not particularly interested in the relative speed of the schooner and the steamer; but his conversation with the boatswain quieted his fears, and he soon became accustomed to the dash of the vessel. Mrs. Arbuckle was rather nervous, but Grace enjoyed the wild scene. Paul had pointed out the steamer ahead, and both of them were watching her. The Josephine was gaining about two knots an hour upon her, and the fair passenger was quite excited by the race. They watched her for an hour, and as the boatswain had prophesied, the schooner went by her long before eight bells.

After the interest attending the race had subsided, Grace again alluded to the "poor creature in the cage." She was really troubled by his presumed sorrows and sufferings.

"When may I see him, Captain Kendall?" she asked.

"When you please," replied Paul.

"I will go to him now," said she, her eyes brightening.

"I am afraid he will convince you that I am an awful monster," laughed Paul.

"O, no, captain!"

"He is an ugly fellow: are you not afraid of him?"

"Not at all; take me to him, and perhaps I can make a good young man of him."

"Perhaps you can; and I hope you will."

"If he will promise to be good, you will let him out — won't you?"

"He will promise anything and everything. When I am satisfied that he really means to obey orders and behave himself, I will release him."

"Then take me to him."

"We will go into the cabin, and I will send for him."

"Thank you."

Paul conducted her to the cabin. All the officers were on deck, and the captain told the steward to pass the word for Mr. Cleats. The boatswain came, the keys of the brig were given to him, and he was directed to bring McLeish into the cabin.

"You will let me talk with him alone — won't you?" continued Grace.

"Alone! I should not dare to have you alone with him," replied Paul.

"I'm not afraid of him. He would not be himself before you," persisted Grace.

"Very well; I will go into my state-room, but Mr. Cleats will remain."

"I will consent to that."

Paul retired to his room, and Mr. Cleats returned with the prisoner, who seemed to be astonished at being brought into the cabin to see a young lady who was a stranger to him.

"Shall I leave you, miss?" asked the boatswain.

"No; the captain said you were to remain," replied Grace, as she bestowed a look of mingled pity and interest upon the ruffian face of McLeish.

The prisoner did not know what to make of it. He looked confused, thrust his hands into his pockets, and gazed upon the carpet at his feet.

"Pray sit down, Mr. McLeish," said she, pointing to a stool in front of her.

McLeish dropped himself upon the seat.

"Won't you sit down, Mr. Cleats?" she added, to the boatswain, who stood at the door with his cap under his arm; but the boatswain never sat down in the cabin.

"You don't know how sad it made me feel when I saw you through the bars of that cage," continued Grace, as she drew her stool a little nearer to the culprit.

"It's no my fault," flouted McLeish. "The nobs here are all Yankees, and I'm a Scotch boy. They hate me, and that makes them insult me."

"Insult you! I hope not," said Grace, mildly.

"That's just what they do," protested the culprit, sourly.

"Won't you be very calm, Mr. McLeish? I persuaded the captain to let me talk with you, for I pity you very much, and I wish to do something for you."

The prisoner stared at her, as though he doubted her interest in him; but she was a very pretty girl, and her expression was so tender and pitying that he could not long doubt the reality of her sympathy.

"Won't you tell me now why you were put into that cage?" continued Grace.

"The brig, miss, if you please," interposed Cleats, to whom it seemed like treason to miscall anything on board the vessel.

"I mean the brig," added the fair questioner.

"I was first put in because I wanted to change my berth," replied McLeish, in a pleasanter tone than he had yet spoken.

"Indeed!"

But Cleats, fully sustaining the discipline of the vessel, was so indignant at this partial statement, that he let the truth all out in half a dozen words.

"Why shouldn't I change my berth if I wanted to?" said the prisoner. "The nob made me mad, and I was bound to whip him."

"Then one of the nobs knocked him over," added Cleats.

"But he didn't fight fair."

Even Grace could not help seeing that McLeish was wholly in the wrong, and she frankly told him so.

"Then the captain robbed me of my money," growled McLeish. "He took three pounds from me."

"But that is one of the rules of the ship," replied Grace. "Mr. McLeish, I am so sorry to find that you have done wrong! but I pity you ever so much. Don't you think it was wrong to make a quarrel, and resist the officer?"

"I was mad."

"That is no excuse."

"They made me mad."

"Mr. Terrill treated you just as he did the others."

"He didn't knock any other fellow over."

"No other one resisted him."

"They were not MacGregors," replied the descendant of that famous name.

Grace laughed in spite of herself at the answer; but she "wrestled" with the culprit until she compelled him to acknowledge that he was wrong, and that all he had done was wrong.

"Do you wish to be forgiven?" asked Grace, in the gentlest and most winning tones.

"I don't know."

"You don't!" exclaimed she, fearing that she had made no real progress in her work.

"Who's to forgive me?"

"The captain and the first lieutenant, to be sure."

"Mr. Terrill?"

"Yes; he is the one you resisted."

"But he knocked me down, and by the blood of the MacGregors, he shall pay dearly for that!" said McLeish, shaking his head.

"It was quite right for him to knock you down, when you resisted. If you had not resisted, he would not have knocked you down," added Grace, who was clearly on the side of law and order; and Cleats was so pleased with her spirit that he could hardly contain himself.

"He didn't fight fair, or he wouldn't have got the better of me," retorted the culprit, resorting to his usual clincher.

"That wasn't the reason why he got the better of you, Mr. McLeish. The reason was, because he was in the right, and you were in the wrong," responded the gentle umpire. "Duty makes us strong, and God gives the victory to the just cause. I have no doubt, if you had been in the right, you would have got the better of Mr. Terrill."

This was rather soothing to the damaged pride of the prisoner, and perhaps the obvious truth of her words made an impression on his mind and heart. It was a plausible explanation of the disaster which had befallen him in his encounter with the first lieutenant; and it was pleasanter to believe that he had made a mistake than to acknowledge even to himself that Terrill on any and all occasions could whip him.

"I think you are right, miss," said he, rubbing his

curly head. "I believe I was in the wrong; if I hadn't been, Mr. Terrill could not have beaten me as he did."

"Then you are willing to be forgiven," said Grace, hopefully.

"I am," he replied with some hesitation.

"Are you willing to ask Mr. Terrill to forgive you?"

McLeish looked at her. Those bright eyes and that winning face were irresistible.

"I am," said he. "Am I to be let off then?"

"That's nothing to do with the matter. I don't know. I can't promise anything," replied Grace. "I wish you to apologize to Mr. Terrill, because it is right for you to do so — because you have done wrong."

"For your sake I'll do it!" exclaimed McLeish, who could not resist her influence.

"No," interposed she, decidedly. "You shall not do it for my sake, but for your own."

"I will! I will!" exclaimed the culprit, who now seemed eager to apologize.

"Then go on deck, and do it," said she, with the air of an empress.

He rose from his seat, and hastened up the steps, closely followed by Cleats. The first lieutenant was standing in the midst of a group of the officers. He was astonished when he saw McLeish approaching him, and still more astonished when the prisoner went through the motion of touching his cap, bowing even humbly as he did so.

"I have come, Mr. Terrill, to say that I was all wrong, and I humbly beg your pardon for resisting you as I did," said McLeish. "I ask your forgiveness, sir."

"I grant it with all my heart," said Terrill, as promptly as a kind and noble heart could express itself. "Here is my hand."

"I promise you I will do all you tal me," added McLeish, taking the offered hand. "I hope you will all forgive me for the wrong I have done," he continued, glancing at the rest of the group.

"All right," replied Pelham. "You shall have fair play."

"Thank you," said McLeish, as he bowed again and retreated to the cabin, still followed by Cleats, who was utterly amazed, though he afterwards said he did not see how the beggar could help doing as he did, with those bright eyes shining into his soul — the boatswain wrote sea-poetry sometimes.

"Well, Mr. Cleats, did he ask Mr. Terrill's pardon?" Grace inquired, as they returned to the cabin.

"Yes, miss; and he did it handsomely too," replied the boatswain; "and not only the first lieutenant's, but that of all the officers on deck."

"And I meant what I said," added McLeish, who certainly appeared to be sincere.

Grace pleaded with him for duty's sake till he was almost in tears, and then sent for the captain. Paul was as dignified as an admiral when he returned.

"Captain Kendall, I've been all wrong, and I hope to be forgiven for it," said McLeish.

Paul bit his lip.

"I only ask to be forgiven, and I'll bear any punishment you put upon me," added the culprit.

"I freely forgive you, McLeish, and I assure you that neither I nor any other officer on board has any ill-will towards you," replied the captain; "I only wish you to do your duty."

"I will do it faithfully; I'll no give you any more trouble from this out," protested the prisoner.

"McLeish, your case shall be carefully considered. If I conclude that it is safe to trust you, I will set you at liberty; but not at once. Mr. Cleats, you will return him to the brig," added Captain Kendall.

"I hoped you would set him free now," said Grace, when the boatswain and the prisoner had left the cabin; and her face glowed with excitement.

"I am not quite ready yet."

"I'm sure McLeish means well."

"We shall see," replied Paul, as he escorted Grace to the deck.

The scene which had taken place on the quarter-deck had already been reported to all hands. The captain and the first lieutenant conferred together in Grace's presence, Mr. Terrill joined with her in pleading for the release of the prisoner, and Paul finally gave the order to set him free.

"Let me go with you, Mr. Terrill," said Grace. "I want to see him when he comes out."

"Certainly," replied the first lieutenant; and he conducted her to the steerage.

The door of the brig was opened, and McLeish directed to come out.

"By order of the captain, you are set at liberty," said Terrill.

"I will do my duty from this out," replied the culprit. "And, miss, you have softened my heart, and I thank you for that, and for getting my liberty for me."

Grace talked to him for half an hour, and with maidenly dignity pointed out to him the destiny of the evil-doer. She told him he could never be happy while he persisted in doing wrong, and could never be satisfied with himself or any one else.

"You have saved me, miss; you have made a good young man of me, and I will die rather than go wrong again," protested McLeish, impulsively.

"I shall hear from you often, McLeish, and I hope nothing bad will be reported of you," added Grace, as she returned to her parents on deck.

"How are you, McLeish!" exclaimed Templeton, as the discharged prisoner showed himself among the crew.

"Don't tampt me, lads, don't tampt me, any of you, for I have promised to be good, and I mean it," said McLeish.

"Eh! What's the matter with you?" demanded Templeton. "Have you become one of the chaplain's lambs?"

"No, but I wish I were one — upon my life I do, for I would like to live in the same heaven with yon young lady."

"Whew!" whistled Templeton.

"O, I'm in airnest, lads; I mean it all."

"He has fallen in love with Miss Arbuckle," laughed one of the seamen.

"I've fallen in love with the goodness in her heart. If there was ever an angel upon earth, she is the one. Dinna laugh at me, lads. With the halp of God, I'll be as good as the best of ye."

"Gone mad!" sneered Templeton. "I say, McLeish, there's a little unsettled matter between us — you remember."

"I don't mind."

"Don't you, indeed? You have a bad memory. Didn't you want to fight me when we were on Loch Lomond?"

"I'll no fight you now," replied McLeish, decidedly.

"Don't back out, man. We have liberty now, and there is a good chance to find out who is the best man."

"I'll no fight you."

"Have you become a coward?"

"Say what you just like, lads; I'll keep to the right path now."

Certainly the convert promised well, and after some of "our fellows" had bantered him for a while, they let him alone. He did not yield to the temptation which the taunts of the evil-minded suggested, and then some of the better boys came to him, and cheered and encouraged him. Grace had exerted a powerful influence upon him, and if he persevered it would be the best day's work a young lady ever did.

The darkness swept down upon the Josephine while she was still leaping over the waves, making an average of twelve knots. The passengers retired, and the vigilant officers paced the deck, watching the compass, the sails, and the weather. Safely she sped on her way amid the gloom and the waves, and at two o'clock in the morning she was off the Bell Beacon, at the mouth of Queen's Channel. Fortunately a pilot was at hand, and while it was still dark the anchor of the Josephine was dropped within hail of the Young America.

"What's the matter?" asked Mr. Arbuckle, as he rushed on deck, roused from his slumbers by the rattling of the cable through the hawse-hole.

"Nothing, sir," replied Paul, cheerfully, for he was on deck, having been called when the schooner came up with the beacon.

"I thought we were going to the bottom. What was all that fearful noise?"

"Nothing but the cable, sir, as the anchor went down."

"The anchor!" exclaimed the passenger. "Have you come to anchor?"

"Yes, sir."

"What for? Is there a storm?"

"No, sir; we have arrived at Liverpool, and have concluded not to go any farther to-night," laughed the young commander, who was in the highest of spirits.

"Liverpool! Bless me, I did not expect to get to Liverpool till to-morrow night. Pray what time is it?"

"Three o'clock, sir."

"You must have made a remarkable passage."

"Pretty fair, sir," replied Paul. "You wouldn't have come much quicker by the mail line."

"Really, it's astonishing."

"The Josephine has done splendidly, as she will any time, if you only give her wind enough. After all, one might have been two or three days about it. I hope the ladies have not been disturbed by the noise."

"I will see them, and tell them we are in Liverpool."

Mr. Arbuckle went below, and after everything had

been made snug on board, all hands, except an anchor watch, turned in. All was quiet below, and the captain was soon sound asleep.

Six o'clock was the hour in the morning at which all hands were called, on board the Young America and her consort, and at that hour the pipe of the boatswain rang through the vessel. The deck was washed down, the yards squared, and every rope was hauled taut. By this time all hands were on deck, and the passengers had come up to taste the morning air. Grace was as fresh as a new-blown rose, and as Paul looked at her, he was sorry he had made such a quick passage.

The Young America lay within a short distance of the Josephine, and after her morning work was done the crew crowded into the rigging. Mr. Lowington was seen on the top-gallant forecastle, and presently all hands in the ship gave three rousing cheers, which were returned by the Josephine. The professor's barge was lowered; the principal, surgeon, and chaplain embarked in her, and were soon on the schooner's deck. Of course Mr. Lowington was surprised to see Mr. Arbuckle and his family on board; but he was not the less delighted to meet them.

CHAPTER X.

THE EXCURSION TO CHESTER.

"WELL, Captain Kendall, how does the Josephine work?" asked Mr. Lowington, after he had congratulated him upon his safe arrival.

"Splendidly, sir," replied Paul, with enthusiasm. "We made the run from Belfast in twelve hours, beating the steamer."

"I think you must have carried sail pretty well," laughed the principal.

"I didn't strain her any, sir; I kept her easy all the time."

"I find no fault; but you must remember that the Josephine's spars are not the heaviest," added Mr. Lowington. "I see that Lynch and Grossbeck are among the crew, and that McLeish is at liberty."

"Yes, sir; we overhauled that brig off the Isle of Man, and our runaways were glad to get away from her," replied Paul, as he proceeded to describe his interview with the brig, and the escape of the deserters.

"I am sorry to have any one run away from us, but I am not sorry this incident has occurred," replied the principal, as Paul finished. "As long as the students have but little money, they cannot go far on shore; but

I have feared they would ship in other vessels. The experience of Lynch and Grossbeck will be a wholesome lesson for them to ponder. The captain of the Prince Alfred is evidently one of the worst specimens of a British ship-master; but, even if kindly treated, our boys would not thrive as common sailors in the forecastle of any merchantman. Salt junk and hard bread would disgust them in a few days, for they have been used to roast beef and plum puddings, to say nothing of hard work, hard bunks, and hard companions. You did not punish them?"

"I gave them no liberty at Belfast, as I did the others. I thought they had punished themselves about enough," answered Paul.

"Use your own judgment," added the principal.

Paul then related the remarkable conversion of McLeish, through the agency of Grace, which, in spite of its serious nature, had some amusing features. The idea of a young lady of fourteen, brought up in ease and luxury, troubling herself about the reformation of an obdurate sailor boy, was not in keeping with every-day experience; but it was a very pleasant incident, and Mr. Lowington expressed his high appreciation of the character of Grace.

"What shall I do with McLeish now, sir?" asked Paul.

"Do what you think proper."

"Shall I deprive him of his liberty?"

"As you deem it expedient," laughed the principal, as he walked away.

Dr. Winstock was happy to see Paul again, and walked through the vessel with him. The chaplain heard the story of McLeish, and endeavored to deepen the impression which Grace had produced upon his mind. As Mr. Arbuckle wished to proceed immediately to London, the gig was prepared for his accommodation.

"I hope I shall see you again, Miss Arbuckle," said Paul, as he escorted her to the gangway.

"We shall be at my uncle's, near London, for a month," replied she, "and I shall depend upon seeing you."

"We shall be in London by the first of next month, I think."

"But you will write to me — will you not?"

"With the greatest pleasure."

"And you will not fail to tell me all about Mr. McLeish?"

"I will not."

Grace gave him her address in London, and he handed her down into the boat, which pulled for George's Landing Stage, in charge of Pelham.

"Everything seems to be lovely on board," said the doctor, as he noticed that Paul's eye was following the boat. "I hope you will not be homesick now that young lady has gone."

"I have too much to do for that," replied Paul, with a blush, as he glanced at the boat again.

"The millennium seems to have come on board of your ship — all rebellions, mutinies, and insurrections repressed, and even McLeish suddenly converted from a demon into an angel."

"I hope it will last," replied Paul.

"I think you will have to employ that young lady

to sail with you; for she seems to have a powerful influence over obdurate youngsters," laughed the surgeon. "As you have no chaplain, you had better engage her. She has conquered the rebels — and the captain too."

"I like her, doctor, and I won't deny it," added Paul, desperately; "and I don't like her any the less for her interest in McLeish."

"It isn't always quite agreeable to have a young lady interested in two young gentlemen at the same time."

"Pooh, doctor! It isn't anything of that kind."

"I suppose not; but I dare say you would not like to have her take too much interest in McLeish."

"The more the better," replied Paul, stoutly.

"I fear you will not always be so disinterested."

"I shall try to be, at any rate."

This bantering was interrupted by the principal, who had business matters to adjust with the captain.

"How many petty officers and seamen have you now, Captain Kendall?"

"Thirty-one, sir; and I would like one more to make even watches."

"You shall have him. That will give you eight in each quarter watch," added Mr. Lowington, consulting his memorandum-book. "My agent in the United States has received more than I supposed, and forty arrived in the steamer. They are now on board the ship. If I send you one, the ship will then have her complement, lacking one, and you will have four berths vacant in your steerage, and four in your cabin. At this rate we shall soon want another vessel."

"Are the instructors for the Josephine on board of the ship?" inquired Paul.

"They are, and very anxious to see the vessel in which they are to sail. We will make these changes at once, and send them on board, for we go to Chester this afternoon."

The barge returned to the ship, and the first cutter was sent off for the professors and the extra hand.

"The first cutter is coming, sir, with the flag-officer on board," reported the fourth master to the captain, in his state-room.

"Man the side," replied Paul, who had already made arrangements for this important ceremony.

Twelve of the crew had been selected to act as side-boys; and when the first cutter reached the gangway, they were drawn up in two lines, facing each other, between which the superior officer was to pass. In the navy the captain of the ship, whatever his rank, or any higher officer, is always received in this manner when he comes on board of the ship. Paul took his place on the quarter-deck, at the end of the double line of side-boys, with his officers standing behind him.

Flag-officer Gordon was the first to reach the deck; and as he passed between the side boys, they saluted him by touching their caps. He was followed by the professors, to whom the same courtesy was extended. Paul raised his cap as the high and mighty flag-officer of the squadron approached him, and all the lieutenants and masters did the same.

"Captain Gordon, I am happy to receive you on board of the Josephine."

"Thank you, Captain Kendall," replied the flag-officer, who could hardly keep from laughing at the stateliness of the ceremony, as he extended his hand. "I congratulate you upon the brilliant success of your first cruise. And between you and me, Paul," he added in an under-tone, "I would rather be in your boots than in my own."

"You can hoist your flag aboard my vessel if you like, Charley," replied Paul, in his ear.

"Captain Kendall, allow me to introduce Professor Hamblin," continued Gordon.

"I am happy to welcome you on board of the Josephine, Mr. Hamblin," said Paul, taking the instructor by the hand, and raising his cap. "Gentlemen, Professor Hamblin," he added to his officers.

"I am glad to meet you," replied the learned man, with dignity enough for the president of a college.

"Professor Stoute," added the flag-officer; and he was received as his colleague had been.

"Glad to see you, boys. Wanted some more ballast — didn't you?" chuckled the fat professor, shaking his sides. "You seem to have a jolly time of it here?"

"We try to be happy," answered Paul.

"I'll help you do that," continued the professor. "Arn't you afraid I shall sink this little vessel?"

"O, no, sir," laughed the captain.

"Between us, Captain Kendall," added Mr. Stoute, in a low tone, "Mr. Hamblin is as heavy again as I am, though I weigh about twice as much as he does."

"Then you will just balance each other," replied Paul. "Mr. Briskett," he continued, calling the head steward, " I'll thank you to show the professors their state-room."

" I must have my berth pretty near the middle of the vessel, or you will have to shift the ballast," added Professor Stoute, shaking his fat sides again. " I used to do duty as chain box for a small steamer on the Sound."

All hands laughed, as much because they were pleased, as because it was a duty to laugh at the schoolmaster's jokes, and the head steward conducted the " brains" of the vessel to the state-room prepared for their reception. Professor Hamblin did not laugh. He appeared to be displeased at the levity of his companion; but the students had already made up their minds to like the fat professor, and to leave the lean one to circumstances.

" Captain Kendall, with the continued assurance of my distinguished consideration, permit me to inform you that I am the bearer of a note from the honored principal of the Academy squadron to the gallant captain of the Josephine," said Gordon, as they retired from the group of officers, and handed Paul a note, laughing as though he regarded the honors paid to a flag-officer as a stupendous joke.

" Thank you, Charley; we will be boys now, if you please," replied Paul, as he opened the note and read, —

" MY DEAR CAPTAIN KENDALL: To save the time and trouble of drawing a lot for one hand, I have concluded to send you a new scholar; but he claims to be a thorough sailor, and to know all the ropes in the ship, besides having other accomplishments, which will doubtless be developed in due time.

Truly yours,
R. LOWINGTON."

"Where's the new hand?" called he to one of the masters. "Send him aft."

The new hand was conducted into the august presence of the flag-officer and the captain. He was a tall, thin young man of seventeen, with an incipient mustache on his upper lip, and an eye-glass suspended upon the bridge of his nose.

"Why, Ben Duncan!" exclaimed Paul, forgetting for the moment the dignity of his exalted position, and grasping the hand of the new scholar.

"I am delighted to see you, Paul," replied the new hand. "I was sadly disappointed when I went on board of the ship to find you were no longer in her. I suppose Mr. Lowington sent me here, though, to oblige you rather than me, for I find the discipline is very strict."

"It is quite as strict in the Josephine as in the Young America," laughed Paul.

Duncan belonged to New York city, and had been a schoolmate and friend of Paul at an academy in Ohio.

"I must return to the ship, Captain Kendall," said Gordon; "and I'll trouble you for a boat. I only came on board this time to introduce the professors."

"Come again, Charley," replied Paul. "I want you on board when we sail."

"Thank you. I'll hoist my flag on board some day," laughed Gordon.

"Man the side!" shouted Paul.

"Confound the side!" added the flag-officer, as the captain escorted him to the lines of side boys, and politely bowed him out of the schooner.

"I am glad to see you, Ben," continued Paul, as he turned again to the new hand. "I had no idea that you were coming."

"I teased my father, till at last he consented, very much against my mother's wishes. This is a fine little vessel you have, Paul."

"Splendid, Ben! I am sorry you did not join the academy before."

"I should if I had had my own way."

"You must work your way up, as the rest of us have, for you can only be a common seaman now."

"I suppose not," sighed Duncan. "My father kept a yacht, and I have sailed in her a great deal, so that I know all about a vessel. I suppose there is a great gulf between us now."

"There is considerable difference between a seaman and a captain, but the offices are open to all who will win them by hard work and good behavior. You are a fine scholar, and your chances are good. The first lieutenant will now give you your berth, and station you."

The new seaman was handed over to the first lieutenant; but before he had disappeared in the steerage, some fellow called him "Specksy," on account of his glasses, and the name clung to him. After he had been berthed and stationed, all hands were mustered for practice. Duncan took his place, and so did McLeish, the former being at the outhaul of the foresail and the foretop-gallant-sheets, and the latter at the throat halyard of the mainsail and at the weather topsail brace.

"Sheet home and hoist away!" shouted the first lieutenant, in the course of the exercise, when the topsails were set.

"Mind your eye, Specksy!" said Templeton, as Duncan did not move.

"Foretop-gallant-sheets!" shouted Pelham, on the forecastle.

Duncan had read this term on his station bill, and he leaped into the rigging, and was half way up the fore shrouds before he could be stopped.

"Avast there, Specksy!" cried the boys; and everybody laughed at the misdirected zeal of the new hand.

"Duncan," Pelham called to him, "lay down!"

Duncan descended, and stretched himself on the deck at full length, achieving the manœuvre with the celerity of a cat, amid the most tumultuous roars of laughter.

"What are you doing?" demanded Pelham, almost choked with laughing.

"You told me to lie down," replied Duncan.

"No, I didn't; I told you to *lay* down, which means come down."

"I beg your pardon," replied the new hand, good-naturedly. "The principal made us a speech yesterday on board of the ship, in which he admonished us all to yield an unquestioning obedience to the commands of a superior officer, even if we did not know the purpose of the order."

"What were you going aloft for?" asked Pelham.

"I am on the foretop-gallant-sheets," replied he.

"Then I think you had better keep off of them. Where do you expect to find the top-gallant-sheets?"

"On the foretop-gallant-sail, I supposed."

"We don't usually go aloft to sheet home."

"O, don't you!" exclaimed Duncan, as if surprised that they did not.

"I thought you said you knew all about a vessel," interposed the captain, laughing at the blunders and the coolness of the new hand.

"So I do, Captain Kendall," replied Duncan, blandly; "but the vessels with which I have had to do, did not carry any topsails or top-gallant-sails. I am acquainted with the nomenclature of the jib, foresail, and mainsail, and I am on familiar terms with the halyards, tack and outhaul of a gaff-topsail; but above and beyond that my knowledge does not extend."

"Ah! then we will instruct you," added the captain.

"Thank you; I shall be under obligations for any information you or your officers may impart to me."

"Mr. Pelham will give you the information you need," said Paul, as he went aft again, choking with laughter at the grandiloquent speech of his friend.

"Mr. Pelham, I am your most obedient servant," added Duncan.

"Specksy's a brick," said Templeton.

"Allow me to insinuate, in the most unaffected manner, that the foretop-gallant-sheets lead down the foremast, and are belayed at the fife-rail."

"I am under obligations to you for this lucid explanation, Mr. Pelham. If I may trouble you to introduce me to the fife-rail, I shall know it when I see it."

"This is the fife-rail."

"I am obliged to you for the information."

"When the order is given, 'Sheet home, and hoist away!' you will pull away on the sheet till it comes home."

"Home — at the end of the voyage?"

"By no means; till you have hauled the corner of the sail down to the end of the yard; or as long as you can get anything by hauling."

"I will not fail to do so," replied Duncan, politely touching his cap to the second master, and then seizing the rope.

"Attention, all hands!" shouted the first lieutenant, through his trumpet. "Sheet home, and hoist away!"

Duncan pulled on his sheet till the corner came home and the topgallant-yard went up to its place. The sails were taken in, and then set again, and the new hand proved that he was an apt scholar. When the drill was finished, the ship's company were called together in the waist, and the proposed visit to Chester was announced. An allowance of two shillings was paid to each student. An early dinner was taken, as the train left Birkenhead at ten minutes before one. That evening, after the return of the excursion, Paul wrote an account of the trip in a letter to Grace, which we shall transcribe, as much to assure the reader that Paul did not put any soft nonsense into the epistle, as to inform him what the party saw in Chester.

"Dear Miss Arbuckle: As I have a state-room all to myself now, you will find that I keep my promise rapidly, for I can write without interruption. After you left this morning, the two new professors came on board of the Josephine. One of them is as thin as the fore royal-mast of the ship, and as stiff as the mainmast. He has not been seen to laugh yet, though lots of funny things have happened. The other is so fat that he jars about like a form of jelly, and he is as jolly as he is fat.

"All hands went to Chester this afternoon — all but McLeish, Grossbeck, and Lynch, for I must keep up my dignity by punishing them a little. If I don't, the discipline of the Josephine will go to the dogs, and I shall wear my two anchors in vain. If they take it kindly this time, I shall punish them no more. So far, McLeish has done splendidly, and is doing honor to the fair reformer who converted him. Almost any fellow would mend his ways with such an advocate.

"We landed in the boats at Birkenhead. This place has grown almost as fast as some of our American cities — not quite. In thirty years it has increased from an insignificant village with only twenty-six hundred people, to a city with fifty-two thousand. Dr. Winstock told me this, as we marched up the street, or I shouldn't have known anything about it; and aware how much you are in love with statistics — [At this point Paul wrote, 'I wish I were statistics,' but his conscience smote him, and as the words were at the top of a new page, he tore it off, and omitted the audacious phrase.] It has any quantity of docks, and they say it will some time rival its neighbor on the opposite side of the river. I don't think that will be till they get a couple of dozen of Yankee ferry-boats to connect the two cities.

"To be candid, when I saw the ferry-boats that ply between Liverpool and Birkenhead, I was ashamed to own that my ancestors came from England. I wish you could see one of the ferry-boats that run from New York to Jersey City or to Brooklyn. These Birkenhead ferry-boats are little old tubs of steamers, just like any other boat, and not at all adapted to the purpose.

"We went to Chester, and as this was the first time I had seen the green fields of England, I looked with all my eyes. It is a fine country, not very different from the north of Ireland. After riding fifteen miles, we arrived at Chester, which, you know, is a very old city, and it looks as musty as my grandmother's house in New Hampshire. The Romans founded the city — though it has been founded two or three times since, and its Roman name was Deva, or 'the city on the Dee.' It was rather inspiring to think that the regular old Romans had walked about on the ground, and it seemed to bring my Virgil and Sallust nearer home to me.

"When the Roman legions left the city, the Saxons, the Northmen, and the Danes destroyed it several times. William the Conqueror gave the city to a fellow whose name I don't remember, with permission to add as much more to it as he could win from the Welsh. He was called the Earl Palatine; and I have come to the conclusion, after mature deliberation, that he built the castle, though it has been built over again within a hundred years or so. If he didn't build it, who did, Henry III. wiped out the Earl Palatine, and annexed the earldom to the crown, which was very obliging and disinterested of him. The Prince of Wales is now Earl of Chester, as well as Baron of Renfrew, Duke of Lancaster, Duke of Cornwall, and I know not what else.

"Chester certainly looks like a very old city. It has a kind of crumbling look. The houses are very odd, and have porticos extending over the sidewalk, under which people travel. The place is a walled town. I have heard about such things, but never saw one before. This wall goes entirely round the city, and we walked about two miles on it. It is from twelve to forty feet high; but as the town became too small for the people, or the people too many for the town, they built houses outside of the walls. There are some towers on this wall, from one of which Charles I. saw his army defeated by the Roundheads, which, our guide said, did not make him feel good. We were shown some stone work of the Romans, which proved that they were good masons, or their work would not have lasted so long.

"The cathedral is the great object of interest in Chester. It is only about three or four hundred years old, — that is not much, — but it is built of soft stone, which crumbles away, and makes it look older than it is. My friend Ben Duncan, who is a poet, went into ecstasies over it, and said it was worth crossing the Atlantic to see. If it is, I am glad he came.

"We also went to St. John's Church and St. Peter's Church, and then through the castle. There is a bridge over the Dee here, with a span of two hundred feet, which the Romans did not build. As we all wanted to see how a great lord lives, we walked out to Eaton Hall, three miles from Chester, to the residence of the Marquis of Westminster. We had to procure tickets to get into it, and Mr. Lowington bought them of the landlord of the Royal Hotel. There is more sense in charging an admission fee in this case than in many others, for I suppose the poor marquis would be overrun with people if he did not put the shilling stopper on them; and besides, the money is given to the poor. We walked nearly all the way through the park, which is covered with fine trees, till we came to the Hall, a splendid building, in Gothic style, said to be the finest dwelling-house in England — not having seen them all, I can't say. It is fitted up on a grand scale, with lofty rooms, fit for a palace, I should judge. I should think the marquis could keep comfortable, and have room to turn round without knocking anybody over. There are some fine pictures in the chapel, dining-room and drawing-room — Duncan almost had a fit over them. I liked the two by Benjamin West the best — he was an American, you know.

"The Chester railway station is a big thing. I never saw anything equal to it in the United States, and that is confessing a great deal. America is a great country, and if we could import two or three of those Roman stations, and transport a few spare cathedrals, Englishmen would think as much again of it.

"We returned to Birkenhead about eight o'clock. I have only room to add, that the boatswain says

McLeish has behaved handsomely, and does not grumble because he was deprived of his liberty. That settles the case with him, and to-morrow he shall go to Manchester with us. Remember me kindly to your father and mother, and believe me ever

   Your sincere friend,

      PAUL KENDALL."

CHAPTER XI.

THE NEW HAND.

ON Thursday an excursion was made by all hands to Manchester, the great cotton manufacturing city of England. It is situated on the Irwell, a branch of the Mersey, and with Salford, on the other side of the river, has a population of nearly four hundred seventy-two thousand, which gives it the third rank among the cities of the United Kingdom. Without Salford, it ranks as the fourth, Glasgow being the third. At first its manufactures were of woollen fabric; but during the last hundred years, cotton has superseded it. It was not till the raw material was obtained in such vast quantities from the United States, that Manchester obtained its importance. The invention of a Connecticut Yankee, Eli Whitney, who furnished a machine for separating the seeds from the cotton, thus rendering the production of the article practicable and profitable, was the foundation of the growth of the city.

Manchester also contains immense manufactories of iron, and is located in the midst of a coal region. It is thirty-one miles from Liverpool, upon which it depends for its supply of cotton. There are six railroads diverging from the city, as well as several canals.

The students divided into parties, and explored the city as much as they could in the brief period allowed for the purpose. McLeish, agreeably to Captain Kendall's promise to Grace Arbuckle, was a member of the party; and so far as the officers were able to observe his conduct, he behaved with the utmost propriety and discretion. Dr. Winstock had a letter of introduction to Mr. Murdock, a wealthy mill-owner in the city, which procured for him and his friends the privilege of going through one of the immense cotton factories. When Captain Kendall was presented to Mr. Murdock, the gentleman seemed to be greatly amused at Paul's "fine feathers," as he called them, alluding to his shoulder-straps, sleeve-bands, and the gold lace on his cap; but the dignity and self-possession of the young commander carried him through the interview, and won the respect of the mill-owner.

"What is the meaning of it all?" asked Mr. Murdock of the surgeon as they were walking over to the mill they were to visit. "Upon my life, these young gentlemen swell up like lords of the admiralty. Are they sailors, do you say?"

"Captain Kendall is commander of the Josephine," replied the doctor; "and I assure you he is not only a gentleman, but he is a better officer and seaman than one half the men who go in command of vessels."

Dr. Winstock explained the system of the Academy Ship and her consort, which strongly excited the interest of the English gentleman, and he asked a great many questions. The doctor answered them all, and described the voyage of the Josephine to Belfast.

"But is it possible the young man took the vessel to Belfast alone?" asked Mr. Murdock, who did not live by the sea, and his wonder was correspondingly increased.

"Certainly he did. I should be entirely willing to cross the Atlantic, or even go round the world, in a ship under his charge."

Mr. Murdock was very attentive and respectful to Paul after this conversation. The mill was explored, and the party, by urgent invitation, went to the house of the proprietor, who insisted upon giving them some refreshment. They were presently ushered into an elegant and spacious dining-room, and after an introduction to the gentleman's family, partook of the lunch. Their host had a son of sixteen, who appeared to regard the young officers with great interest, and bestowed much attention upon them.

"Have a glass of sherry, Captain Kendall," said Spenser Murdock, filling a couple of glasses.

"You must excuse me," replied Paul, pleasantly; "I never drink wine; we are not allowed to take it."

"Ah! teetotalers — are you?" laughed the young man, as he drained the glass without a rebuke, or even a question, from his father.

Mr. Murdock then proposed to drink the health of Captain Kendall; but the doctor interposed, and explained the rules to which the ship's company were subjected. Spenser conducted the young officers to the drawing-room, where one of the ladies sang and played for them, leaving Dr. Winstock with the host in the dining-room.

"I have been thinking a great deal about your institution, Dr. Winstock," said the host. "It seems to me to be really a very fine thing to give health and vigor, as well as a good education, to our young men."

"It has been very successful thus far," added the surgeon.

"You will be in Europe a year or two, I dare say."

"A year, at least; perhaps two years."

"There is that son of mine — he is not a bad boy, but he has given me a deal of trouble. Is it possible for him to be entered in your Academy Ship?"

"I am unable to say, sir."

"Spenser isn't a bad boy," repeated Mr. Murdock; "he's only wild."

"That's the case with most of our boys," laughed the doctor, who thought it quite probable that Mr Spenser Murdock was another McLeish; for fathers and mothers find it hard to believe that their own sons are ever bad boys.

"I sent him to Rugby; but the rules were so strict there, the poor boy could not stand it. Then I had a private teacher for him; but he walloped his tutor one day when they had a difference," laughed the father, who seemed to think this was to the boy's credit.

"I fear our discipline would be too strict for the young man," suggested Dr. Winstock.

"Perhaps so; but you have so much excitement in going from place to place, and knocking about the sea, that there is always something to interest the boy. I hope you understand my meaning. Spenser is not a bad boy; he has a good heart, but he has given me a deal of uneasiness. A few weeks ago the lad broke into the counting-room of the mill, and took fifty pounds from the drawer; but it was only done for the fun of the thing. The poor boy has plenty of money; indeed, he gave the half of what he took to a miserable fellow who was distrained for his rent. He has a good heart, the lad has; but he is wild."

The surgeon thought he must be wild; and he took the liberty to hint that Spenser was spoiled by over-indulgence.

"Not at all; I am quite strict with him," protested the father. "I don't permit him to be out of the house after twelve at night, and I allow him only twenty pounds a month for pocket money. I increased it from ten to twenty pounds after he broke into the counting-room, to keep him from indulging in such wild freaks."

"And I suppose, if he should break into your counting-room again, you would raise it from twenty to forty pounds," laughed Dr. Winstock.

"Possibly not. I told him his conduct was dishonorable and disgraceful, unworthy the character of a gentleman."

"Did you tell him it was immoral and criminal?"

"No, I didn't tell him that. You see the lad only did it for fun, as a mere freak, and I did not wish to injure his self-respect."

On all other topics Mr. Murdock was a sensible man. He controlled his mill with judgment and skill, and governed his operatives with stern decision. If a poor girl stole half a pound of raw cotton, she was at least discharged. It was not regarded as a "freak" on her part. Dr. Winstock was grateful to his host for his kindness, and invited him to visit the ship at her moorings in the Mersey; and the invitation was eagerly accepted.

The excursion party returned to Liverpool, and went on board of the vessels. The next morning, the classes were organized, and the regular studies pursued. In the forenoon, Mr. Murdock and his son visited the ship, and both of them were delighted with everything they saw. Mr. Lowington explained the operation of his system, and invited the guests to visit the Josephine after dinner.

"I fear the discipline of the ship would not suit your son," said the principal, when the guest had applied for Spenser's admission.

"He seems to be delighted with everything he sees," added Mr. Murdock.

"To oblige a friend in Greenock, I took his son on board. The young man has seen a great deal of trouble, and spent most of his time in the brig."

"The brig! What is that, sir?"

"The ship's prison."

"A prison!" exclaimed Mr. Murdock, exhibiting some alarm.

"A place of confinement. Of course we do not have stone walls on board a vessel. But I am happy to say that the lad I mention is now doing well."

When the session of the school was closed, the brig was exhibited to the guests. Wilton and Monroe were still its occupants. Mr. Murdock did not like the looks of the place. He thought it would be degrading to be committed to the prison, and damage the self-respect of the prisoner. Mr. Lowington regarded the culprit's evil deeds as more degrading than the punishment, and insisted that discipline should be vindicated, that the self-respect of others might not be damaged.

Mr. Murdock dined with the faculty, and Spenser with the officers in the after cabin. As McLeish had thought when he was a passenger, it was all very fine, and the English boy was quite as anxious as the Scotch lad had been to be enrolled among the students. The principal did not wish to receive him; there had been trouble enough with McLeish. The barge was ordered to the gangway to convey the guests to the Josephine, and they were received by Paul, who with pride and pleasure exhibited the vessel to them.

"Mr. Murdock, we sail for Whitehaven this afternoon," said the principal. "I should be happy to have you accompany us."

"I should be delighted to do so!" exclaimed the guest.

"You can return by railway at your own pleasure."

"Thank you. I am so interested in your institution, that I cannot deny myself the satisfaction of seeing more of it. We must have something of this kind in England."

"I am glad that the idea meets with your approbation."

"Unless I can prevail upon you to receive my son, I shall attempt to get up an Academy Ship at Liverpool."

"Then perhaps it would be better for me to decline

your application. You may not think so well of the plan after you have seen more of it, for I assure you it is not all sunshine. These young men are generally the sons of wealthy people, and many of them have acquired bad habits by the indulgence of their parents."

"Doubtless," added Mr. Murdock, rather coldly.

"Some of them require severe discipline."

"But this vessel, you tell me, is controlled by the boys," added Mr. Murdock, glancing at Paul, who stood near talking with Spenser.

"This is an experiment; but Captain Kendall is really in command of her, though he may call upon me for help if he requires it. Now, sir, you and your son may take passage in the Josephine, or in the Young America, as you prefer."

"If you please, Mr. Lowington, we will go in the small vessel. Do you think it entirely safe?"

"If I did not, I should not permit the young gentlemen to handle her," laughed the principal.

"Then I will go in her, for I am anxious to see the young captain handle his vessel."

Mr. Lowington returned to the ship, leaving his guests and the surgeon, who had decided to go in the Josephine, on board. In half an hour the signal for getting ready to sail was hoisted on board of the ship. The boatswain's whistle sounded, and all hands sprang to their stations. The sails were shaken out, the anchor hove short, and the pilot came on board.

Mr. Murdock and his son were filled with astonishment and delight as they witnessed these evolutions of seamanship.

"I must certainly join this vessel," said Spenser to his father.

"Could you endure the discipline?"

"It would be fun," replied the young gentleman, with enthusiasm.

"Would you like to pull those ropes?"

"I would; I should enjoy it."

"Or be sent up where those lads are?" added Mr. Murdock, pointing to the seamen on the top-gallant yard.

"That would be the best part of it."

"You can't be an officer, you know, and live in the cabin."

"I would rather be a seaman."

"That would make you an inferior, and you must obey the orders given you."

"I could do that."

"And when you go on shore, only a couple of shillings or so would be allowed for pocket money."

"But I can have my own money."

"No; your money would all be taken from you, and doled out to you in shillings."

"I should'nt like that, but I could endure it, if the rest do; though I don't think I should be without money a great while," added the hopeful young gentleman, significantly. "I have been talking with some of the lads, and I think they understand the matter."

"But you must do your duty if you join, and you may be captain, or something of that sort."

"I intend to do my duty; but there can be no harm in having my spending money."

"They take it from you when you join."

"Let them; but of course you would send me my allowance every month in a letter."

"I think my friend Mr. Lowington is needlessly strict in this matter," added the father, in a tone which seemed to indorse his son's idea that this stringent regulation might be evaded.

"Now she goes!" exclaimed Spenser, as the jib was run up, and the Josephine swung round. "I'll never be anything but a sailor."

"Perhaps you will change your mind before morning," said Paul, who happened to come near enough to hear the remark.

"O, no!"

"Were you ever at sea?"

"Never, except I crossed to Dublin once, and went in a steamer from Liverpool to Bristol; but I know I should like it."

"Would you like it to be turned out of your berth in a dark and stormy night, and then be sent aloft to reef topsails?"

"I think it would be fun."

"If you think so, probably it will be," added the captain, who always put a cheerful face upon hard and disagreeable work.

The Young America had tripped her anchor a little before the Josephine, and went down the river ahead of her. It was evident to the officers of the schooner that the ship was not as well handled as usual; but this was not to be expected, for one half of her crew were green hands, who had been drilled but a couple of days, and did not know the difference between a topmast and the cook's galley. The "greenies," as they were called on board, had been mixed in with the "old salts," so that there was always an experienced hand near to tell them what to do.

Off the entrance to Queen's Channel, the pilots were discharged, and the two vessels headed north by east, by the compass. The wind was moderate from the west-north-west, and the ship and the schooner went off close-hauled. It was soon evident that the Josephine was beating her consort, and could easily go a point closer to the wind while the Young America's topsails were almost shaking.

Anything that looked like a race produced an excitement on board. The Josephine carried all sail as well as the ship, and though she was a good mile astern when the course was given out off the Bell Buoy, in an hour she was within hail of her.

"We shall pass her," said Terrill to the captain.

"Yes, pass her, but go to leeward of her," replied Paul.

"We can lay a point closer, and easily go by her to windward."

"That would not be respectful. We must not take the wind out of the flag-officer's sails."

"Why don't she go faster?" asked Spenser Murdock.

"She can't when she is close-hauled," replied Paul. "With the wind on her quarter, or abeam, she is a very fast sailer, and perhaps would beat us."

The schooner was kept away a little, and in a short time passed the ship. When the two vessels were abeam of each other, the students ran up into the rigging and cheered lustily.

"Take in the foretop-gallant-sail, Mr. Terrill," said Captain Kendall, when the Josephine was a mile ahead of the ship.

"What is that for, Captain Kendall?" asked Spenser Murdock.

"I don't wish to run away from the ship," replied Paul.

"Man the foretop-gallant clewlines and buntlines! Stand by the braces!" shouted the first lieutenant when the hands had been piped.

"All ready, sir," reported the third lieutenant.

"Clear away the sheets! Clew up!" added Terrill.

The sheets by which the corners of the top-gallant-sail were hauled down to the end of the topsail-yard were let go; the corners of the sail were then hauled up to the yard by the clewlines, and the middle, or bunt, of the sail by the buntlines.

"Settle away the topsail-halyards!" continued the executive officer. "Square away!"

By the halyards the yard was lowered down on the cap, and as it descended, the spar was hauled round square by the braces.

"Lay aloft and furl the foretop-gallant-sail!" said Terrill; and the hands who were stationed on the top-gallant-yard went aloft, rolled up the sail, and wound the gaskets around it.

As the schooner seemed to be still gaining, the main gaff-topsail was taken in, and then the flying-jib. Finally the foresail was lowered, and then the Young America gained rapidly upon her. As she approached the Josephine, nine cheers were given, and the foresail was reset. With the foretop-gallant-sail, gaff-topsail, and flying-jib furled, the speed of the two vessels was about equal.

Paul entertained his guests handsomely in the cabin, and made them quite at home. Spenser Murdock was seasick in the evening, and was obliged to turn in at an early hour, in spite of his assertion that he meant to stay on deck all night, and see how the vessel was handled. When he turned out in the morning, there was a pilot on board, and the Josephine was following the Young America into the harbor of Whitehaven; and in due time both of them were moored in the second basin.

"Perhaps you have had sea enough," said Paul to the younger passenger, when he had given the order to furl everything. "People who are sick don't like the sea."

"But I like it; I dare say I shouldn't be sick again," replied Spenser, who was as chipper as a bird, now that the ugly motion of the sea had ceased.

"Do you really think you would like to be a sailor?"

"I do; I know I should; and I'm going to sea at all events. If your principal won't take me, I shall run away to sea on my own account."

"Don't do that. You will find that life in the forecastle of a ship, to one who has lived in a parlor, as you have, will be as bad as anything can be."

"I dare say; but I hope I shall be permitted to join this vessel."

"Not this one; if Mr. Lowington receives you, it will be in the Young America. We have none but old sailors here," added Paul.

"It's all the same to me."

The gig was lowered, and sent to the ship with Dr. Winstock and the passengers. Mr. Murdock renewed his application to the principal on behalf of his son. He was even more anxious than at first to procure his admission, for he had been strongly impressed by the system of discipline he had observed in the squadron. The appeal was successful at last, and Spenser was delighted beyond measure when informed that he had been admitted. He was in haste to put on his uniform, and commence his career as a sailor.

A suit of clothes was served out to him by one of the pursers, berth 66 was assigned to him, and he was sent below to make the change in his dress. A seaman pointed out his quarters, and then hastened on deck, where all hands were busy observing the new scene just opened to them. Spenser's berth was in the second tier from the cabin bulkhead, and the entrance was directly opposite the brig. The stewards were preparing the tables for breakfast; but there was no one else in the steerage.

The new hand made haste to clothe himself in his sea togs; and when he had done so, he felt as smart as though he had just donned a new suit from London. He went out into the passage-way, and surveyed his person in the small looking-glass which hung by the bull's-eye. He looked "salt," and felt so. Satisfied with his appearance, he picked up his shore suit, and took the contents of the pockets from them before tying them up in a bundle. His monthly allowance had been paid to him a few days before, and he had not yet spent any of it; he even had two sovereigns and some silver left from the previous payment.

He stood in the passage-way with the four bank notes and the specie in his hand, thinking what he should do with them. To him almost the only disagreeable thing in the discipline of the ship was being deprived of his pocket money. He had talked with several of the crew of the Josephine, one of whom told him how McLeish had managed; and he had decided before his admission to save his funds, especially as his father was ready to " wink " at his plan, and even supply him with his usual allowance. It would not do for him to say he had no money when asked by the principal, for he believed that a lie was dishonorable, rather than immoral, and was to be avoided when possible without the sacrifice of too much personal comfort.

While he was trying to make up his mind whether to put the notes in his stocking, as McLeish had done, or hide them in the berth, he became conscious that a couple of pairs of eyes were fixed upon him. Wilton and Monroe were both staring at him between the pales of the brig.

" I say, Greeny," called Wilton, in a low tone.

" Whom do you call Greeny? " demanded Murdock, displeased by the appellation.

" Hush! " added Wilton. " Come over here."

The new hand went over to the door of the prison.

" What do you mean by calling me Greeny? " he continued.

" That's a title of respect we give to new fellows — no harm intended. How are you off for stamps? "

" Stamps? "

" Have you any money? "

"I have — twenty-two pounds, and some odd silver. What's that to you?" said Murdock, still holding his money in his hand.

"They'll take it all away from you, and that will be the last you will see of it," replied Wilton.

"I don't want to give it up. I'm going to hide it in my berth."

"That's played out; the officers will search your berth after you have put everything to rights."

"I'll put it in my stocking, then."

"One of the lambs will see it when you turn in, and blow on you."

"Who are the lambs?"

"The lambs of the chaplain's fold."

"I don't understand you."

"Those that feed on water gruel and pipe to prayers twice a day in their berths. Give me the money, and I'll take care of it for you."

"You! What are you in there for?"

"For resistance to tyranny; because we wouldn't stand it to have our money taken from us."

"Is that all?"

"That's all. Hush! some one's coming down to fish your trousers pockets."

"Take it then," said Murdock, hastily, as he thrust the four five-pound notes through the bars, keeping back the specie.

One of the students came down the steps, went to his berth for something, and then returned to the deck, followed by Murdock.

"Well, he is a Greeny," said Wilton, as he glanced at the bills when the owner had gone.

CHAPTER XII.

THE CONSPIRATORS IN THE BRIG.

HAVING satisfactorily disposed of the young man who had given him so much uneasiness, Mr. Murdock left the ship, and hastened back to Manchester. Probably he did not even yet suspect that his own weak indulgence had spoiled the boy; but now he was in no danger of breaking into the counting-room, and stealing fifty pounds "for fun."

"Monroe, it's about time for us to get out of this place," said Wilton, after Murdock had gone on deck, and he had concealed the bank notes in his clothing.

"That's what I have been saying for ten days," replied Monroe.

"But I'm not going to make any confessions, or beg anybody's pardon, as Gus Pelham did."

"Then you may stay here for the rest of the cruise."

"I can get out of this place any time when I'm ready," added Wilton, compressing his lips, and shaking his head, to signify both his decision and his ability to do what he said.

"Why don't you do it, then?"

"Because I'm not ready. I don't want to go ashore without any money. I've got some now, and I'm going to turn my attention in that direction."

"Well, what are you going to do?" asked Monroe, doubtfully.

"I'm going to get out when I'm ready."

"What's the use of talking? You can't get out!" sneered Monroe, who had not much confidence in the boasts of his companion in confinement.

"Yes, I can."

"How?"

"It's easy enough; but I'm going to pay off old Lowington, for keeping me here so long, about the time I take my leave of the ship."

"You get out! I've heard you brag before."

"Brag! Do you think I can't do what I say I can?"

"I do think so. You wouldn't have staid in here ten days if you could have got out."

"I told you I wasn't going without any money," replied Wilton, impatiently. "Now I have some money, I'm going to do something."

"You don't mean to use that spoony's money — do you?"

"I'm going to borrow it of him for a brief period. I haven't any doubt there is money for you and me now in London. When we get it, we will pay off this fellow."

"Just as you paid that twenty pounds you borrowed from the safe!"

"See here, Ike Monroe; if you say another word about that, there'll be a row within a thousand miles of where we are. What's the use of talking about that any more? I mean to pay it, and I shall pay it; you may bet your life on that."

"Well, drop that then," added Monroe, who was not disposed to quarrel with any one, even on a matter of principle. "You don't tell how you intend to get out?"

"I don't mean to tell you till you show more spirit than you have yet," said Wilton, reproachfully.

"That's cool! Haven't I staid in this place ten days just to please you?"

"Yes; and if it hadn't been for me, you would have gone down on your knees to old Lowington, and thrown yourself into the arms of the chaplain, and piped to prayers with Shuffles and the rest of the lambs. It was all I could do to keep your back stiff. Now you want to brag of your spirit."

"I haven't bragged of it; but I have stood by you from the beginning, even when you made a fool of yourself."

"Where would you have been, if I hadn't put you through? Who helped you out of the policeman's hands in Edinburgh?"

"And who helped me into the policeman's hands in London?" retorted Monroe, galled by the boasts of his friend.

"Never mind, Ike Monroe; it's no use to help you out of trouble. There is nothing like gratitude in you."

"You have helped me into trouble twice where you have helped me out once."

"No matter; that's the way you treat a fellow after he has done everything for you," said Wilton, as he walked over to the farther corner of the prison, and sat down on his stool.

"What's the use of getting mad, Wilt? If you are

going to keep punching me in this way, I shall make my peace with Lowington, and get out as soon as I can."

"You want to quarrel with me."

"I don't want to quarrel. It's you."

"No, it isn't I! You keep twitting me about the safe, or something of that sort," growled Wilton. "I wish I had a good fellow in here with me. I'd end up this old Academy Ship in less than ten days."

"What would you do?"

"Do you suppose I would tell such a milk-and-water sop as you are what I'm going to do? There is no more backbone in you than there is in a fish-worm."

Monroe felt reproved for his want of firmness. He was silent for a time, and the crew were piped down to breakfast. There was no chance to say anything more till afternoon, when all hands were on deck drilling in seamanship. By that time both of them had cooled off, and the kettle ceased to call the pot black. There had been half a dozen such disputes between them since they had been in the brig. Monroe, though he had a strong desire to escape from confinement, had not the courage to send for the principal, and declare that he was sorry for what he had done, and was willing to do better. The taunts and jeers of his friend were too much for him.

"I don't see how you can get out," said he, after they had talked conciliation a few minutes.

"If you say you are willing to stand by me till the end, I will tell you," replied Wilton.

"Of course I shall stand by you, whether you tell me or not," added Monroe, magnanimously.

"Now you speak like a good fellow!" said Wilton, warmly. "Didn't you see Adler talking with me yesterday?"

"Yes."

"Well, we fixed it then."

"Fixed what?" asked Monroe, when the other paused.

"Fixed the plan to get out, of course," replied Wilton, in a whisper.

"What is it?" demanded Monroe, his curiosity excited.

"When I am ready, he is to bring me the carpenter's saw, and nothing can be easier than to saw off one of these pales."

"I suppose not; but how long do you think you could saw before some one would hear the noise?"

"O, you are a blockhead, if there ever was one!" exclaimed Wilton.

"Perhaps I am; but if my head is a block, you can't saw it with that kind of nonsense."

"Do you think I'm going to saw it off when all hands are in the steerage?"

"There's always somebody round."

"When the fellows go ashore, the boatswain, carpenter, and sailmaker always go with them to take care of the boats — don't they?"

"They do; and while they are gone, all the boats are gone — are they not?"

"Well, they are generally; but I can manage that. I haven't told you a quarter part of my plan yet?"

"Tell the rest of it then."

"I will, if you will keep your mouth shut and hear

what I have to say. When I go next time, I'm going to take twenty or thirty of the fellows with me."

Monroe laughed at this extensive arrangement.

"Don't you believe it?" asked Wilton, taking a slip of paper from his pocket. "Look at that!"

Monroe did look at it. On the paper were written in pencil the names of twenty-five of the crews of the Young America and the Josephine. But this list failed to convince the sceptic of the practicability of the plan suggested.

"Do you see that?" demanded Wilton, in a tone of triumph, as though he had established his position.

"I see it; but any fellow could write out a list of names."

"No, he couldn't — not such a list of names as that. This thing has racked my brains for a week, and it means something, I tell you."

"Well, what does it mean?" asked Monroe, whose curiosity was wrought up to a high pitch.

"I have been thinking this thing over while you lay there whining."

"You didn't say anything to me about it."

"I know that. I wasn't going to talk about it till I got things ready; besides, I wanted some money to work with. It took some gumption, I can tell you, to make out that list. It isn't every fellow that could have done it."

"I don't see it."

"Don't you? Have you looked at those names? Have you considered who and what they are?"

"They are all our fellows," replied Monroe, glancing at the list again.

"That's so; every fellow whose name is on that paper is just as true as steel. I've worked over that list, Ike Monroe, you'd better believe. I weighed every fellow in the balance, and if there was a doubt against him, I threw him over. I rejected the names of a good many fellows."

"I have no doubt there was a good deal of talent displayed in getting up that list. I'm willing to grant that it is a big thing."

"It is a big thing."

"What of it?" asked Monroe. "That's what I want to know."

"Those are the fellows who are going with us when we leave the ship," replied Wilton, in a whisper, as though he was afraid the crew, who were at that moment in the rigging, would hear him.

"How do you know they will go?"

"Don't I know the fellows?"

"Have you spoken to them about it?"

"Of course I haven't yet."

"That's like one of your plans, Wilt!" laughed Monroe; "you have got it all fixed before a single fellow has agreed to take part in it!"

"Don't I tell you I know the fellows?"

"So do I know them; but I am not so sure they will be willing to run away from the ship with you."

"You are an ignoramus, Ike Wilton! You don't know beans!"

"I know peas, if I don't know beans," replied Monroe, alluding to former experiences.

"You haven't heard half the plan, and begin to condemn it."

"If you have anything more that is half as hopeful as what you have told me, I don't believe you will set the river afire with your nonsense."

"Do I understand you to say that you won't go in with me?" demanded Wilton, chilled by the cold water which had been thrown upon his scheme.

"Don't understand anything of the sort! I have staid in the brig ten days to please you, and now I will do anything, if it is to knock the bottom out of the ship, with you."

"That sounds more like it," replied Wilton, mollified by this unequivocal manifestation of devotion on the part of his friend.

"I am willing to go it blind, capture the ship, set her on fire, or anything else," added Monroe, desperately.

He had been bullied into resisting his convictions of duty, and though he had exaggerated his devotion to the cause of his friend, he was doubtless ready to do anything rather than endure his painful confinement much longer.

"All right, my boy!" added Wilton with enthusiasm. "You are just where I want you to be, and just where I am. Do you think I am going to join the lambs and submit to Lowington's tyranny? Not if I know it!"

"Bully for you!" replied Monroe, whose spirit seemed to have improved under the cunning castigation of his fellow-prisoner. "I am ready to stand by you, whether you go up to the moon or down to the bottom of the sea. Now tell me what it's all about?"

"When we leave, we shall go off in the Josephine," whispered Wilton, giving due emphasis and dramatic effect to the astounding revelation.

Monroe was not much astonished, and would not have been if his companion had told him he intended to make his escape in one of the mail steamers in the harbor, to be chartered or captured for that purpose. While he was desperate enough to undertake anything, he had not much confidence in Wilton's strategy or ingenuity. He was willing to do the worst thing that could be done, and then abide the consequences.

"What do you think of that?" demanded Wilton, with a sensational flourish, when his friend relapsed into silence.

"Put it through! I'm with you."

"I suppose you think it can't be done," added Wilton, who courted a little opposition in order to present his case with due effect.

"I don't know but it can," said Monroe, looking over the paper which was still in his hand. "I don't see the name of any officer on this paper."

"Not an officer; and you won't, while I have anything to do with it. They put on too many airs. It was the quarrel between Shuffles and Pelham which used up the Chain League."

"Half of these fellows are in the Josephine."

"I know they are; and that's just where I want them. Now I will tell you just how the whole thing is to be done," continued Wilton, dropping his voice to a whisper. "Half the fellows are in the ship, and half in the consort. On a certain day fixed upon beforehand, all these fellows will cut up so as to lose their liberty when the ship's company go ashore. Adler says they never use but two or three of the Josephine's boats, and there is always one at the davits. Just as soon as all hands have left, the fellows on board of the schooner will send the boat to the ship, and we will all go on board of the consort, slip the cable, make sail, and be off. Don't you see how easy it is all done?"

"I see how easy it's all done in words," replied Monroe. "Who's to be captain of the Josephine when you get off? I suppose you are, though."

"No; I don't understand navigation well enough. Tom Perth is to be captain. Every fellow likes him, and he can handle a vessel as well as Haven or any of the rest of the officers."

"Perth's a good fellow."

"It's plain enough; there is a heap of work to do before this thing can be carried out, and we may not get away for a month yet."

"A month! Do you mean to stay in the brig a month?"

"I don't know; I think Lowington will get tired of keeping us here."

"I'm tired of it now, and I don't care about waiting for him to get tired of it. We can operate twice as well outside as we can in this cage."

"I don't know about that. Don't be in a hurry, Ike, till we see how the land lies."

That night Wilton contrived to have a talk with Adler, to whom he revealed his plan, after obtaining a pledge of secrecy.

"I'm ready, for one," replied Adler, with refreshing promptness; "but so far as the Josephines are concerned, it's all in your eye."

"No, it isn't," protested Wilton.

"But I tell you it is. You have been shut up in the brig ever since the fellows went aboard the Josephine, and you haven't cut your eye-teeth yet. If I had a place in the consort, I wouldn't get into any scrape — not I. The fellows are treated like gentlemen there. They don't have any one to watch them when they go on shore. It's no use of talking about the Josephines; they won't have anything to do with the affair; and if you say a word to any fellow, he'll blow on you, as sure as your name's Wilton."

"Do you mean to tell me that Lynch, Grossbeck, and Sanborn won't go in with *me?*" demanded Wilton.

"I know they won't; and I wouldn't, if I were in their place. All the old fellows on board would join the lambs to-day if they could get into the Josephine by it. Mind your eye! There comes an officer."

Adler edged off out of sight till the danger was passed, and then returned to his former position between the pantry and the brig, where he could easily get out of sight when any one appeared.

"I'll tell you what to do, Wilt," said he; and it was evident that he had been thinking of the hopeful scheme during his brief absence.

"Well, what?" asked Wilton, who, however, was not prepossessed in favor of any scheme in opposition to his own.

"Make up your crew out of the ship."

"But half the best fellows have gone into the schooner."

"Don't you believe it. There are lots of tip-top fellows among the greenies."

"I don't know them."

"I do; and I know a dozen of them who will go in with me into anything I say."

"They are not sailors."

"They will be before long; but the old fellows can go aloft, and these greenies can pull and haul well enough. Don't you let a word be said to any of the Josephines. You might as well take the speaking-trumpet, and blow it into Lowington's ears. All the old fellows are mad because they can't go in the Josephine; and because McLeish and a chap with specs on were sent to her, instead of a couple of us. Who's going to be captain of the Josephine when you get her?"

"We can't get her on your plan," growled Wilton.

"Yes, you can. If twenty-five or thirty of our fellows cut up so as to be left on board when the fellows go ashore, one of the boats will be left at the davits. I could manage this thing first-rate myself."

"I suppose you could; every fellow thinks he could. Where's Tommy Perth?"

"On deck."

"Tell him I want to talk with him — will you, Adler?"

"Just so — I see," replied Adler, with a knowing look. "He is to be the captain."

"That's so. What do you think of it?"

"First-rate! All the fellows like Tom Perth."

It is to be regretted that Perth, who was really a clever fellow, but without any balance-wheel, consented to see the reprobate of the ship. In the shades of the evening, he managed to have a long chat with Wilton; and flattered by the honor of being captain of the Josephine, which was to be conferred upon him, accepted the leadership in the wild scheme, and promised to "organize victory" out of the available material. Wilton appointed himself first officer.

"See here, Perth," said Wilton, when the details of the scheme had been well considered; "we don't want any more Chain Leagues, or anything of that sort — not if we know it."

"It don't answer to tell all you know," added Perth.

"No; you and I must work the thing up ourselves."

"How do you mean?"

"No fellow shall be allowed to know who joins us and who don't, till the last moment. We can fix twenty-five or thirty of them, and when we are all ready, we will tell them what to do."

"That's the idea," added Perth. Then a fellow won't know who belongs and who don't. I'll go to work on it this very night, and I'll ring in three before we turn in."

"Look out, and don't make a mess of it," said Wilton, earnestly. "There are four of us in now; about twenty more will do the business."

"Don't be afraid of me," replied Perth, as he walked away to commence his mission of mischief.

"I think we might as well repent now, and get out of the brig," said Wilton, jocosely, when Perth had left him.

"That's what I've been saying before," replied Monroe.

"I don't know about it, though. I'm afraid you would back down if you got out."

"Not I."

"To-morrow will be Sunday, and we will see what can be done. I suppose, if we should join the lambs, and pipe to prayers with Shuffles, we shouldn't be half so likely to be suspected, if any of the officers should happen to hear a word or two that was not intended for their ears."

There are degrees of evil as well as of good. Some bad boys are worse than other bad boys. Even Monroe, whose standard of morality was low, revolted at the idea, needlessly, and for the success of a vicious scheme, of putting on the guise of the hypocrite. He was not willing to be a "lamb."

Sunday passed away in the usual manner. All the Josephine's officers and crew attended divine service on board the ship in the forenoon and in the afternoon. It was a stormy day, but no one was allowed to be absent. On Monday, after the lessons were disposed of, the crew of the ship were drilled till dark in reefing, furling, and making sail; and by this time the "greenies" were tolerably perfect in the parts assigned them in the station bills. They were practised at "all hands," by watches, and by quarter watches, but hardly any of them knew anything more than was absolutely required of them. They could not do the work of others. One whose station in tacking, was at the main clew-garnets and main tack, would not have known what to do if told to let go the head-bowlines, as any of the old sailors would. It would be months before the green hands would know all the ropes in the ship.

On Tuesday, after recitations, Mr. Lowington explained to the ship's company of the Young America the object of coming to Whitehaven, which was to devote a couple of days to the Lake District of England; and for this purpose two days of vacation would be granted. He told them that Mr. McLaurin, the kind friend who had rendered them so much service in Scotland, had made arrangements which would enable them to see most of the objects of interest in this attractive region in the time allowed for the purpose.

Orders had been sent to Captain Kendall, and by two o'clock the students were in the railroad station at Whitehaven, seated in the carriages. Very much to the disappointment of Monroe, his companion in the brig decided not to make any confession or promises, and they were compelled to remain in confinement until the return of the excursion. Lynch and Grossbeck were also compelled to stay on board the Josephine, in charge of the boatswain. The party were in their usual high spirits, and in about two hours arrived at Keswick, which is situated in the northern portion of the Lake District. At this place they found Mr. McLaurin, who was delighted to meet Pelham again, and immediately conducted him to his room at the hotel where his family were.

Keswick is a small town, situated near the foot of Skiddaw, a lofty mountain, and not far from Derwentwater, one of the beautiful lakes of this region. The town itself was of no interest, but Mr. McLaurin conducted the students to Greta Hall, a little out of the town, which was the home of Southey, the poet. It was a plain building, with vines running over it, but nothing very fine about it. The library of the poet, and the room in which he died, were shown, and the party wandered about the grounds. A fine view of the lake was obtained near Castle Rigg. It is a beautiful sheet of water, surrounded by embosoming mountains, with several little islets, which made it a pleasant scene for the eye to look upon.

Following the eastern shore of the lake, the party, after a walk of three miles, arrived at the Falls of Lodore, about which Southey wrote his "gleaming and streaming and steaming and beaming" poem, very melodious and very amusing, which makes the reader feel something like a waterfall. The heavy rains of Sunday had given the fall its best appearance, though at low water the cataract is quite tame. The stream which forms it flows between two lofty crags, and its whole descent is about one hundred and fifty feet. At the village of Rossthwait, where Mr. McLaurin had provided accommodations, the travellers spent the night.

The next morning the company started to walk to Ullswater, the second in size of the British lakes, though it is only nine miles in length by one in width. On the way they "climbed the dark brow of the mighty Helvellyn," which the tragic death of Charles Gough, a young man who was killed by falling from a precipice, and watched over by his faithful dogs for three months, has made memorable in the poems of Scott and others. The Red Tarn, Striding Edge, and Catchedecam were familiar names, because the poem of the Scottish bard was in the school readers.

The excursion party arrived at Patterdale, where they dined, and embarked in a small steamer for a trip through Ullswater, a lake surrounded by mountains, and abounding in picturesque scenery. On their return to Patterdale, they proceeded in wagons to Grasmere, the home and the burial-place of Wordsworth, the " poet of nature," and where he often had with him Southey, Coleridge, Scott, Lamb, and Wilson. The lakes Rydal Mere and Grasmere were pretty sheets of water, and everything seemed to be sanctified by the spirit of the gentle bard, who had celebrated every spot in the vicinity by his pen and his presence.

But only a couple of hours could be spent in this delightful locality, and the wagons moved on to the Low-Wood Hotel, on the banks of Windermere, the largest of the English lakes. The next morning the officers and seamen were photographed in a group on the lawn in front of the hotel, by an artist who was taking views of this picturesque region.

CHAPTER XIII.

CAPTAIN KENDALL'S STATE-ROOM.

THE last day of the excursion was spent in exploring the scenery of Lake Windermere, which, though tame and wanting in the grandeur of the other lakes the students had visited, was soft and pleasing in its aspect. The region is a type of that in the vicinity of Lake Champlain, though the lakes are not so large, nor the mountains so high, in the former as in the latter.

Small steamboats ply on Lake Windermere, and the boys had an opportunity to visit every part of it — not a difficult task to be accomplished in a single day, as the lake is only ten miles long, and not more than a mile in breadth. The lakes of the district are all of this character, their width being small compared with their length. Lake George is thirty-six miles in length, but does not exceed four in breadth. The length of Lake Champlain is rather more than ten times its width, while the same is true of numerous sheets of water in the Adirondack region.

Scawfell is the highest mountain in the Lake District, or in England. It is three thousand two hundred and eight feet high. Mount Marcy, the highest mountain in the lake district of New York, is five thousand four hundred and sixty feet. If we could plant Whittier, Longfellow, and Bryant in the Adirondack country, we should have a "lake district" in New York more sublime than any England can boast; for it needs only the inspiration of the poets to invest it with the needed charm. In natural attractions, the country west of Lake Champlain is far richer than the much-lauded Lake District of England, beautiful and picturesque as is the latter.

Lake Windermere is principally fed by two streams — the Rothay and the Brathay, both of which rise in the mountains, and unite their waters about half a mile before they enter the lake. Windermere is full of trout and charr, the latter being the English smelt. In the spawning season both of these fish start in company to go up stream, and swim together up the river till they reach the junction of the two mountain streams, where they separate, all the trout going up the Rothay, and all the charr up the Brathay. Not a trout or a smelt makes a mistake, and goes the wrong way. This singular exhibition of instinct has excited a great deal of attention.

During the excursion, the students had abundant opportunities to wander about in small parties, and from the time the boys began their tramp down the shores of Derwentwater, Tom Perth had been busy enlisting the recruits who were to take part in the capture of the Josephine. Those of "our fellows" who were left in the ship were in a state of discontent. They were jealous of the privileges which had been accorded to the crew of the Josephine, and the rebel captain found the commission he had accepted easier than he supposed. When the party took their places in the train at Windermere to return to Whitehaven, he had actually pledged nine of the old sailors to act with him. This number, added to those already secured, made up half the required crew.

At eight in the evening all hands were on board their vessels, tired enough to sleep without an opiate. The next afternooon was spent in visiting the coal mines of Whitehaven, which are said to be among the most extraordinary in the world. They are nine hundred and sixty feet in depth, and extend for some distance under the bed of the sea, and beneath the town. There are five entrances to these mines on the north and south sides of the place, which are called Bearmouths; but the descent through them is so gradual that horses can go down. In driving times as many as fifteen hundred tons of coal are taken every day from the mines.

After recitation on Saturday, the signal for sailing was hoisted at the peak of the Young America. The pilots came on board, and by two o'clock the ship and her consort were standing out of the harbor, bound for Holyhead. The wind was light, and at dark the little squadron had not made forty miles. In the night a dense fog settled down upon the sea, and the two vessels parted company. Paul did not leave the deck of the Josephine that night. On Sunday morning the weather was clear, but the Young America was not to be seen, and the young commander, after ordering the officer of the deck to "crack on" for Holyhead, turned in. At twelve o'clock she came to anchor within the breakwater at the port of her destination. Three hours later the ship came in, and moored near her.

Monroe, in the brig, was out of patience with Wilton, and was almost ready to get out on any terms, even by sacrificing his companion, and exposing his daring scheme. Perhaps he would have done so, if a circumstance had not occurred, after the ship came to anchor, which forced Wilton to change his tactics. At every opportunity he could obtain, Tom Perth held a consultation with the chief conspirator; for, having received his appointment of captain from him, that honor which is said to exist among thieves would not permit him to ignore his principal. It had been agreed between them, that if Perth was caught in the act of communicating with the prisoners, he should declare he was persuading Wilton to repent and do his duty.

"What are you doing there?" demanded Foster, the fourth lieutenant of the ship, as he discovered Perth talking with Wilton through the bars of the brig.

"He called me," replied Perth, with feigned humility.

"No matter for that; you had no right to speak to him," replied Foster, as he went on deck. "You will report to the first lieutenant at once."

Perth followed the lieutenant, and was reported to Goodwin for speaking to a prisoner. Goodwin reported the case to the captain, and the captain to the principal, before whom the delinquent was summoned.

"He hailed me," pleaded Perth.

"What did he want of you?"

"He wanted to talk with me, and I told him he was a fool to spend a fortnight in the brig," replied Perth.

"Did you, indeed?"

"I did, sir, and I advised him to behave himself."

"That was good advice, and it was only strange that it should come from you," added Mr. Lowington. "Perth, what trick are you up to now?"

"No trick, sir. I haven't been in any scrape for a good while," protested the culprit.

"But I think you are planning one now."

"No, sir!"

"You actually asked Wilton to behave himself."

"Yes, sir."

"What did he say?"

"He said he was really sorry he had run away, and if it wasn't for the fellows laughing at him, he would own up, and turn over a new leaf."

"Well, what then?" asked the principal, deeply interested, even while he had no confidence in the rogue before him.

"I told him the fellows were sorry for him, and wouldn't laugh at him. I advised him to make a clean breast of it."

"Are you telling me the truth, Perth?"

"You can ask Wilton, sir."

"I will ask him; and if you have told me a falsehood, Perth, you shall spend your spare hours to-morrow on the cross-trees."

Mr. Lowington led the way to the steerage, where he sent a steward to his room for the key of the brig. Peaks was directed to bring Wilton before him. The principal had been sadly troubled by the obstinacy of the prisoners in the brig. While they refused even to promise better behavior, he could not let them out; and he felt that their confinement, so long continued, would be an injury to them. He hoped, therefore, that they were in a frame of mind which would permit their release, though their punishment was to be continued by depriving them of their privileges for at least a fortnight longer.

"Did you call to Perth?" asked Mr. Lowington.

"Yes, sir. I was going to send a message to you, saying that I wanted to see you," replied Wilton, promptly.

"Did you wish to see me?"

"Yes, sir."

"What for?"

"To ask you to let me out."

"Did you expect me to let you out?"

"I didn't know; but I wanted to tell you I was sorry for what I had done, and meant to do better."

"Do you mean that?" asked Mr. Lowington, encouraged by the prospect.

"Yes, sir, I do; and I never meant anything half so strongly before," replied Wilton.

"How long have you felt this?"

"Ever since I was first put into the brig."

"Why did you not say so? You are aware that I do not keep any student in the brig unless he is obstinate and rebellious, as you were."

"I didn't like to say so, though I felt so," answered Wilton.

"Why not?"

"I was afraid the fellows would laugh at me."

"Perth, when a prisoner in the brig speaks to you, there is no necessity for you to hold any conversation with him," added Mr. Lowington, turning to the rogue. "If one in the brig wishes to speak to me, he can call upon an officer."

"That's what I was going to do," said Perth.

"But that is what you did not do. You may go now."

Perth went; and for half an hour the principal talked with Wilton and Monroe, both of whom promised to observe the rules of the ship, and submit to whatever further punishment was deemed necessary. They were at once discharged from arrest, but were not to be allowed to leave the ship till further orders.

"That was well done," said Wilton, as he went on deck with Monroe.

"It ought to have been done a fortnight ago," growled Monroe.

As soon as Mr. Agneau, the chaplain, learned that the prisoners had been released, and were in a penitent frame of mind, he hastened to give them such counsel and instruction as their case required. The hypocrite Wilton was prepared for this, but Monroe was silent under the infliction, as he regarded it. The former promised everything, and talked like one of the "lambs." He declared that he had been led to see the error of his ways, and he had reformed. The chaplain was earnest and faithful in the discharge of his duty.

"We must take care of him, and surround him with good influences," said the simple-hearted chaplain to Shuffles, when he had left the supposed penitents.

"I will do what I can for them; I used to be very intimate with both of them," replied Shuffles, in whose change of heart, life, and purpose there was no sham.

Shuffles improved the first opportunity to speak a kind word to Wilton and Monroe. They had all been students of the Brockway Academy together under Mr. Baird; indeed, Shuffles and Monroe had been the indirect cause of the establishing of the Academy Ship.

"Wilton, I suppose you won't believe it, but I enjoy myself ten times as well now as I used to when I was always getting into scrapes," said Shuffles.

"I do believe it," responded Wilton.

"I mean to be a good man; and this desire makes me happy."

"I mean to be so too," protested Wilton. "I have had a long time to think over these things while in the brig."

"I am glad to hear you say so."

"I'm going to be one of the lambs," added Wilton.

Shuffles looked at him, and had a doubt of his sincerity.

"Do you think I don't mean it?" demanded Wilton.

"I hope you do."

"But I do; I am ready to pipe to prayers with you and the rest of the lambs."

"You must not use those sneering terms, if you mean what you say," added Shuffles, mildly.

"I didn't mean anything," continued Wilton, fearful that he had been overdoing the matter, as hypocrites generally do.

Shuffles talked with the penitents for some time; but he understood human nature better than Mr.

Agneau, and he had grave fears in regard to them, though he hoped for the best.

The next morning it was noised through the ship that Wilton had joined the "lambs;" that he had actually attended a private prayer-meeting with the chaplain, Shuffles, and a few others. The hypocrite did not deny it; on the contrary, he declared it was all true, though the prayer-meeting was an exaggeration of the interview between himself and the chaplain.

"Ah, my lad, I'm glad you got out," said Spenser Murdock, as they met on deck.

"Thank you," replied Wilton. "I'm glad to get out."

"And the lads say you have reformed your life and manners, and become one of the lambs. If that's so, I'll trouble you for the twenty pounds I placed in your keeping."

"Twenty pounds!" exclaimed Wilton, vexed at the demand, with which it was no part of his purpose to comply.

"Ay, twenty pounds. Don't you remember?"

"Hush up!" whispered Wilton, as an officer passed them.

"Won't you give me the money?" demanded Murdock, when the officer was out of hearing.

"What money?"

"I see you mean to cheat me out of it," added the new hand, indignantly. "You are not a lamb, after all, for the lambs don't do such things."

Wilton could not help seeing that if he denied having the money, it would not be in keeping with the character he had assumed. He must be consistent, outwardly, at least.

"Did you have any more money?" he asked.

"What if I had?" replied Murdock, angrily.

"What did you do with it?"

"I gave it up when the principal asked for it, and he gave me a receipt."

"Did he ask you if that was all you had?"

"Of course he did. What business is that of yours?" said the new hand, impatiently.

"Of course he did; and you told him you had twenty pounds in my keeping," added Wilton.

"No, I didn't; I told him I had no more, and I hadn't; and if I trust to your honesty I'm not likely to have any more."

"You told him you had no more," repeated Wilton.

"What else should I tell him? To be sure I told him so."

"That was a wicked lie," said Wilton, gravely.

"You may be a lamb, but you can't pull your wool over my eyes. Give me my twenty pounds or I'll choke it out of you."

"Consider, my dear friend, what a fearful thing it is to utter a deliberate falsehood."

"Will you give me my money?"

"I dare not do it after the falsehood you have told. I shall be obliged to hand it to Mr. Lowington, and state the circumstances to him."

"You will!" exclaimed Murdock, aghast at this proposition.

"I am sorry to expose you, but I must do my duty. You would call me a hypocrite if I did not give this money to the principal."

"Or if you did, either," replied Murdock, hitting the nail squarely on the head.

"I am willing to suffer any reproaches that may be heaped upon me. The chaplain told me I should be sneered at and reviled; but I didn't expect it so soon."

"Give me my money then."

"You can't help seeing that my duty will not permit me to do that. I hate to expose you and get you into trouble."

Spenser Murdock was decidedly opposed to having his conduct laid bare to the principal.

"I see you mean to cheat me out of my money, and I suppose I can't help myself," added he, more mildly. "If that's what the lambs are made of, I would rather have veal than mutton."

"Don't you see my position? I don't want to cheat you out of your money, as you call it, and I don't want to expose you to the principal. What shall I do?"

"Give me my money, and then you will neither cheat me nor expose me."

"It wouldn't be right for me to do that," replied Wilton, meekly. "Perhaps we may make a compromise."

"What's that? It's something mean, I dare say."

"I must get rid of the money somehow. It don't belong to me."

"There's a glimmer of truth."

"It would be wrong for me to give it to you, because you have told the principal a falsehood. It would be wrong for me to keep it, because it don't belong to me. I'll tell you what may be done."

"Well, what may be done?" demanded Murdock.

"We can give it to the poor."

"I dare say we can," added the new hand, dryly.

"Then the money will do good, and nobody will be in the wrong. It will save you from exposure, and me from sharing in the guilt of your deception."

"I'll do it!" exclaimed Murdock, who concluded that it was better to lose his twenty pounds than to be exposed to the principal.

"Very well; then the matter is all settled," said Wilton.

"Settled? I think not. I thought you said we were to give the money to the poor," interposed Murdock.

"Certainly."

"Who's going to give it to the poor?"

"I am, of course."

"I prefer to do it myself."

"But I can't trust one who has been guilty of telling a wilful falsehood."

"O, you can't!" ejaculated Murdock. "Then I suppose I am to trust you."

"I see no other way, unless you prefer that our good friend the chaplain should be informed of the circumstances, and requested to give the money away for you."

"He would tell the principal."

"Probably he would," replied Wilton, candidly.

"But I won't trust one of the lambs."

"Very well; then I will wait upon Mr. Lowington and state the case to him;" and Wilton walked aft towards the quarter-deck, where Mr Lowington was.

"Do as you like about it — give the money to the poor yourself," said Murdock, following him.

"Very well," replied Wilton. "I'll give it to the poor," he muttered to himself; "but I don't know of any one that is any poorer than I am."

Murdock gave up his money as lost, though he was tempted to go to Mr. Lowington, expose the rascality of the young "lamb," and confess his own fault. But he had not the moral courage to do this. Accustomed as he had been always to have money in his pocket, he felt poor now. After recitations, when all hands were piped to go ashore, he did not care to join them. He had not a penny in his possession, and the shilling which was allowed each student seemed to be only an aggravation of the misery to one who had hardly ever put his hand in his pocket without finding at least a sovereign there.

"Young gentlemen," said Mr. Lowington, when the crew gathered on the deck of the ship, "I have informed Captain Kendall that we shall visit the Josephine to-day, and on our way to the shore we will spend half an hour with him."

This was welcome intelligence to the boys, for an opportunity had not before been presented for them to visit the consort, which they were very desirous of examining. Mr. Lowington consented to the visit because he had promised it, rather than because it was expedient to do so. The students had Josephine on the brain; and if she had been a beautiful young lady, she could hardly have been more adored. All the hands in the ship, even to the officers, wanted to get into her; and a visit to her would not have a tendency to render them any more contented with their lot in the Young America. As she was so popular, Mr. Lowington entertained serious thoughts of disposing of the ship, and procuring in her place two small vessels like the consort. He had even spoken to Mr. Fluxion on the subject, and the matter was still under advisement.

"If you please, sir, I would like to be excused from going on shore," said Spenser Murdock, as the principal descended from his rostrum.

"Why so?"

"I have been all about Holyhead several times, and it makes me tired to walk about so much," replied the new hand.

"Very well; we will not compel any one to go ashore."

"But if you please, sir, I would like to visit the Josephine."

"You may remain on board of her till a boat comes from her to the ship. The stewards are going back and forth occasionally."

Agreeably to these arrangements, the boats pulled to the Josephine. Flag-officer Gordon and the faculty were received with all the honors, and formally welcomed by Captain Kendall. The crew of the ship were allowed to explore every part of her except the cabin, to which none but officers were admitted. The visitors were as much fascinated by the trim little craft as her own officers and crew were, and envied those who were attached to her. After remaining half an hour on board, the boats started for the shore, to be followed by those of the Josephine as soon as the honors had been rendered to the departing guests.

Captain Kendall was in a hurry, but at the last moment one of the acting pursers had reminded him that there was not small silver enough on hand to pay the allowances to the crew the next time they went ashore. He had settled his accounts with the principal on Saturday, as he was required to do every week, and one hundred pounds in Bank of England notes had been paid to him. While the purser was standing at his door, he had opened his iron box, and taken therefrom twenty pounds to be exchanged for shillings, half crowns, and florins on shore.

Paul was usually very careful in the charge of his financial affairs, but in his hurry on this occasion he made a bad mistake. He handed the bank notes to the purser, leaving the key in the safe.

"What is to be done with McLeish?" asked Terrill, when the captain appeared at the door. "He is in the first cutter, ready to go on shore."

"I stopped his liberty this morning," replied Paul, rather sharply. "You will order him out of the boat. If he does not obey promptly, request Mr. Cleats to take him out."

Paul's thoughts were fully occupied with this case of discipline, and painfully so, we may add, for he could not help considering how much regret it would give to Grace Arbuckle to learn that her penitent had fallen from his high resolutions, and been impudent to no less a person than the captain himself. He closed the door of his state-room, the safe driven from his mind by the affair of McLeish, and locked it, but left the key in the door, according to his usual custom. He went on deck soon enough to hear Terrill order the impudent hand on deck.

Somewhat to his surprise, McLeish yielded a prompt obedience. As he came on deck he met Paul, and touched his cap, with no evidence of being stubborn and refractory in his manner.

"I stopped your liberty this morning when you were impudent to me," said Paul, mildly.

"I did not understand you, sir," replied McLeish, with more than usual gentleness. "I did not mean to be impudent. I was quick, and did not mind what I said. I'm very sorry; indeed I am."

"You must stay on board this time; and I hope there will be no occasion to deprive you of your liberty again," added Paul, kindly.

"I hope not. I am willing to be punished; but as I didn't mean to be impudent, I hope you will not tell the young lady," said McLeish, touching his cap again.

"You shall not suffer in her estimation as long as you try to do well, though you occasionally fail," continued Paul, as he went over the side into his gig.

The boats pulled for the shore, and McLeish watched them till they disappeared behind a ship at anchor. In the forenoon Professor Hamblin had complained of him to the captain for inattention at the recitation, after giving him several black marks.

"I'm doing the best I can," growled he, snappishly. "I'm a fool I suppose, but I'm no the only one where you are."

"Your liberty will be stopped again," replied the

captain, expecting that the next thing would be to order McLeish into the brig.

McLeish was impulsive, and had spoken without consideration. The captain's remark recalled his good resolution, and he was silent. He was truly sorry for what he had done, and intended to apologize to the captain at the first convenient opportunity. He understood the captain to say that his liberty would be stopped if he persisted in his course, not that it had been.

When he turned from the boats he saw Spenser Murdock looking at him. They were strangers to each other, and as McLeish did not care about talking with any one in his present frame of mind, he ran up the fore rigging, and took a seat on the topsail-yard to think of his case. Murdock, finding he was avoided by the only student on board, walked up and down the deck a while, and then descended to the steerage to examine more minutely the accommodations of the crew. The boatswain and carpenter of the Josephine had gone on shore to take charge of the boats, while the party were seeing the sights in Holyhead; and there was no one on board but the cook and stewards, who had done their work and were idling on the forecastle.

Murdock walked through the steerage, looked into the brig, and into the pantry. Then he opened the door leading into the cabin, where all seamen were forbidden to go, which may have been the particular reason why he desired to enter it. No one was present, and he walked through the passage into the cabin. He had spent a day there as a passenger, and was familiar with the place. He looked into everything with more than Yankee curiosity, not neglecting even the sacred precincts of the captain's state-room, the goal of every student's ambition. He looked into Paul's berth, and into his lockers. Before he had fully examined everything, his eye rested upon the iron box, with the key in the lid.

He opened it — of course he opened it, for he was a " wild boy." He saw the bank notes; he picked them up, and counted them. There were eighty pounds in the package. As Spenser Murdock always did wicked things " for fun," he thought it would be a good joke if he should put the notes in his pocket. He did put them in his pocket, for the pressure of poverty which rested so heavily upon him did not permit him to resist the temptation.

Closing the lid of the strong box, he began to exercise what cunning he had in regard to the disposal of the key, which he was satisfied had been left in the safe by accident. If found there it would show the means by which the money had been purloined. On the berth lay the captain's overcoat. He put the key into one of the pockets of this garment. He had seen several of the officers take their overcoats into the boats, for they seldom went on shore without being caught in a shower. Probably Captain Kendall had intended to take his, or why should it be lying on his bed?

Murdock took the overcoat and put it on the table in the cabin. The captain was expected to believe, when he returned, that he had put the key of the safe into the pocket of his overcoat, and left the garment on the cabin table; or, if he did not believe it, the facts, as he found them, ought to convince him that such was the case.

The new hand was satisfied with what he had done to cover up his amusing deed, and, having locked the door of the state-room, returned to the steerage. He had robbed the counting-room of the mill, once, and been detected; but more than once had he pilfered small sums from his father without detection, — always "for fun," of course, — and he was so much accustomed to this jocose criminality, that the deed did not seriously disturb him. He walked about the steerage for a few moments, when McLeish came down, tired of the fore-yard. By this time the young Scotchman felt more social, and the two students had a chat. While thus engaged, they heard the noise of lowering a boat on deck. Of course they wished to know what was to be done, and hastened on deck. The cook, by permission of the captain, was going on board of the Young America, in the boat, with two of the stewards, to visit her cooks; and Murdock obtained a passage with them. The bank notes were warm in his pocket, and he could not feel easy till he had disposed of them.

CHAPTER XIV.

THE KNIGHTS OF THE RED CROSS.

MURDOCK was more troubled to know what to do with the eighty pounds in his pocket than he was about the consequences of the crime he had committed. When he went on board of the ship, he saw Wilton and Monroe sitting on the rail, engaged in conversation; but he noticed that they stopped talking when he approached them. He was satisfied they were engaged in forbidden schemes, but he was too much occupied with his own affair to trouble himself with theirs. He went down into the steerage.

One of the cooks had opened the scuttle, and gone to one of the store-rooms in the hold for provisions. Murdock looked down. The place was as dark as Erebus; but curiosity, as well as the desire to find a hiding-place for his ill-gotten treasure, induced him to descend the ladder. He had hardly reached the foot of the steps before he saw the cook, with a lantern and a basket of stores, approaching the scuttle. Retreating behind a row of water-casks, the man did not observe him, and, going up the ladder, closed the scuttle after him.

Murdock had some matches in his pocket, and he lighted one of them so as to enable him to find a suitable place for the money. There are always plenty of holes and corners in the hold of a ship; and after he had burned half a dozen matches, he found one which suited him. Near one of the store-rooms, he saw a quantity of empty bottles, labelled "Congress Water," one of which he took, and having satisfied himself that the inside was dry, he rolled up the bills and thrust them into it. He then concealed the bottle in a crevice between the water-casks. It was not probable, in his opinion, that any one would think of searching the hold for the lost money, much less the inside of a bottle.

Lighting another match, he made his way back to the ladder. The scuttle was not fastened down, and he raised it far enough to ascertain that no one was in the steerage, before he came out. He raised it a little higher; no one was to be seen, but he heard voices in one of the mess-rooms. Crawling out with the utmost caution, he closed the scuttle, and for the first time since he left Captain Kendall's state-room, he felt safe. He had eighty pounds in store for a good time when he desired to have one.

Creeping on tiptoe to his mess-room, so as not to disturb the persons whose voices he had heard, he brushed the dirt from his clothes, and congratulated himself upon his own cunning. It was true that no human eye had seen him; but the All-seeing Eye had been upon him all the time. Though he might conceal his evil deed from the eyes of men, yet he could not conceal it from himself and from Him who knoweth the secrets of all hearts.

Murdock heard the low murmur of voices still, and

he concluded that Wilton and Monroe had retired to the steerage to discuss the mischief they were plotting. He had a serious grudge against Wilton for cheating him out of his money, and he wanted to know the subject of their private conversation. One who was not above stealing, even for fun, was surely not above listening, mean as such a practice generally is. He crept out of his room, and stole up to the gangway leading to Wilton's mess-room.

"Knights of the Red Cross — that's the name we'll take," Murdock heard Wilton say, in a low tone. "I have somewhere heard the term, but I can't tell where."

"Knights of the Red Cross!" sneered Monroe; "that's a bigger humbug than the Chain League. I thought you were not going to tell the fellows anything about it till all was ready."

"Neither am I; but when the time comes, we want to know who's who," replied Wilton.

"Do you expect it will come before we leave Holyhead?"

"No; we have only thirteen fellows in yet. I hatched up this idea to-day, and it's a first-rate way to know who our fellows are. There is plenty of red chalk on board to make the crosses with."

"I don't see what you want to make any crosses for, if you don't want the knights to know each other."

"Tom Perth says they must know each other; they won't stand it if they don't. Greenway says he won't have anything to do with it, if Perth don't tell who's going in."

"Then the whole thing will be blowed in a short time."

"You are always croaking, Ike Monroe. Don't you see the fellows will think more of it, and keep the secret twice as well, if we make a big thing of it, and give it a high-sounding title, like the Knights of the Red Cross?"

Monroe always grumbled, but he always did what he was told to do by his leader. He consented to become a Knight of the Red Cross, and Wilton explained that each fellow in the ring would wear a red cross on the left lapel of his jacket.

"Any fellow can put that on his jacket, and every fellow will see it, and want to know what it means," Monroe objected.

"If two wearing the red cross meet, one must place his forefinger across the forefinger of the other. When I meet you I cross your forefinger, and say, 'Are you a Red-Cross Knight?' You reply, 'I am.' I ask, 'Has your back been chalked?' You answer, 'It has.' I ask, 'Who chalked it?' You say, 'A Red Knight of the Red Cross chalked it red.' Then you are all right."

Monroe was rather pleased with this form; and the two Knights of the Red Cross went through the dialogue till they could say it perfectly. So could Murdock; but the enterprise in which the Knights were to engage was not explained, and he was disappointed in not being able to learn the nature of the mischief to be accomplished, when "the time came."

"Where's Murdock?" asked Monroe, when the means by which one Knight was to know another had been fully rehearsed. "How do you know he hasn't heard what we have been saying?"

"We have spoken in a low tone. The last I saw of the greeny, he was on deck," replied Wilton.

Murdock, from motives of delicacy, thought it was time to withdraw, and he crawled back to his room, threw off his jacket, and rolled into his berth. Wilton was an active Knight, and when it was suggested that the secrets of the fraternity had been overheard, he wished to satisfy himself on this important point. Before going on deck, he looked in Murdock's mess-room. There he lay in his berth, sound asleep apparently, and it was not possible that he had heard anything. Wilton examined the sleeper; but one who was cunning enough to rob his father's counting-room, even "for fun," was in this instance smart enough to be "caught napping;" and the conspirator did not even suspect that he was wide awake. He was satisfied, and went on deck with Monroe.

Murdock remained in his berth thinking of the Knights of the Red Cross, and wondering what they were going to do when the time came; but he was determined, as soon as he saw any student with the cross on the lapel of his jacket, to join the association, and pretend to know all about it.

The boats of the Josephine pulled for the shore, where Paul joined Dr. Winstock, and explored the place. Holyhead is on a small island, separated by a narrow strait from the larger island of Anglesea, which is itself separated from Wales by the Menai Strait. It is the point of Great Britain which lies nearest to Dublin, and derives its importance principally from this fact. It is the terminus of the railway from Chester, by which all the quick travel to Ireland is carried on. As a harbor of refuge for ships bound in or out of Liverpool, Holyhead has obtained a national importance, and upwards of half a million pounds has been expended upon its improvement. An immense breakwater has been extended before the place, and a large portion of Holyhead Mountain, which frowned uselessly above the town, has been moved into the sea, to protect the shipping from the north-west gales which blow remorselessly down the Irish Sea.

Except the breakwater, the pier, and the harbor, there was not much in Holyhead for the boys to see. At the entrance to the pier there is an arch built of Mona marble, to commemorate the landing of George IV. in 1821. On the western part of the island is the South Stack Light-house, the point for which a ship from the United States to Liverpool runs, after leaving Tuskar.

The distance across the channel, from Holyhead to Kingstown, is sixty-three miles, and the passages of the mail-steamers vary from four to four and a half hours. There are three boats a day to Kingstown, and the whole distance from London to the Irish metropolis is accomplished in less than fourteen hours.

At the appointed hour, the boats of the Josephine pulled for their vessel, but those of the ship had to wait for some of her crew. Paul had not thought of the key to his iron box during the afternoon, but in the boat he happened to put his hand into the pocket where he usually kept it, and then missed it. He was startled at first, but when he considered that all hands had been on shore, he was confident that his valuables could not have been disturbed.

When he went on board, he hastened down into the cabin to ascertain what had become of his key. On the table he saw his overcoat. He did not remember that he had left it there. Taking the garment on his arm, he entered his state-room. The safe was in its place, securely locked, but the key was not to be seen. He felt in all his pockets again, and examined every part of his room. While he was searching for it, the purser came to the door with the small silver he had procured in exchange for the notes.

"I've lost my key," said Paul, who was now suffering from anxiety.

"Lost it!" exclaimed Ritchie, the acting purser.

"I cannot tell what has become of it."

"Perhaps you lost it while you were on shore."

"I don't think it is possible. If I had been turning somersets, or anything of that kind, it might have slipped out of my pocket; but I hardly sat down while on shore, and I don't see how it could have jumped out," added the captain, as he took his overcoat out of the berth where he had thrown it, and hung it upon a hook.

Something had struck against the partition as he did so, and thrusting his hand into the side pocket of the coat, he drew forth the lost key.

"Here it is!" exclaimed he; and a gleam of pleasure lighted up his face. "I didn't see how it was possible for me to lose it. I'm fortunate this time; but I'm going to have this key tied to me, so that I can't lose it if I try."

"I'm glad you have found it," replied Ritchie, as he handed Paul the silver he had brought off.

The young commander was happy now, for a heavy burden of anxiety had suddenly been removed from his mind. What would Mr. Lowington say if he had lost that key? Would it not prove that he was not fit for the responsible position in which he had been placed? Paul was disposed to judge himself more harshly than he judged others; and this, within reasonable limits, is a safe policy. But if he had lost the key, he would have done no more than the principal himself. It was an inexpressible relief to find the key, and it was a better fate than had attended that of the Young America's safe.

Poor Paul! How soon was all this self-gratulation to be exchanged for a state of feeling bordering on despair! He opened the safe, and looked in as he was about to deposit the silver in it. He had left the bank notes on the top of the loose gold. He did not see them where he had placed them in his hurry. He pulled the safe out from under the berth, raised the papers it contained, and the cold sweat stood on his brow as he realized that the bills were not there. He was appalled at the discovery. If it had been his own money, though the loss of it deprived him of any coveted joy, he would not have suffered half so much. He took the silver from the purser, and dropped it into the box.

"Ask Mr. Terrill to come to me, if you please," said he, dropping upon his sofa, as though life had no further joys for him.

Ritchie saw that something was the matter with his

captain, but he knew not what. Being a good officer, he asked no question of his superior, but hastened to obey the order. Paul tried to think; to recall what he could in regard to the key; but he was stunned by the loss, and his mind was confused. Perhaps there was some mistake, after all, as there had been about the key. He was willing to believe that in his hurried departure from the vessel, he had put the key into the pocket of his overcoat, instead of his pants, where he was in the habit of carrying it. He remembered nothing about it, and he could only take the evidence of the facts as he found them. It did not seem possible that any one had stolen the money.

Opening the safe again, he took out the papers, unfolded them all, and assured himself that the money was actually gone. Whatever was strange, there was no doubt about this disagreeable fact. He had found the safe locked, and the key in his overcoat, where he had doubtless left it. Overwhelmed by his misfortune, and forgetting the unswerving kindness of Mr. Lowington, he gave himself up to despair. The tears started in his eyes, and he concluded that he was not fit to command the Josephine. While he was thus weeping, and thus feeling that he had sacrificed all claims to the consideration of Mr. Lowington, the first lieutenant entered the state-room.

"Terrill, I am ruined!" he exclaimed, in tones which left no doubt in the mind of the executive officer that something terrible had occurred.

"Why, Captain Kendall, what is the matter?" demanded Terrill, astonished and alarmed at the aspect and the words of the commander.

"I left eighty pounds in Bank of England notes in the safe when I went on shore, and now they are gone," replied Paul, with a kind of gasp which startled the executive officer.

"Gone!"

"Gone! Eighty pounds, in Bank of England notes, gone, — about four hundred dollars."

"Do you mean that the money has been stolen?"

"I don't know whether it has been stolen or not; I only know that it is gone," replied Paul, with a shudder. "I had a hundred pounds in bills, besides the gold and silver. I took out twenty pounds for Ritchie to exchange for small silver, and put the rest back into the safe. It is gone now."

"But how can it be gone, if you had the key?" asked Terrill, fully sympathizing with his commander in the distress of the hour."

"I don't know, — I can't understand it. I only know that I left the money in the safe, and now it is gone," answered Paul, not at all comforted by the dismay of Terrill.

"Did you find the safe locked, as you left it?" asked the first lieutenant.

Paul stated all the circumstances as he understood them; that he had locked the safe and put the key into the pocket of his overcoat, instead of his pants, as was his custom; that he had forgotten to take his overcoat with him, and had left it on the cabin table, where he had found it on his return.

"It is clear enough that somebody has fished your pocket during your absence, opened the safe, and taken the money," replied Terrill, when he had listened to the captain's statement.

"Of course the money did not leave the safe without some help," replied Paul. "None of those who went on shore with us could have taken it. Now, who was left on board?"

"No one but McLeish," replied Terrill, who did not know that Spenser Murdock had spent half an hour in the Josephine after the boats left.

"Would McLeish do such a thing?" asked Paul, anxiously.

"I don't know. I shouldn't like to charge him, or any other fellow, with such a thing without some evidence."

"We must look into this matter without delay," added the captain. "Where is Mr. Briskett?"

"He is in the cabin."

"Send him in, if you please."

The head steward, who had not left the vessel that day, informed Paul that Spenser Murdock had been on board by permission of the principal, and returned in the boat which conveyed the cook to the ship. Captain Kendall did not know that the new hand had robbed the counting-room of his father's mill "for fun," and was not disposed to suspect him of so serious a crime as the stealing of the money.

"Where was McLeish during the afternoon?" asked Paul.

"He was in the steerage most of the time, I think; at least I saw him there several times," replied Mr. Briskett.

"Where were you?"

"I was on deck part of the time, and in the cabin part of the time," answered the steward, uneasily, for the captain had not yet told him why he asked these questions.

"How long were you on deck?"

"I can't tell precisely how long; perhaps two hours after the boats left the vessel."

"I only wish to ascertain what you know in regard to the movements of the two students who were on board," added the captain, when he perceived that the steward was fretting under the examination.

"I did not particularly notice them, Captain Kendall," replied Mr. Briskett, with a more cheerful aspect when he was satisfied that he was not himself suspected of a wrong act. "Murdock was not on board more than half an hour. I was on the forecastle talking with the cook when the boats left the schooner. Murdock walked about the deck a while, and then went below. McLeish was on the fore-topsail-yard; but he soon came down and went below. The cook told me he had permission to visit the ship in the third cutter, and I sent the two steerage stewards with him. While we were getting out the boat, both of the students came up, and Murdock went off in the boat."

"Did either of them come into the cabin?" asked Paul.

"I don't know that they did. Neither of them could have been in the cabin when the cutter was lowered, for we had hardly touched the falls before both of them came on deck."

"How long had Murdock been below when McLeish went down?"

"Not more than ten or fifteen minutes, I should say, but I did not take particular notice."

"After the third cutter left, where was McLeish?"

"He went below again. When I went down, in about two hours, he was writing at a mess table."

From all this evidence, it appeared that Murdock had not been on board more than half an hour after the boats left; that he had been below alone not more than fifteen minutes, and that he had come on deck with McLeish when the stewards began to lower the cutter; that McLeish had been in the steerage alone about two hours. Paul then told the head steward that eighty pounds had been taken from his safe.

"I hope you don't think I took it, Captain Kendall," added Mr. Briskett, with a blush.

"Certainly not; such a thought never entered my head. You will not mention what I have told you to any one at present."

"I will not, Captain Kendall; but I would rather have given a year's salary than had such a thing happen on board. McLeish must have stolen it," added the steward.

"Why McLeish?"

"Because it is not possible that any one else could have done it. I am sure that none of the men went into the cabin during the afternoon, except myself. I am certain of that; so the loss of the money lies between the two students and me."

"Of course I have not the remotest suspicion that you took the notes, Mr. Briskett," added Paul, troubled by the manner of the steward. "It lies between the two students."

"I know that I didn't take them, Captain Kendall. Murdock was on board only a short time; not long enough, it seems to me, to find that the safe-key was in your coat pocket, that your safe was under your berth, and that it contained money. It would have taken him some time after he found the key in the coat on the cabin table to discover what it belonged to, and then to open it, take out the bills, and put things as he found them. I don't believe it was Murdock."

If Paul had known that he left the key in the safe, it would have changed the whole aspect of the affair. It followed, therefore, from the testimony of the steward, that McLeish was the guilty one. He was bad enough to do anything. Perhaps he was preparing to run away. It was even possible that he had been impudent for the purpose of being left on board, and had gone into the boat in order to manifest an anxiety to visit the shore. Paul, while willing to give the reprobate every opportunity to reform, had not had much confidence in his good resolutions.

But the evidence against him was all negative in its character. There was nothing to show that he had entered the cabin. As the theft lay between him and Murdock, it was only more probable that McLeish was the guilty one. Paul went on deck, and sent for the presumed culprit. Without making any charge against him, he asked where and how he had spent the afternoon. The answers were all straightforward and direct. McLeish detailed minutely where he had been and what he had done.

"Did you go into the cabin this afternoon?" asked Paul.

"No, sir; I did not," answered McLeish, as square as a brick.

"Have you seen my overcoat anywhere?"

"I have not. Have you lost your overcoat?"

"No; that is all, McLeish."

"I hope I'm not charged with anything bad," added the Scotch boy.

"I have not charged you with anything," replied Paul, perplexed beyond measure by the square answers of the supposed culprit. "Mr. Terrill, have the gig manned, if you please," he continued, turning to the first lieutenant in order to avoid McLeish, who began to exhibit some signs of wrath when he felt that he was suspected of something without being informed what it was.

Paul stepped into his gig, and directed the coxswain to pull for the ship. Arriving on board, he had an interview with Mr. Lowington in the main cabin, and with a woful expression on his handsome face, and occasionally with tears in his eyes, told him all about the loss of the eighty pounds.

"Don't take it so sorely to heart, Captain Kendall," said the principal, kindly.

"It was all my own carelessness, sir."

"Perhaps you were a little careless; you certainly were, if you left the key of the safe in your overcoat on board when you went on shore," added Mr. Lowington, mildly, and with a pleasant smile.

"I think I had better resign my place as captain of the Josephine," added Paul, bitterly, as the tears coursed down his cheeks. "Or perhaps you will remove me."

"My dear Paul," said the principal, taking him by the hand, "if we are all to be judged as harshly as you judge yourself, I think none of us can stand up any longer. The truth requires me to say that you were careless, but it is worth more than eighty pounds for you to learn the lesson which the loss of it has taught you. Great battles have been lost by a little carelessness; nations and dynasties have been swept away by it. I do not reprove you, Paul. By a similar act of carelessness on my part, sixty pounds was taken from the ship's safe. Do you think I ought to resign because I was careless then?"

"It is different with you, sir."

"Perhaps it is, but I will not judge you more harshly than I judge myself. I do not know to this day how Wilton got into the ship's safe; but I have no doubt I left the key where he found it."

Mr. Lowington opened the safe and took eighty pounds in bills from it, which he handed to Paul. He spoke words of comfort to him, but he could not entirely remove the sense of guilt which weighed down the young commander. He was deeply moved by the kindness of the principal, and felt that he did not deserve so much consideration. He was instructed to inform all his officers of the loss of the money, and direct them to be on the lookout for any suspicious circumstances that might transpire, but on no account to permit any of the crew to know that the safe had been robbed. He was advised to use the strictest vigilance to prevent the culprit, whoever he was, from running away; for this would doubtless be his next step. Paul returned on board, Mr. Lowington declining to express an opinion in regard to the guilt of McLeish.

The principal was greatly annoyed at the event which had transpired on board of the Josephine; but, knowing the antecedents of Murdock, he was not so sure that he was not the guilty party. After thinking of the unpleasant affair for a time, he sent for the new hand, and questioned him very closely in regard to his movements while on board of the Josephine. Murdock had not expected to escape questioning in regard to the money, and he had carefully schooled himself to give the right kind of replies. He told just where he had been on board of the schooner, only denying that he had been in the cabin, and declaring that he had spent all his time on deck or in the steerage. He had not seen Captain Kendall's overcoat — did not know that he had any overcoat.

"The safe of the Josephine has been robbed of eighty pounds in Bank of England notes, Murdock," added the principal.

"Has it, indeed?" replied Murdock, opening his eyes with well-feigned surprise.

"As you were on board, I thought it possible you might know something about it."

"Do you think I took the money, sir?" demanded the new hand.

"Who took it is still an open question," added Mr. Lowington. "Did you see any one go into the cabin?"

"No, sir, I did not. I hope you will search me and my things, sir; for I don't wish to be accused of an act I'm not guilty of," protested Murdock.

"I do not accuse you. I desire information."

"You should search me, sir."

Mr. Lowington declined to go through with such a useless formality, and dismissed Murdock.

The principal had directed Paul not to allow any of the crew of the Josephine to be informed that the money had been stolen; but he had himself told one of the crew of the Young America. He was satisfied that, if Murdock was innocent, he would communicate the fact of the robbery to others, and within a few hours the information would be patent to every student on board; while, if he were guilty, he would not be likely to mention it to any person. He intended, before any one went on shore again, to inform the officers of the ship of the theft, and, as they mingled with the crew when off duty, they could inform him whether the secret was known or not.

It had been announced, since the return of the party, that on the following day, after recitations, the students would start upon a three days' trip into Wales. Murdock wanted the money he had concealed in the hold for this excursion; but he watched vainly for an opportunity to obtain it. Somebody seemed to be looking at him all the time, and the scuttle was not raised when there were not twenty students in the steerage.

After the regular studies had been disposed of, and dinner was over the signal, for "all hands, attend lecture," was hoisted at the peak of the ship.

CHAPTER XV.

A TRAMP THROUGH SNOWDONIA.

AFTER dinner, when the signal for the lecture had been displayed, the principal assembled the officers in the after-cabin, and informed them of the robbery; but not one of them had heard a word about it before. He instructed them not to mention it to any seaman, and required them to keep a close watch upon the hands. Mr. Lowington was a just man, and the fact that Murdock had not mentioned the theft was, in his estimation, insufficient evidence upon which to charge him with the crime; but it justified him in causing a strict watch to be kept over the suspected person, He was not to be accused till better evidence was obtained, but all his actions were to be carefully noted, and their significance observed.

"Have you obtained any further information, Captain Kendall, in regard to the money?" asked Mr. Lowington, when Paul came on board.

"No, sir, none at all, I am sorry to say. All the officers think McLeish did it," replied the young commander. "They all wanted to have him searched."

"Don't permit it to be done, and make no charges against him till you have consulted with me," added the principal.

"McLeish is quite surly to-day."

"I am not surprised at that, after the questions you asked him yesterday. He evidently thinks he is suspected of something, and don't know what. Let your officers treat him kindly, and not notice any surliness which does not amount to positive disrespect. If he is innocent, he feels hurt by the suspicions your questions indicated."

"He told some of the hands that he had been accused of stealing my overcoat."

"That remark is in his favor. This is very delicate business, and we must all be cautious while we are vigilant."

All hands were piped to the steerage to hear what Professor Mapps had to say about Wales. The map of Great Britain hung upon the foremast, but the learned gentleman appeared to be nervous, and complained that he had but half an hour for his lecture, and he could not possibly do justice to the subject in that time. Wales was a very interesting country, and he could hardly allude to Owen Glendower, the last of the Welsh chieftains. The professor did what many eminent men do who are allowed but a brief period to make a speech — he used up one sixth of his time in regretting that he had so little time. But the students, with their bags and blankets ready for a start, thought that half an hour was long enough; and most of them would have voted that any professor who occupied more than half an hour at one time, in his lecture, ought to be committed to the brig on bread and water for twenty-four hours.

"Young gentlemen, what is Wales?" asked Mr. Mapps, when he had finished his exordium.

"Where they strike ile," replied Duncan, the new hand of the Josephine, who appeared not to have the fear of professors before his eyes.

"No levity, young gentlemen!" added the professor, rather sternly.

"I've always heard that oil came from whales," replied Duncan, meekly, as he adjusted his eye-glass, and looked gravely at the instructor.

"Bully for Speksy!" whispered Lynch; and most of the students laughed.

"Silence, young gentlemen!" exclaimed Mr. Mapps. "I asked what Wales was."

"It's what a fellow finds on his back when he has had a licking," replied Little, one of the "greenies."

"No more of this, young gentlemen," interposed the principal; and his word was sufficient, though that of the professor was not always heeded.

"Wales is a part of Great Britain," answered one of the students.

"Is it, indeed?" replied the professor. "You must have burned the midnight oil to learn that."

This was spoken in a sneering way, and the boy who had given the answer in good faith was hurt in his feelings by its tone. Mr. Lowington frowned upon the teacher, for he would not permit an honest answer, however foolish, to be ridiculed, for sneers are always discouraging to a boy who is trying to do his duty. To a careless, indifferent student, a little ridicule is sometimes wholesome and beneficial.

Everybody was silent, for no one knew what the professor meant. It was a question which could be correctly answered in a dozen different ways.

"Wales is a principality," continued Mr. Mapps, more mildly — for he had probably seen the frown upon the face of Mr. Lowington — " deriving this name from the fact that its ruler, even before it was subjugated by Britain, was a prince. Wales is about one hundred and forty miles long from north to south, and about ninety in breadth from east to west. Its area and population are about the same as those of Massachusetts. It has three hundred miles of coast line, having the waters of the Irish Sea on the north, of St. George's Channel on the west, and of Bristol Channel on the south. It contains twelve counties, and is entitled to twenty-nine members in the House of Commons.

"Wales is wholly a mountainous region, and abounds in the richest mines of coal, iron, zinc, lead, copper, and silver; and mining is the chief branch of industry in the principality. More iron is manufactured in Wales than in all the United States.

"The climate of Wales is very moist; the annual fall of rain is forty-five and a half inches, the average of the British Isles being only thirty-two inches. I am glad to see that you have your overcoats and blankets ready, young gentlemen, for you will find the weather among the mountains quite chilly, even at this season of the year.

"Swansea and Merthyr Tydvil are the largest towns in Wales, the latter having about fifty thousand inhabitants, and the former forty thousand. The Latin name of the country was Cambria. Most of the people of Wales are of Celtic origin. While the English call them the Welsh, they choose to call themselves the Cymri. They are a brave and generous people, as their traits of character appear in the history of their country; but they are quick-tempered, impulsive, and given to superstitions. The progress of education has improved the people very sensibly, and their manners and customs have greatly changed for the better, though some of their superstitious practices are still retained, one of which I will mention as an illustration.

"The fanaticism of the 'sin-eater' is said to be still in vogue in some parts of Caermarthenshire. When a person dies, the relatives send for the sin-eater of the district. After he arrives, a plate of salt, on which a piece of bread is placed, is deposited on the breast of the corpse. The functionary then repeats some mystic phrases over the bread, and finally eats it. By this ceremony he is supposed to eat the sins of the deceased. A fee of two and sixpence is paid to him, and he makes haste to retire; for having taken upon himself the sins of the dead of his district, of course he must be a very wicked man, and the friends banish him with kicks and blows from their presence.

"At Tenby, near Milford Haven, a very pleasant New Year's custom was formerly prevalent. The children of the neighborhood gather together on the morning of the first day of the year, and visit the houses in the vicinity of their homes. Having knocked and gained admission to a house, they sprinkle the furniture with water, singing, at the same time, a couple of fantastic verses, which I shall ask Mr. Modelle to read to you."

Mr. Mapps handed a book to the professor of elocution, and he read these stanzas:—

"Here we bring new water from the well so clear
  For to worship God with this happy new year.
  Sing levy dew, sing levy dew, the water and the wine,
  With seven bright golden wires, and bugles that do shine.

"Sing reign of fair maid with gold upon her toe;
  Open wide the west door, and turn the old year go.
  Sing reign of fair maid, with gold upon her chin,
  Open you the east door, and let the new year in."

"There is much in Wales to interest the antiquarian," continued Mr. Mapps. "Twenty-eight cromlechs are to be found in Anglesea alone, and the remains of ancient British customs are to be seen in all parts of the country. There are also a number of Roman stations, and some evidence that the Romans mined gold from the mountains of Cambria has been discovered.

"The people of Wales take pride and pleasure in their ancient origin, and cling earnestly to their peculiar customs and traditions. Though English is spoken in the larger towns, the people of the mountains and farming districts confine themselves to the Welsh tongue. Within six hours' ride of Holyhead, you will find people who do not know a word of English, and who will answer your respectful inquiry with a '*Dim Saesneg*,' uttered in short, curt tones, as though the Welsh language was the only one fit to be spoken. The phrase means ' No English.'

"Of the history of Wales only a little need be said, even if I had time to say it. The Cymri, a Celtic tribe, had possession of the whole of South Britain when the Romans first invaded the country

They were driven by the Latins into the region west of the Severn River, but were never wholly conquered. When the Anglo-Saxons had conquered Britain, they found the Cymri to be a brave and powerful enemy, and they never were able to dislodge them from their strongholds in the mountains, though they wrested from them the territory lying between the Severn and the present eastern boundary of Wales.

"In the tenth century, King Athelstan of England partially conquered Wales, and received an annual tribute from the people. They declined to pay this tax to William the Conqueror, and he invaded their territory, and reduced them to submission. This is the period from which the kings of England claimed the supremacy of Wales; but for hundreds of years the Welsh continued to struggle for their independence. In the thirteenth century, a civil war broke out between the ruler of North Wales and his son. The father appealed to the King of England, Henry III., to assist him in recovering his authority. The request was granted, with the condition that the prince should become the vassal of England. The compact was kept by the ruler and his immediate successor; but the next prince was refractory, and a war ensued, in which Edward I., then King of England, subdued the rebel. In a subsequent rebellion, the disobedient vassal was killed, and Edward cunningly obtained the consent of the Welsh to the creation of a Prince of Wales, who should be a native of their own country.

"Queen Eleanor, wife of Edward I., resided at Caernarvon Castle, in Wales, when her son Edward was born. The people claimed him as a Welshman, and his father made him Prince of Wales, since which time this title has generally been conferred upon the eldest son of the sovereign of England.

"Other rebellions, in which the Welsh have vainly attempted to obtain their independence, have occurred, — the most important of which was the insurrection of Owen Glendower, in the fifteenth century. He was a descendant of Llewellyn, the last reigning Prince of Wales. He studied law in London, but took to the profession of arms, and followed the fortunes of Richard II., till he was deposed, when Glendower retired to private life in his own country. Henry IV., who succeeded Richard, construed his absence from the court as disloyalty, and confiscated his estates. Forced by this act of injustice to take a hostile position he proclaimed himself Prince of Wales.

"Glendower allied himself with several disaffected noblemen of England, the principal of whom were the Percys of Northumberland, and struck some heavy blows at the power of the king. The confederates divided the kingdom among themselves, — the Welsh chieftain taking Wales, of which he was formally crowned Prince at his capital. In 1403 the prince and his allies met Henry in battle, near Shrewsbury, and were badly defeated, Percy being killed in the action.

"After this event Glendower formed an alliance with the King of France, and two armies of French soldiers were at different times sent to his aid, with which he fought several battles with varying success. Being compelled to retreat into Wales, the French left him, and for a few years he waged a guerrilla and predatory warfare upon the English. Though his power was broken, he was still a formidable enemy, and Henry V. offered a free pardon for himself and his followers, if they would return to their allegiance. While the negotiation for the pardon was in progress, Glendower died.

"It has been the aim of the rulers of England to remove the ancient landmarks of the Welsh, and assimilate them to their more powerful neighbors. There is now no material distinction in the privileges of the people of the two countries."

Mr. Mapps finished his lecture, and with the description of Wales fresh in the minds of the students, the order was given to pipe into the boats. The ship's company took the train at Holyhead, and in an hour were at Bangor, on the Menai Straits, near the northern entrance. This arm of the sea, which separates Anglesea from the main land, is twelve miles in length, and the region through which it passes presents some very attractive scenery. The woods on both sides extend down to the water's edge, relieved at intervals by rugged steeps. The northern portion is lined with beautiful cottages and villas, used for permanent or summer residences of wealthy people.

A walk of less than two miles brought the students to the Menai Bridge. At different points the straits are crossed by five ferries; but the navigation is very difficult and dangerous, owing to the rocky character of the shores, and to the fury with which the tide sweeps through the narrow channel, and more than fifty years ago, the attention of the government was directed to a project for bridging it. The Menai

Bridge was commeenced in 1819, and completed in 1826. It is a suspension bridge, supported by chains one hundred feet above high-water mark, so that vessels may sail under it. The suspended part, over the straits, is five hundred and sixty feet long. But the bridge, though it was the wonder of the world for a time, is by no means the most remarkable in the world. There is one in Switzerland, and there are several in the United States, which exceed it in span and height.

Half a mile below the Menai is the Britannia Tubular Bridge, which, until it was rivalled by the Victoria Bridge over the St. Lawrence, at Montreal, was the most peculiar and wonderful structure of the kind in the world. It was built for the use of the Holyhead and Chester Railway, and cost half a million pounds. The structure consists of two rectangular tubes, placed side by side, through which the up and down trains pass. The location of the bridge was chosen on account of a rock in the middle of the straits, which afforded a foundation for the middle tower. The tubes were constructed in a convenient place, and each floated on pontoons, at high tide, to a position beneath its permanent resting-place, from which it was elevated at the rate of six feet a day by hydraulic pressure,— the masonry being carried up at the same rate to support it until the requisite height was reached.

It was a difficult undertaking, for the tide, in the straits, rises and falls twenty feet, and often flows at the rate of eight miles an hour, and it reflects the highest credit on Stevenson, the distinguished engineer who planned and executed the work.

The students spent the night at the George Hotel, near the Menai Bridge. After supper, Perth and Adler operated for the Knights of the Red Cross, and initiated the eight boys who had already pledged themselves to engage in the desperate enterprise which Wilton had devised. The ceremony consisted only in instructing the candidates in the dialogue by which he was to prove that he was a Knight, and which Murdock had committed to paper on the preceding day, so as not to forget it. Only the most daring and reckless fellows in the ship's crew had been approached on the subject of joining the organization, and all of these had been members of the Chain League. They were delighted with the idea of a secret society — a fancy which seems to be very fascinating to young men in their teens.

Murdock was too cunning to take any notice of certain movements on the part of Perth and Adler, which were intelligible to him, but not to those who were not possessed of the secret of the Red Cross. He expected an invitation to join the organization; if it did not come within a reasonable time, he was determined to have his fun, at the expense of the valiant Knights.

In the course of the excursion into Wales, Perth made four more additions to the force of the desperadoes, who were to capture the Josephine. These were new hands; for among the old crew, there were no more whom it was deemed prudent to admit to the ranks of the knightly band. Ten more could easily be obtained when the time was found to state the scheme fully to each one, for it required at least an hour of private talk to relate the particulars of the enterprise, and initiate the convert.

The next morning the party proceeded by train to Caernarvon, and after viewing its castle — in which a room in the Eagle Tower is shown as that in which Edward II. was born — started on a pedestrian tour to Llanrwst. After they had left the town behind them, and entered the mountain defiles, the country became exceedingly interesting. Then, for the first time, they saw Wales. A guide accompanied the excursionists, and pointed out the objects of interest on the way, and told who lived in each residence seen from the road. Several small lakes were pointed out, and their names given. In Wales, a lake has the term "Llyn," as Llyn Padarn, Llyn Peris. "Moel" is applied to smooth conical hills, and Moel Eilio was shown. "Llan" means a church, and is thus used as a prefix to numerous Welsh villages, as Llangollen, Llanrhaiadr.

Most of the Welsh proper names are unpronounceable by an American, because they have so many syllables which contain no vowels — Tanybwlch, Craigddrwg. The boys cracked their jaws in vain attempts to utter words they saw in print on the maps and in the guide-books. At the Victoria inn, in Dolbadarn, they stopped to dine. At the village of Llanberis, about ten miles from Caernarvon, they halted for the night. The capacity of the lodging-houses was not sufficient to meet such a demand as the tourists made upon them, and a large portion of the boys were obliged to sleep on the floors of parlors and dining-rooms — no great hardship, however, to sailors, though some of the new hands grumbled.

The next day they ascended Snowdon, at the top of which they found hotels, restaurants, and stalls for the sale of trinkets, — the Welsh exhibiting not a little of the Yankee desire to make a trade, even under the most difficult circumstances. Snowdon consists of several peaks and spurs, the highest of which is Moel-y-Wyddfa, whose extreme summit is only a few yards in diameter; and on a clear day part of England, Scotland, Ireland, and the Isle of Man, may be distinctly seen. When the students ascended, the weather was admirable; indeed, it was this favoring circumstance which induced the principal to undertake the ascent.

The descent was made by a different route, as much to obtain a fresh prospect as to gain time on the journey. Passing over the most northerly ridge, called Crib-y-Ddysgwyll (we mention the name that our readers may pronounce it when they have the toothache; possibly it would cure this distressing malady, for it means the "Toothed Dish"), the excursionists followed a zigzag and steep path, requiring the utmost care, for a single false step would oftentimes roll the incautious traveller over ragged precipices to certain death. After a walk of nine miles from the summit of Snowdon, nearly half of which was on the turnpike, the tourists arrived at Capel Curig, where they lodged under the same difficulties which had attended them the previous night. But they were too tired, after climbing the rugged steeps, to complain even of the "soft side of a pine board."

The forenoon of the following day was spent in visiting the cataract of Pont Glyn Diffwys, the lakes, and the mountain passes in the vicinity of Capel Curig, which is one of the most attractive spots in Snowdonia, as the region for a dozen miles around the mountain is called. After an early dinner — or rather lunch, for a meal taken at meridian can hardly be called a dinner in the United Kingdom — the party started for Llanrwst, ten miles distant. A halt was made to enable the students to see Rhaiadr-y-Wenol, or Swallow Fall, which, after rainy weather, is considered the finest cataract in Wales. In Bettws-y-Coed the travellers took another rest. The place is a favorite resort of tourists, especially anglers and artists; and the students saw more of Welsh customs and manners than at any former stopping-place. Four miles more brought the party to Llanrwst, where those who were not too much fatigued were permitted to visit the old church of St. Grwst, and other places of interest in the town, till the departure of the train which was to convey them to Conway, twelve miles distant, on the Holyhead and Chester Railway.

"What station is this?" asked Paul Kendall of the guard, when the train stopped a few miles from Llanrwst.

"Trevor," replied the guard.

"Trevor," repeated the captain, consulting his guide-book. "I don't see it."

"Don't you?" laughed the doctor. "There it is;" and he pointed to a name on the page.

"That isn't it. He said Trevor, and this is Trefriw," added Paul, spelling out the word, which, however, was not generally of much use in making out Welsh names.

"That is the local pronunciation of the word," added Dr. Winstock. "The names of several English places hardly differ more widely from the orthography than these in Wales. You pronounce Birmingham with the primary emphasis on the first syllable, and a secondary emphasis on the third — Bir′ming-ham′. The lowest class of people call it Brumajum, or something like that; but the word is said to be spelled in one hundred and fifty different ways, and one of them is Bromwycham. A well-educated Englishman calls it Bir-ming-ham, with no secondary emphasis on the third syllable. Many cultivated people call London *Len-den*, or *Lend'n*."

"I heard an Englishman, in Liverpool, say a *pay-ound* for a pound, as a Vermonter calls a cow a *caow*."

"Hardly with the same accent," replied the doctor. "Give the *a* its long sound, and leave out the *y* — pāound. In many parts of this country, Welshmen hold occasional meetings, at which prizes are offered for the best performance on the harp, and the best piece of poetry. These gatherings are called *Eisteddfodd*, or *Cwmrygyddion*. How would you pronounce this last word?"

"I shouldn't pronounce it. I should as soon think of swimming across the Atlantic as uttering such a word," laughed Paul.

"It is pronounced Coom-re-gith-i-on," continued Dr. Winstock.

"My jaws ache now with the efforts I have made to pronounce Welsh names," replied Paul, whose attention was attracted by a small steamer going down Conway River.

22*

At Conway the tourists took the train for Holyhead, and at dark were on board their respective vessels, glad of an opportunity once more to sleep in their own beds, but delighted also with the views of Welsh scenery, and Welsh manners and customs, they had obtained in their tramp through Snowdonia.

CHAPTER XVI.

THE BANK OF ENGLAND NOTES.

THE students had seen a specimen of North Wales, and as soon as the recitations were completed on the following day, the vessels sailed for Milford Haven. The weather was fine, but the wind was very light, and it was not till Sunday afternoon that the little squadron came to anchor in the harbor of its destination. Divine services were held on board both vessels, Professor Hamblin officiating in the Josephine.

Though the officers had carefully observed the movements of the students on the tramp through Snowdonia, no bank notes were seen or heard of, for the simple reason that none of the party had any. Murdock had been unable to enter the hold to obtain any of his ill-gotten spoils, and had been forced to confine his expenses to the five shillings allowed for the trip. Wilton and Monroe were not allowed to go on shore, and the twenty pounds the former had "borrowed" of Murdock was not taken from its hiding-place.

So far as the outward requirements of discipline were concerned, McLeish behaved with propriety; but he was cross, and rather surly. He was suspected of something, — stealing the captain's overcoat, he believed, — and he fretted sorely. He was making a mighty struggle to do well, and demanded all the credit which belonged to his good intentions. The officers watched him very closely, as they did Murdock, for the reasons which have already been indicated; and though nothing was said or hinted to him, the supervision did not always escape his notice.

He was tempted to abandon his good resolutions, and strike hands again with Rossfeldt and Templeton; but the remembrance of what pretty Grace Arbuckle had said to him, and the terror of meeting her again after he had "fallen from grace," deterred him. He could face the principal and Captain Kendall, but he could not hold up his head in her presence, if he should prove false to the promises he had made to her. Perhaps he might never see her again; and under the consciousness that he was watched and suspected of something which it had never entered his head to do, he was vibrating between the right and the wrong, doubtful which way to turn.

Mr. Lowington was very much perplexed by the circumstances attending the loss of the eighty pounds. Murdock had not said a word to any of the crew about the theft, so far as he could learn, and his means of information were good. On Sunday evening, after the ship came to anchor at Milford Haven, he called Murdock to him on the quarter-deck, and had a long conversation with him about the matter. The new hand was too cunning to betray himself, and positively denied all knowledge of the money. The principal compelled him to relate all his movements on the afternoon that the students went on shore at Holyhead, to tell what boys he had spoken with in the Josephine and the Young America.

Murdock, as before, told the exact truth concerning all his time, except the fifteen minutes he had spent in the cabin of the schooner, though he did not think it best to say anything about the Red Cross Knights. While he was explaining his movements, Wilton happened to be in the waist, and Murdock pointed to him, saying that he had spoken to him on his return from the Josephine. It was of no consequence what he had said to Wilton, and Mr. Lowington seemed to be no nearer the truth than before. The new hand was dismissed, and the guilt still lay between him and McLeish.

Just at dark, Captain Kendall visited the ship in his gig. In coming to anchor, Havenshaw, one of the best seamen in the Josephine, had received an injury in his foot, in trying to remove a kink from the cable, and Paul had come on board for the doctor, as well as to obtain instructions from the principal. Dr. Winstock was just going on shore with the chaplain to attend a vesper service in one of the churches; but he hastened to the schooner in the professor's barge as soon as he was informed that his services were required. As Captain Kendall's gig was to wait until he had had his interview with Mr. Lowington, the crew were permitted to go on board of the ship. Havenshaw, the injured seaman, belonged to the gig's crew, and McLeish had been ordered to take his place.

"I smell a mice, Ike," said Wilton, just before the gig came alongside.

Standing in the waist, he had observed with interest the long talk that was taking place between the principal and the new hand. It troubled him; and when Murdock pointed to him, it excited the direst fears in his breast. Being a "lamb" would not save him from condemnation, if Murdock told that he had borrowed his money; and this was what Wilton believed he was doing. This was the "mice" he smelt.

"What's the matter now?" demanded Monroe.

"Matter enough. That greeny has told old Lowington that I borrowed his twenty pounds," replied Wilton, excited by his ticklish situation.

"How do you know he has?"

"Saw him do it, and saw him direct Lowington's attention to me while I stood in the waist. Here's a pretty kettle of fish; and they'll make me out an old sheep, instead of a lamb, within twenty minutes."

"In another scrape!" growled Monroe, almost in despair. "Another term in the brig."

"Not yet; don't give it up. We'll get out of the scrape some how or other. Murdock didn't give me any money. Don't you know he didn't?"

"But he did."

"No, he didn't. If two of us stick to it that he didn't, it will be no use for him to stick to it that he did. Understand, Ike?"

"I understand; but you have the money sewed into your jacket; and of course you will be searched."

"That's so," replied Wilton, with a troubled look. "Come down into the steerage, and we will fix things."

Monroe followed Wilton to his mess-room, where the latter took the notes from their hiding-place in his jacket, and put them into an envelope.

"We must get rid of them at once, even if we have to throw them overboard," said he.

"It's a pity to do that," added Monroe, thinking what a heap of luxuries could be purchased for twenty pounds.

"I would rather do it than be caught. It won't do to have the money anywhere in the steerage, for they will look into the mattresses, and everywhere else. I fancy that Gus Pelham told the principal all that I ever said to him about the safe-key and the sixty pounds."

Pelham did nothing of the kind. His sense of honor would not permit him to expose a comrade who had told him anything in confidence, even to save himself from punishment.

"Perhaps we can find a place on deck to hide it," suggested Monroe.

When they went on deck in search of such a place, the Josephine's gig was alongside.

"I'll tell you what we can do," said Wilton, as the gig's crew came up the accommodation ladder. "We can give it to one of the Josephine's fellows to keep till to-morrow. Then it will not be in the ship."

"Whom will you give it to?" asked Monroe.

"I don't know. Let me see who they are. There's that Scotch fellow. They say he is a brick."

"But he has joined the lambs, they say."

"So much the better. He don't mean it, any more than I do. Templeton told me about him the night we were put into the brig. They say he hates Lowington and Fluxion, and has had a jolly row with all the officers of the consort. He's the fellow for me."

Perhaps this course of reasoning was fully in keeping

with Wilton's former exhibitions of judgment and discretion. He knew very little about McLeish. When he and Monroe had been committed to the brig, the Scotch rebel had come to them, expressed his sympathy, and offered to help them. This prompt offer of assistance had prepossessed them in his favor as a good fellow. Since McLeish had been transferred to the Josephine they had not seen him, though they had been informed of his plucky conduct, as they regarded it, with Terrill, and had heard the boys laughing about his reformation, or, in the phrase of " our fellows," of his " joining the lambs."

" How are you, McLeish? I'm glad to see you," said Wilton, walking up to the Scottish hero.

" Well, I thank you. How is it with yourself?" replied McLeish, not very cordially; for he was still in a cross mood.

" You are a good fellow, McLeish: everybody says that; and what everybody says must be true. I am sorry you went into the Josephine, for we don't see much of you now."

McLeish softened, for this was the kind of stuff to feed him with.

" You got out of the brig, lad, I see," said he.

" Yes, after a while; but I expect to go back again soon," answered Wilton, lightly.

" Do you, man? Why so?"

" One of the fellows is trying to get me into a scrape. There comes an officer; don't say anything now;" and Wilton walked away from McLeish, fearful that the interview might be charged against him, if anything happened afterwards.

As he crossed the deck, he encountered Murdock, in deep thought, brooding over what the principal had said to him.

"What were you saying to Lowington?" asked Wilton, as they met.

"What was I saying to him?" replied Murdock, who was not prepared to answer this question, and thus acknowledge that he was suspected of stealing eighty pounds from Captain Kendall's state-room.

"Yes, what were you saying to him?" repeated Wilton, sharply. "And what were you pointing to me for?"

"Pointing to you?"

"That's what I said. You are not deaf — are you?"

"I'm not aware that it concerns you to know what we were talking about," answered Murdock, embarrassed by the fear that his shipmates would find he was suspected.

"Yes, but it does concern me. I know what you were talking about."

Murdock was really alarmed now. How should Wilton know that the principal had almost accused him of stealing the money; or, at least, had hinted it so strongly that his guilty conscience interpreted his words as a direct charge?

"If you know, what do you ask me for?" replied Murdock, with a weak effort to bluff him off.

"You can't deny it."

"Perhaps I can't."

"If you can, why don't you?" demanded Wilton, warmly.

"What am I expected to deny?"

"O, you needn't talk! Didn't you tell Lowington that you let me have twenty pounds? O, you needn't deny it!" added Wilton, shaking his head at him.

Murdock was relieved.

"If it isn't any use to deny it, I won't do so," replied Murdock, mildly. "It was a mean trick you played upon me; and you may thank yourself if you get into any trouble on account of it."

"Then you have owned up to Lowington that you lied to him when you told him you had no more money."

"That's my affair. If you wish to give up the money now, I will make it all right with the principal."

"Give up the money! Do you labor under the delusion that you handed me twenty pounds?"

"I certainly do."

"It's all in your eye. You didn't do anything of the kind; and I can prove that you didn't," added Wilton, emphatically.

Murdock was so pleased to find the real secret was not suspected, that he was not disposed to quarrel about his twenty pounds. He had given up the money as lost; but his companion's mistake suggested that he might work upon his fears till he recovered it. Wilton did not wait to argue the matter any farther, but returned to McLeish, who was waiting to hear in what manner some one was to get him into a scrape.

"You were a good friend of mine when I was in the brig," said Wilton, without explaining who his enemy was. "I want you to help me a little now."

"I have promised to keep out of all scrapes, and to behave well! and I mean to do it," replied McLeish.

"This will not get you into any scrape — it can't. I only want you to keep this envelope for me till I see you next time," said Wilton, slipping it privately into McLeish's pocket.

"What's in it?"

"Never mind what is in it. You needn't know, and then you certainly will not get into trouble. Don't let any one see it, or know that you have it."

"All the gigsmen, pipe down!" called the coxswain of Captain Kendall's boat.

"Keep still, and don't say a word. Don't open the envelope, and don't let any one suspect that you have it. When I see you again I'll tell you all about it," said Wilton, hastily, as McLeish moved off.

Wilton called Monroe as soon as the gig had gone, and they had another interview with Murdock. Both of them stoutly denied all knowledge of the twenty pounds, and the new hand, if no one else, was satisfied that Wilton was more snake than lamb. While he was disappointed that he had not been able to intimidate the rogue into returning his money, he congratulated himself that he was not known as a suspected person by his companions.

As for Wilton, he was in momentary expectation of being summoned to the bar of the principal's justice for not giving up the twenty pounds intrusted to his care. He was prepared to deny that any bank notes had been handed to him, and to fall back upon his character as a young lamb to sustain him. He expected the chaplain would be his friend, and help convince the principal that Murdock wished to injure him because he had turned over a new leaf. No summons came from the principal, and he was surprised that it did not come.

He waited nervously for the summons, till all hands were called to evening prayers, and still it did not come. He concluded that the case was reserved for the next day; but on Monday the exercises of the Academy passed off as usual, and after dinner all hands went on shore. Not a word was said about the bank notes, and Mr. Lowington did not even look at him. It was very strange, and he could not account for it. The principal never passed over any alleged wrong without an investigation, and he continued to anticipate the summons.

In the mean time, McLeish, with the envelope in his pocket, returned to the Josephine. The surgeon had dressed the wound on Havenshaw's foot, and assuring the patient that it would be well in a few days, left for the shore to attend the vespers.

McLeish was not a Yankee; neither were the several Mrs. Blue Beards Yankees; but he was as anxious to know what that envelope contained as they to know what the mysterious room contained — which proves that curiosity is not an exclusively American vice. McLeish was troubled about two things: first, he was sorry he had accepted the keeping of the envelope, and second, he desired to know what it contained. It was sealed, and nothing was written upon it.

His strongest impulse was to carry it to Captain Kendall, who would open it, and thus at the same time expose its contents, and relieve him from all blame.

But a second thought assured him it was mean to expose a friend who had confided in him, and he had not the courage to follow what his reason convinced him was the proper course.

On the afternoon of Monday all hands went on shore, but returned at an early hour; Mr. Lowington found he was behind time in the carrying out of his programme, for he had intended to be in London by the 1st of August, and it was now the 25th. The delay had been occasioned by the non-arrival of the new pupils at the time they were expected, and the necessity of training the crew of the ship. He found it requisite, therefore, to use the nights, so far as practicable, in going from place to place. As a quarter watch was generally sufficient to handle either vessel, the officers and seamen were not deprived of any considerable portion of their sleep, those who served two watches having had six hours of continuous rest below. When the squadron came to anchor before six in the morning, those who had been on duty were allowed to "sleep in" till they had made up their eight hours.

At six o'clock in the afternoon, with Bristol Channel pilots on board, the ship and her consort sailed for Cardiff, where they arrived after a brisk run of twelve hours. At two o'clock in the afternoon, after the regular studies had been disposed of, all hands embarked in the boats for the shore. Cardiff is one of the most important towns in Wales, though there is nothing of especial interest to attract the attention of the tourist. It is the port from which the iron brought from Merthyr Tydvil and other places, by railway and canal, is shipped. It is also an immense depot for the shipment of coal. The extensive docks planned by the Marquis of Bute, and constructed at his own expense, have wonderfully increased the commercial prosperity of the place.

A walk through the town satisfied the boys, and they took the train for Merthyr Tydvil, famous for the number and extent of its iron works, and its coal mines. An opportunity was afforded to the students to see the Welsh operatives in the mines and manufactories, and to compare their condition with that of men in similar employments in their own country. The place is situated in a region celebrated for its romantic beauty; but the boys saw but little of the scenery, except from the windows of the railway carriages.

With the Bristol Channel pilots still on board, the ship and her consort sailed for Bristol. Though the distance was only about thirty miles, the wind was so light that it required all night to make it; and steam tugs were employed in going up the Avon River. For the first time the vessels went into a dock, if that at Bristol may be called by such a name. The water was diverted from the Avon, and its tributary, the Frome, and their original beds converted into a "floating harbor" by the erection of dams and gates at either end of the enclosure. About two miles in length of the Avon was thus converted into a dock, affording sufficient room for a thousand vessels to float. Between the termini of the dock, a deep canal was made, so that the waters of the river could pass without going through the enclosure. The average rise and fall of tides in Bristol is nearly thirty feet, the spring tides being thirty-four. The Josephine was moored alongside of the Young America, so that the crews of the two vessels could mingle without the use of a boat — an experience as pleasant as it was novel.

McLeish still carried the envelope in his pocket, as it had been given him by Wilton; and if it had been a coal of fire, it could not have annoyed him more than it did. He did not even dare to look at it, or to take it from his pocket, lest some one should see it; and just as soon as an opportunity was presented, after the vessels were moored together, he went on board of the ship for the purpose of getting rid of it. If there had been no mystery about it, probably it would have annoyed him less. He wished to know what it all meant quite as much as to avoid the responsibility of having it on his person.

He found Wilton, who was still dreading a summons to the mainmast, where all questions of discipline were settled, for Mr. Lowington tenaciously adhered to naval practices. Wilton did not want the bank notes yet; the danger had not passed away; but when he saw McLeish approaching him, he understood what he wanted, and had a plausible explanation ready to induce him to retain the funds.

"I don't care to keep the paper any longer," said McLeish, when the conspirator had conducted him to a secure place for the interview.

"Why not? It don't harm you, and can't get you into any trouble."

"I don't know that."

"Upon my word and honor, it can't get you into any trouble. If it would, I'd tell you so."

"You didn't tal me what the envelope hald," suggested McLeish.

"I'll tell you all about it now," added Wilton, in a whisper. "You know I went to London."

"I haird you did."

"My father sent me twenty pounds, which I sewed into my jacket when those beggars of detectives caught me. The money was in four five-pound notes, and they are now in the envelope."

"Is this the truth?" asked McLeish, suspiciously.

"Of course it is! You don't think I'd lie about it — do you?"

"Why do you wish me to keep it for you?"

"A fellow got mad with me, and I expect he has told Lowington I have the stamps about me."

"Who is the fellow?"

"He's one of the new fellows. I expect to be searched soon, and if I am, Lowington won't find the money upon me. I'll do a good thing for you, McLeish, any time when you need it."

McLeish did not wish to keep the money any longer, but Wilton's rhetoric finally overcame his scruples, and he agreed to retain it for a few days more.

"You are a first-rate fellow, McLeish," continued Wilton, who had one more favor to ask.

"That means that you want something more of me," added McLeish, laughing.

"That's so; and when a fellow has a good friend like you, he don't hesitate to ask him to do a good turn for him. I want to get rid of those bank notes. I'm afraid they'll get wet and be spoiled. I have no liberty, you know, and you have. You will go ashore this afternoon, and you fellows in the Josephine are not watched at all. Now, if you could just change those bills for gold, at some store or banking-house, you would do the best thing for me that ever one fellow did for another; and I'll do five times as much for you any time you ask me. I will, whether you ask me or not."

"I'll just do it," replied McLeish, who could see no great harm in the simple act required of him.

The money was Wilton's, sent to him by his father. Doubtless it was against the rules of the ship for him to retain it in his possession; but McLeish felt that he had nothing to do with his violation of the regulations. Mr. Lowington did not countenance tell-tales, and no student was required or expected voluntarily to report the misdeeds of his companions. If questioned, he was to tell the exact truth, whoever suffered thereby; but, in ordinary cases, no one was considered to be under obligations to expose the faults and foibles of his associates.

McLeish promised to exchange the paper for gold, and in the afternoon, when the students went on shore, he separated himself from his shipmates, as he supposed, and entered Stuckey & Co.'s banking-house, in Clare Street, where the exchange was effected.

The officers of the Josephine, jealous of the integrity of the ship's company, had not forgotten the instructions given them by the captain at Holyhead. Every one of the four lieutenants and masters, who believed that McLeish had robbed the captain's safe, was watching him with the utmost care. Pelham saw him separate himself from his companions, and cautiously followed him into Clare Street, where the bills were exchanged for gold. As soon as McLeish had left the banker's, Pelham entered, and wrote down the numbers of the notes which the suspected student had presented.

CHAPTER XVII.

BRISTOL TO THE ISLE OF WIGHT.

"THAT proves plainly enough that McLeish stole the money — don't it?" said Pelham, when he had related the incident in Clare Street, in which he had taken part, to Captain Kendall, after their return to the Josephine.

"I think it does," replied Paul, sadly; for nothing was more painful to him than the evidence that any of his ship's company had been guilty of crime.

The fact that McLeish had exchanged four five-pound notes for gold had been communicated to the officers, who were directed to watch him very closely until Mr. Lowington could be informed of the circumstances; for the principal had gone to the railway station to make the arrangements for a trip to Birmingham and Stafford on Avon. The twenty pounds in McLeish's pocket felt heavy, and not only heavy, but hot. He wanted to give up the money; and as soon as he had reached the deck of the schooner, he hastened to find Wilton, in order to get rid of his uncomfortable burden.

Not less than four of his officers followed him to the deck of the ship, and their eyes were all fixed upon him. He went forward, but they dogged his steps.

He went below, and they went below. He returned to the consort, and they returned. He tried again, and this time six of them attended his steps, not in a body, but scattered about, so that whichever way he turned, he encountered a lieutenant or a master. He was foiled again, and not only foiled, but alarmed, for it was almost certain to him that the movements of the officers were not accidental. He was tempted to drop the gold over the side of the vessel into the dock; but so closely was he watched that he could not even do this without being detected.

This strict surveillance continued for half an hour longer, when Mr. Lowington came on board. Paul, almost as much grieved as though he had been convicted of the crime himself, related to the principal the evidence which had been obtained.

"I did not believe McLeish was the guilty person before," replied Mr. Lowington; "but this testimony is direct, though not conclusive."

"I do not see where he could have obtained twenty pounds in bills, unless from the safe," added Paul.

"I am afraid there is not much doubt in regard to his guilt. You will direct Mr. Cleats to arrest him, and bring him into your cabin," said Mr. Lowington, as he led the way below.

The order was given to the boatswain, and he found McLeish walking up and down the deck, waiting for a chance to communicate with Wilton.

"You are wanted, McLeish," said Cleats, touching him on the shoulder.

"Who wants me?" asked the alleged culprit, startled by the summons.

"The captain!"

"What does he want of me?"

"I don't know; I never ask any questions. I'm ordered to take you into the cabin."

"I'll not go," replied McLeish, his bad temper getting the better of him.

"See here, my hearty: don't make a fool of yourself. The young miss won't pity you, if you behave silly."

"I'll go," added he, subdued by the reflection that Grace Arbuckle would hear of his misconduct. "I'll go, but I've not done anything wrong."

"All right, my lad. If you haven't, you may be sure it will come out right; for the captain was as sad as though he had lost his grandmother when he ordered me to take you down. He's sorry for you, whatever is the matter."

McLeish was touched by this evidence of sympathy on the part of the commander of the Josephine, and followed the boatswain into the cabin, where he saw the principal and Paul seated at the table, waiting for his appearance.

"Do you know why you are sent for, McLeish?" asked Mr. Lowington, when Cleats had retired.

"I do not, sir. I haven't done anything," replied McLeish.

"Are you quite sure you have done nothing wrong?" demanded the principal, mildly.

"Very sure, sir. I may have broken some rule, but I've no done anything very bad."

"You were on shore this afternoon, with your shipmates?"

"Yes, sir."

"Have you any money about you?" demanded the principal, squarely.

"I had sixpence left from my allowance," replied the culprit, turning red in the face; for he now understood what was coming, though he could not for the life of him imagine how the principal should know anything about his affair with Wilton.

"Have you only sixpence?"

McLeish was troubled. Experience had taught him worldly wisdom, if not much absolute morality. If he denied that he had twenty pounds in gold, the big boatswain was within call, and his pockets would be turned out only to prove that he had added falsehood to indiscretion, for he regarded the keeping of the money for Wilton only as an indiscretion. He could not believe there was anything very bad about it, and he decided to tell the truth.

"I have more than sixpence about me," he replied, after a pause which looked bad for the boy who had turned over a new leaf.

"How much have you?" asked Mr. Lowington, in the same quiet tone in which he had thus far conducted the examination.

"Twenty pounds in gold; but it does not belong to me, sir?"

"To whom does it belong?"

Two weeks before, McLeish would have betrayed his best friend as readily as he would have turned his hand. Lynch and Grossbeck had lectured him soundly on this tendency, for they had suffered by it. He had caught from his companions something of that spirit of boy honor, which, though based on a genuine nobility of purpose, is often put to base uses, and is carried to an extent which involves actual dishonor and vice.

"I'll no tal," replied McLeish, firmly, but not in a disrespectful tone.

"I think it is your duty to tell, McLeish," added Mr. Lowington.

"I'll no be a tal-tale."

"You will leave me to infer that the money in your possession does not belong to another, but to yourself."

"It's not mine, sir; but a MacGregor never betrays a friend," added McLeish, who had proved that, however true his ancestors were to their associates, the present generation had sadly deteriorated.

The principal then stated that the safe of the schooner had been robbed of eighty pounds in bank bills.

"Do ye tal me that I robbed the safe?" demanded McLeish, now highly excited by this new phase of the case.

"I give you the opportunity to defend yourself by informing me who gave you the bank notes, if any one did."

"A MacGregor never betrays a friend," repeated McLeish, warmly.

"You will remember that you were questioned while we were lying at Holyhead," added the principal.

"I remamber; and I was accused of stealing the captain's overcoat — a thing I naver did in my life."

"The overcoat was not stolen. You were questioned in order to ascertain if you knew anything of the robbery of the safe. Now, McLeish, this looks like a plain case. The safe must have been robbed by you, or by another student, whose name I will not mention. You have exchanged twenty pounds in notes for gold. It is at least proper that you should explain how the twenty pounds came into your possession."

McLeish considered. It seemed plain enough to him that Wilton was the robber. New converts are proverbially zealous, and having set up his artificial standard of honor, he was obstinate enough to become a martyr in adhering to it. Though the principal kindly explained his position to him, and gave him every opportunity to free himself from the charge, McLeish positively refused to betray his friend.

Mr. Lowington had some doubts. The fact that Murdock had not spoken of the theft was against him, and it was possible that he had employed McLeish to exchange the money for him; but as long as the apparent culprit refused to give any information in regard to the person who had intrusted the notes to him, the principal could not do otherwise than commit him to the brig. Cleats was called, and this was done after the gold had been secured.

The prisoner's berth, bag, clothing, and all his effects, were very thoroughly searched for the remaining sixty pounds purloined from the safe, but of course without finding the money. McLeish felt like a martyr now. He was not guilty, and imprisonment did not seem as it had before. He was innocent, and his native obstinacy caused him rather to glory in his martyrdom. He was a strange boy. By and by it would be proved that he was not the guilty person, and he could revel in the thought that the principal had made a blunder. Under the influence of this stupid fanaticism, his imprisonment became a positive joy to him.

To all intents and purposes he was the thief while he refused to explain how the twenty pounds came into his possession; or, to take the mildest view, he was the accomplice of the thief — the accessory after the fact. He could not see this; he did not want to see it.

Wilton was terrified when he heard of the arrest of McLeish, and expected every moment to be called to an account; but the next afternoon the officers and crews of both vessels started for Birmingham, and not a word had been said to him, or about him, so far as he knew. The party did not return till the next night, and he found an opportunity, as he and Monroe had the run of both vessels while they lay alongside each other, to have a talk with McLeish.

The prisoner proudly rehearsed his fidelity to his employer, assuring him that a MacGregor never betrayed a friend, and that he would rot in the brig before he would open his mouth.

"But, Wilton, you cheated me," said he, reproachfully. "You told me I could not get into any scrape."

"I didn't mean to get you into any scrape. I didn't know the safe of the Josephine had been robbed," replied Wilton, earnestly.

"You didn't, lad! Yes, you did! Didn't you tak the money yourself?" interposed McLeish.

"No, I did not. I'm certain none of the fellows in the ship knew that the safe had been robbed. I'm sure I didn't."

"It's no use, lad, for you to tal me that."

"When was the safe robbed?" asked Wilton.

"At Holyhead."

"Then you may know I didn't do it. I never put foot on the Josephine till we moored in this dock yesterday. You know I couldn't have meddled with her safe. Did you see me aboard the consort while we were at Holyhead?"

"That's true, lad; and it couldn't have been you, any more than it was me," answered McLeish, convinced by this argument.

"I told you the truth about the money — I did, upon my word and honor," protested Wilton.

"All richt, lad; I believe you now, and I feel easier. I didn't like to stay in here for a fallow who had been stealing money; but if you are no guilty, you may trust me till the end of the world."

"I'm not guilty."

Wilton was selfish enough to let the prisoner remain in durance as long as the offence required, which he believed would be only a few days longer; for Perth had informed him that the ranks of the Red Cross Knights were full, and as soon as the Josephine reached a port where she could go to sea without a pilot, he intended to put the grand scheme into execution. It was understood that the squadron would next sail for the Isle of Wight, and this would be a good locality for carrying out the enterprise.

The chief conspirator did not consider it safe to tell

McLeish what was in contemplation, but he assured him that something would happen in a few days which would set him at liberty. The prisoner teased to know what it was, but Wilton kept his secret, and a footstep on the deck drove him away from the brig before his constancy was very severely tried.

After a three hours' ride by fast train the students arrived at Birmingham at about six o'clock — in season to see a specimen of the city before they retired. In thirty years this place has tripled its population, being now next to Glasgow in size. It contains nothing of special interest to the tourist, except its manufactories of hardware. After another walk through the town, the excursionists went to Stratford on Avon, the birthplace of Shakspeare, twenty-two and a half miles from Birmingham by railway.

Ben Duncan, the poet, went into ecstasies when the party entered the house where the immortal bard was born. He "spouted" Shakspeare in quantity, and declared that he had lived long enough. The house has been purchased by subscription, and is kept in as nearly its original condition as possible. The boys wandered about the town for an hour, and some of them were susceptible enough to realize that they were in the midst of scenes on which the master poet of England had gazed, and to be moved by the fact. Ben Duncan did not recover from his raptures till the train stopped on the verge of the city of Bristol, to enable the guard to pick up the passengers' tickets.

As it was but five o'clock in the afternoon, and the train stopped near the Ashley Road, Mr. Lowington decided to visit Mr. Müller's Orphan Asylum, located in this quarter of the town. The founder of this institution has a world-wide reputation as a philanthropist, and his history is without a parallel in the annals of benevolent enterprise.

George Müller was born in Prussia, in 1805. While a student at the university in his native land, he consecrated his life to preaching and piety, and determined "to go about doing good." He went to England, and applied for a place in the East where he might preach the gospel. He lived for a time at Teignmouth, in Devonshire, proclaiming the truth to the poor, and living upon the scanty contributions of a few friends. In connection with Mr. Craik, a Scotchman, he opened a small chapel for the poor at Bristol, where his attention was attracted by the wants of the indigent children, and he established an institution for the purpose of instructing them in their religious duties. He commenced the enterprise when he and his friend possessed only a shilling between them.

Mr. Müller afterwards established his large "Orphan Houses," in which he has clothed, fed, and educated upwards of a thousand children. His life was a life of prayer. If he wanted anything, he prayed for it, and it always came. Sometimes it happened that there was not a penny in the treasury of the institution to buy bread for the children; but Müller did not borrow — he prayed for help. He never applied in person to any human being for money or assistance; and he fully believed that the means to carry on his work came to him in answer to his prayers. In this manner he has received more than one hundred and fifty thousand pounds.

Müller's story was told to the boys by the chaplain, who regarded the philanthropist as a "remarkable man of God." The students were interested in the institution, and no better lesson of goodness and piety could be presented to them than this visit afforded.

At seven o'clock all hands were on board. Mr. Lowington paid a visit to McLeish before he went to his cabin; but he found him as obdurate as before. Supper was on the table in both vessels, and after it was disposed of, though the students were very much fatigued by the journey of the day, the order was given to unmoor, and work out of the dock, for it was full tide at eight o'clock. A steam tug had been previously engaged to tow them down to the channel, and before ten they were clear of King's Roads, at the mouth of the river. The weather was pleasant, and a moderate breeze from the southward indicated a prosperous beginning for the voyage.

It had been the intention of the principal to put in at Plymouth, Cowes, and Folkestone; but he was so far behind time, that he proposed to run direct for the Thames. Paul Kendall hoped he would stop at Cowes, and Mr. Lowington consented to do so, at his request. The young commander blushed as he asked this favor, and felt compelled to state the reason of it, which the principal had deemed sufficient.

After the watch had been set that evening on board of the Josephine, Paul went to his state-room, and took from his pocket several letters which had been received at Bristol. There was one from Grace Arbuckle, which he read more than once. It informed him that Mr. Arbuckle and his family had gone to the

Isle of Wight to spend a week with the friends with whom they were staying near London. A previous letter had announced that they expected to visit Cowes. She hoped to see him there, and Paul hoped so too. What would she say when she learned that McLeish was in the brig again? For her sake he took more interest in the young reprobate than he otherwise would have done. As he thought of the fair reformer, he went into the steerage, and directed the prisoner to be brought before him. Taking him into his stateroom, where they could be entirely alone, he talked very kindly, but very plainly, to him.

"I didn't steal the money, Captain Kendall," protested McLeish, with so much earnestness that Paul was almost persuaded to believe him.

"I do not say that you did, McLeish, though I believe you did," replied Paul, gently, but candidly.

"It's no fair for you to believe it, Captain Kendall, when I tal you I did not."

"Then tell me where you got the twenty pounds."

"How can I tal you without betraying the secret of another?"

"You are under no obligations to keep such a secret. You are simply defeating the ends of justice, and in doing so you become the accessory of the thief. You are screening him, if there is any such person, from punishment. McLeish, Miss Arbuckle will probably come on board of the Josephine at Cowes. What shall I say to her when she asks for you."

"Tal her I suffer myself rather than betray a friend," replied the prisoner, proudly.

"Very well; if you choose to persist in your present course, I cannot help it."

"You will find out, Captain Kendall, to your sorrow, some day, that I am innocent."

"It will not be to my sorrow, for I shall say to you, as I say to you now, that it serves you right. If you are not guilty, you have only to say who gave you the money, and if your statement is proved to be correct, you will be immediately discharged."

"I'll no betray my friend," added McLeish. "It's no right to keep me in the brig without proving the chairge upon me. Can you show that the bills I changed for gold were the ones you lost?"

"No, I cannot prove it; but you are not kept in the brig for stealing, but for refusing to explain where you got the twenty pounds, since it is against the rules of the Academy for any student to keep so much money about him."

"I'm content to stay in the brig till I die on that chairge," added McLeish, with something like defiance in his tones.

Paul, satisfied that nothing could be made out of the prisoner, ordered him back to the brig. Pelham had supposed that, when he took the numbers of the notes in Liverpool, he had furnished the means for identifying them; but neither Mr. Lowington nor Paul had noted down the numbers of the bills, as very many people in England do when they receive them. Pelham's memorandum of the numbers had been carefully preserved, and it was hoped that the banker in Liverpool, who had paid them to the principal, would be able to inform him whether they were received from him. He had been written to on the subject, and his reply was expected at London.

Wilton was beginning to breathe easier. He was not called to account for keeping Murdock's bills, and before the ship reached Land's End, he concluded that the new hand had not said anything to him about the matter.

"Now own up honestly, Murdock, that you didn't say anything to Lowington," said Wilton, as the ship was going through the channel between Land's End and the Scilly Islands.

"Ah, but I did tell him all about it," persisted Murdock, who did not consider it safe to take the back track — it would damage his veracity, if nothing else.

"What's the reason Lowington hasn't hauled me up, then?"

"The principal knows what he is about," replied Murdock, mysteriously. "I suppose he expects you to deny the charge."

"Of course I shall, because you didn't give me any money."

"Mr. Lowington is waiting till he can prove it, I reckon," added Murdock. "No doubt he will be able to prove it. Do you happen to know why McLeish was put in the brig the other day at Bristol?"

By this time the robbery of the safe was patent to all in both vessels, and Wilton gave the reason, as he understood it.

"That's not the reason," replied Murdock. "He was put in the brig for refusing to tell who gave him the twenty pounds, which he exchanged for gold. Do you know Mr. Pelham took the numbers of those notes at the bankers' in Bristol?"

"What if he did?" asked Wilton.

"You can't see half an inch beyond your own nose," added Murdock, contemptuously.

"Perhaps I can't, but if my nose were as long as yours, I ought not to be expected to see a great ways beyond it; at least not without a spy-glass," retorted Wilton.

"I thought you could smell a mice when there was a mice round."

"So I can."

"No, you can't; your smellers are worse than useless, or you would know what the principal is waiting for."

"What is he waiting for?"

"Do you think I don't know where McLeish got the twenty pounds?"

"If you do, why don't you tell, and get him out of the scrape?" demanded Wilton, uneasily; for the odor of the mice was beginning to be apparent to him.

"You don't know that I haven't."

"Haven't what?"

"Told where McLeish got the money."

"Well, where did he get it?" asked Wilton.

"It was my twenty pounds, of course, and you gave it to him to get it changed for gold. Just as soon as my father sends down the numbers of the bank notes he paid me, your head will go on the block, Mr. Wilton, and you will find out just how mean it is to cheat a fellow out of his money."

Wilton tried to laugh and look unconcerned, but the effort was a failure. He felt as though he had been suddenly plunged into a tank of hot water, which was even then scalding him.

"When will your father send down the numbers of the bank notes?" he asked.

"When we get to London."

"All right," thought Wilton, who intended to be at sea in the Josephine before that time; but he said nothing.

"Your time will come, my lad," added Murdock.

"So will yours," answered Wilton, determined, if possible, to get even with his tantalizer. "Though I cannot see the length of your nose, I can see the length of my own."

"What do you mean by that?" asked Murdock, disturbed in his turn.

"Who robbed the safe? That's the question," sneered Wilton.

"Who did?"

"It was done by you, McLeish, or the mainmast of the Josephine, and neither McLeish nor the mainmast did it," retorted Wilton, as he turned on his heel and walked away.

Wilton had really no idea who had robbed the safe. Since the theft had come out, it had been thoroughly discussed among the students; and they, like the principal and the officers, had come to the conclusion, from their knowledge of the circumstances, that the theft lay between Murdock and McLeish. The new hand had a cold sweat. He felt that, after all the cunning and care he had used in covering up his tracks after the robbery, his crime was almost sure to find him out.

He was confident that the bills McLeish had exchanged, were those of which Wilton had defrauded him. If the prisoner explained where the notes came from, he would be discharged, and the crime would then be charged upon him — where it belonged. He was in despair, and was fully resolved to run away the very next time he was allowed to go on shore; and in anticipation of this event, he followed one of the cooks down into the hold that day, and recovered the stolen money, which he had deposited in the bottle, smashing it on a cask to get at its contents.

On Monday afternoon the two vessels passed near enough to Eddystone Light-house to enable the students to see this wonderful structure, and being favored with a fair and fresh breeze, came to anchor the next morning in the harbor of Cowes, which is the principal seaport of the Isle of Wight.

CHAPTER XVIII.

AROUND THE ISLE OF WIGHT.

"OUR time has come, Perth," said Wilton, impressively, to the future captain of the Josephine, after the sails of the ship had been furled. "We mustn't put it off another day," he added, as he chalked a red cross on the lapel of his companion's coat, when he had already made one on his own.

"I am ready, and so are our gallant crew," replied Perth, briskly. "The two vessels lie first rate for the undertaking, and I don't see anything to prevent a perfect success."

"Nor I, if the fellows move quick and obey orders; but we must have our arrangements all made, so that we can move without a moment's delay."

"That's so; but I know every fellow, and can give him his instructions in two minutes," added Perth.

"How many are there?"

"Twenty-five, besides myself."

"In the first place," continued Wilton, "we must all be left on board this afternoon, when the ship's company go on shore."

"That's the difficult matter," said Perth.

"What's the difficulty about it? We have only

to cut up sharp enough; or rather you have, for Ike Monroe and I will have to stay aboard any how."

"What shall we do?" asked Perth. "There are twenty-five of us, and it is not an easy thing for us to cut up just enough to be left on board."

"I'll tell you how to manage it. In the first place, you must chalk every fellow's back this morning."

"Chalk every fellow's back on the lapel of his jacket, you mean," laughed Perth.

"Of course; that's the meaning we give to the words; and if we understand it, that's enough."

"Go on; what shall we do?"

"At half past one, the lessons will all be finished; and before the fellows leave the steerage, Lowington will announce, as usual, that an allowance of two shillings will be paid to each student, and all hands will go ashore at two o'clock. The professors will go to their state-rooms to put on a clean dickey. Lowington will take his place in the main cabin to mark the orders, and all the fellows will form a line to march round the main cabin to receive their money. Don't you see?"

"Yes, I see; that's the way it is always done. What then?" demanded Perth, impatiently, for the matter was becoming exciting to him.

"Then all the Knights, except Ike Monroe and me, will quietly slip up the ladder to the deck."

"But they won't get their two shillings."

"What odds does that make? We shall find all the money we want in the Josephine — two or three hundred pounds, at least. You don't want the paltry two shillings."

"Go ahead; it is almost seven bells, and we shall be piped to breakfast before you get through, if you don't hurry up."

"Don't interrupt me, then. The boats will all be ready at the swinging boom; for when they are going ashore in the afternoon, the boats are always lowered at recess, so that there shall be no delay. As soon as you get on deck with the Knights, make a rush over the side, and get into the captain's gig, or the professor's barge, whichever one lies most convenient to the accommodation ladder."

"But the boats will be at the swinging boom."

"So they will. Well, one of you must drop down from the boom, cast off her painter, after sliding down into her, and run her up to the gangway."

"We can manage all that."

"As soon as you get into the boat, up with your oars, and pull away."

"Suppose we should find Peaks or Bitts, or both of them, on deck," suggested Perth.

"Tell them Lowington wants to see them in the steerage. As soon as you get off in the boat, some one will be likely to observe you; and there will be a big row. Two boats will be sent after you, and, of course, you will be caught and brought back. Just say, when Lowington hauls you up, that the Josephines have more liberty than we do, and you were going ashore to have a good time on your own hook. You can be penitent, and snivel as much as you have a mind to — the more the better. Then you will be sentenced to stay on board while the rest of the fellows go ashore; which will be just the thing we want."

"Hush up! There's Murdock," said Perth, as the new hand approached them.

"I hate that fellow!" replied Wilton.

Murdock jumped upon the top-gallant forecastle, where the conspirators were discussing their plan, and took a survey of West Cowes, and the beautiful yachts which were moored near it. He glanced at the pair of Red Cross Knights, and observed the insignia of the order upon the lapel of their jackets. While he stood there, all hands were piped to breakfast. Murdock fully intended that this should be his last day on board. McLeish would "cave in" before many days, and this event would be likely to fasten the robbery upon him. It would not be a very difficult matter to slip away from the chaplain, who had the charge of the shore squad, to which he belonged, and then take a steamer for Southampton. But he was deeply interested in the affairs of the Red Cross Knights, and in spite of the fears which disturbed him, he could not resist the temptation to have some fun at their expense.

As he went down to breakfast, he took one of the red crayons used for map-drawing at the blackboards, and made the red cross on his lapel. In the course of the morning, before the studies were commenced, every true Knight was duly chalked, and his instructions given him. At recess, Murdock looked about him, and saw who they were. The boats were lowered, and dinner disposed of. By this time the Red Cross Knights were as thick as rain drops in a thunder shower; for Murdock had been busy, even in school hours, with his crayon. Not less than half a dozen of the officers had their "backs" chalked.

Just before the students were summoned to the steerage to finish the exercises of the day, Howe, a genuine Red Cross Knight, walked up to him with his fore finger extended in index form. Murdock promptly crossed it.

"Are you a Red Cross Knight?" said Howe.

"I am."

"Has your back been chalked?"

"It has."

"Who chalked it?"

"A red Knight of the Red Cross chalked it red."

"All right; but I didn't know it before. Are you one, though?" demanded Howe, puzzled by the promptness and the correctness with which the cross had been made, and the questions had been answered.

"Haven't I proved that I am one?" replied Murdock.

"You have, but your name isn't down on the roll."

"It ought to be."

The call to recitations disturbed the conference before Murdock had obtained the information he wanted. Perth and Wilton had been appalled at the number of Red Cross Knights which appeared at recess. They and other members of the order had elevated the fore finger in position to be crossed, but the signal had not been answered by any one except Murdock.

"There's a traitor among us," whispered Wilton, as they went below.

"Not a bit of it," replied Perth; "I tried half a dozen of them, but not one could make the signal."

"But more than fifty fellows have their backs chalked."

"It's only a joke. Some fellow noticed the cross, and marked the others. It is all right, and we will put things through as we arranged."

When the recitations were finished, Mr. Lowington made the usual announcement that the ship's company would go on shore; and the students were required to form the line, and present their orders. The genuine Red Cross Knights obeyed their instructions, going on deck, some by the main hatch, and some by the fore hatch, and only one at a time, so as not to attract attention. By the time the students in the steerage had written their orders and formed the line, all the Knights were on deck, and one more.

Murdock had not ceased to watch Perth and Howe, who, he knew, were Knights; and, as it was evident that "the time had come," he was determined to know what it all meant. Peaks, the boatswain, was not on deck, but was mending the foretop-gallant shrouds, which had been chafed on the passage from Bristol. Bitts, the carpenter, was "planking" the deck in the waist. Perth politely informed him that Mr. Lowington wished to see him, and he hastened below, leaving the deck without an officer.

Howe ran out on the swinging boom, and sliding down on the rope to which the barge's painter was made fast, cast off, and worked the boat up to the gangway. The rest of the conspirators tumbled in as fast as they could. The oars went up, and the boat pushed off. Murdock, as soon as he saw the Knights creeping up on deck, followed them, and tumbled into the boat with the others.

"Avast, there! What's up now?" shouted Peaks

from aloft, satisfied by the confusion with which the students had embarked that the proceeding was irregular.

He hastened down, and rolling into the main cabin, where Bitts was waiting, cap in hand, for Mr. Lowington to say what he wanted, —

"Beg pardon, sir; but did you or the officers send the boat away?" inquired Peaks.

"What boat?" demanded Mr. Lowington.

"The barge, sir. She just left the ship with more than twenty in her; but I didn't see any officers," added Peaks.

"Who was in charge of the boats?"

"Mr. Bitts, sir. I was aloft."

"I was in charge of the boats, sir," interposed the carpenter; "but one of the lads just came to me, and said you wished to see me. I have been standing here waiting your orders."

"I sent no one to you," replied the principal, who readily perceived that some mischief was in progress.

All hands were piped to muster, the money boxes put away, and the business of the hour suspended. The crews of the gig and first cutter were sent over the side, and with Mr. Fluxion in one, and Peaks in the other, they started in pursuit of the deserters. The barge was pulling up the river, instead of to the nearest shore. For the sake of keeping up appearances, Perth ordered the oarsmen to pull with all their might; but half of them were green hands, disposed to "catch crabs," and the race was a short one. When the two pursuing boats came up, the runaways ceased rowing, and surrendered at discretion, according to the programme. Mr. Fluxion and Peaks stepped into the barge.

"Well, what are you going to do now?" demanded the professor of mathematics.

"We don't have fair play," growled Perth, who was in the stern-sheets.

"You will probably get fair play now."

"All the Josephines have their liberty when they go on shore, and we would like the same privilege."

"Where were you going?" asked Mr. Fluxion.

"On shore, sir."

"What for?"

"Only to enjoy ourselves. We intended to come back before night," answered Perth.

"Pull for the ship," said Mr. Fluxion, sharply. "Take the helm, Mr. Peaks."

The boys pulled again, and the boatswain steered for the ship. Murdock, who did not understand the programme, was the only one who was disappointed. With eighty pounds in his pocket, he was ready to leave, and to enjoy himself as long as he could on his ill-gotten treasure. He supposed the conspirators intended to land when they got into the boat, and the opportunity just suited his case. Perth told him they did not want him, but he would not leave, and delay would be fatal.

"Murdock is not one of us; let no fellow say a word," called Perth, as soon as the boat put off.

Thus cautioned, no one did say a word, and Murdock was left ignorant of the real purpose of the apparent deserters.

"Take their names before they come on board, Mr. Fluxion," said the principal from the gangway, as the barge approached the ship.

The list of the Red Cross Knights, including Murdock, was written down by the professor, and the runaways sent on board. They were hauled up at the mainmast, in due form, and stated their excuse for deserting, as they had to Mr. Fluxion.

"Your liberty is stopped till further orders," said Mr. Lowington, just as Wilton had planned the affair.

The excuse which Perth had given troubled the principal. It certainly was not fair that the crew of the Josephine should have greater privileges than the crew of the ship. Yet the former had an inducement to keep them orderly, which the latter did not have, and it would not be prudent to permit the half-disciplined recruits of the Young America to visit the shore without any restraint. There was no remedy at present, for as long as the Josephines did not abuse their liberty, it was not fair to deprive them of it. The matter was left for future consideration and correction.

The business of paying the allowances proceeded in the steerage; but before it was finished, Captain Kendall appeared, and announced that Mr. Arbuckle, his family and friends, had just arrived on board of the consort.

"There's going to be a race between two yachts this afternoon, sir," said Paul, with no little excitement in his manner.

"I am willing," laughed the principal.

"Mr. Arbuckle and his friends have come off to our vessel to see them start," added Paul.

"I am still willing, and I hope you will entertain them as well as your means will permit."

"I will, sir; but I want to follow the race, for there is a piping breeze, and I believe I can beat either one of the yachts," continued the young commander, with enthusiasm. "Our officers and crew would rather run with the race than go on shore."

"I am willing, Captain Kendall. Do you propose to enter for the race?"

"No, sir; the race is between those two yachts, and no others enter. Captain Dashover, one of Mr. Arbuckle's friends, is an old yachtman, and knows all about the course, which is round the Isle of Wight. I did not dare to invite them without your permission."

"It would not have been proper for you to do so; but you have my permission. But, Captain Kendall, none of our ship's company, except the doctor, have even sailed in the Josephine, not even myself. Perhaps you will be willing to invite us," added the principal, with a smile.

"I should be delighted to have the whole ship's company!" exclaimed Paul.

"I thank you, and I will put it to vote. If the officers and crew prefer to accept your invitation rather than visit the shore, I will allow them to do so."

Paul hastened back to the Josephine, invited his party to follow the race, and ordered his first lieutenant to bend on the fore square-sail. On board the ship, all hands were piped to muster, and the question put to them whether they would go on shore, or make the excursion in the Josephine. The decision was unanimously in favor of the race, especially as the ship's company were to have a sail in the Josephine, which they had desired ever since they saw her.

"What do you think of that?" demanded Tom Perth, as soon as the vote had been taken.

"Our cake is dough again!" replied Wilton, disgusted with the proceedings of the majority of the students.

"As usual!" snarled Monroe.

"A pretty scrape you have got us into!" exclaimed Howe. "Instead of having a good time in the Josephine, we have to mope on board the ship all the afternoon. I would rather have followed that race than be commander of the schooner in a runaway cruise."

"This is what we had our liberty stopped for — is it?" added Greenway, "Just to stick on board while the rest of the fellows are having some tip-top fun."

"It is not my fault," replied Perth.

"Nor mine," said Wilton. "If the rest of the fellows had gone ashore, as we supposed they would, we should have got off in the Josephine, as sure as you live."

"Perhaps we should," sneered Howe.

"It's no use to grumble, fellows," continued Wilton, recovering his equanimity in some degree. "The fellows will go ashore to-morrow, if they don't to-day, for the queen has a palace here, and they all want to see it."

Perth and Wilton, after considerable argument, partially reconciled the Knights of the Red Cross to the disappointment. They assured the Knights they would be deprived of their liberty the next day, when the ship's company went on shore; and an opportunity would be offered for the execution of the grand scheme. They cautioned the members of the valiant order to beware of Murdock, and not give him the slightest hint. He had probably heard others repeat the dialogue, and had learned it; and during the afternoon, while the conspirators were moping about the deck, the machinery of the Knights was entirely changed. A new dialogue was invented, with new signs and signals.

Murdock was more thoroughly disgusted than any of the real conspirators. In ignorantly following the Knights he had defeated his own purpose; and while his companions in misfortune were reorganizing their mysterious band, he went into the hold, and concealed the bank notes in another bottle, as he had done before. He was vexed and disheartened. There was no way to get on shore, and the grand crash which would expose him could not long be deferred.

The boats transferred that portion of the ship's company which had not been deprived of their liberty to the Josephine, and the adult forward officers returned to the Young America with the boats. Paul Kendall was in a blaze of excitement. Grace Arbuckle was on board his vessel with her friends. The anchor was at a short stay, and they were waiting for the yachts to start. The run was to be around the Isle of Wight, about sixty-three miles.

The contending yachts were two English cutters; that is, they were sloop-rigged, with a topsail. Both were of about the same tonnage as the Josephine. The gun was fired, and the cutters slipped their moorings. The Josephine had previously got under way, and was standing out of the harbor. At the mouth of the river, she lay to till the yachts were abreast of her. The wind was on the port quarter, and coming very fresh. The fore square-sail was set, and some of the liveliest sailing the students had ever beheld followed as the schooner stood down the Solent, which is the name given to the westerly part of the channel that divides the island from the main land, while the eastern section is called Spithead.

The two cutters were probably not of the fastest class of sailing vessels in the Royal Yacht Squadron, for the Josephine outsailed them, because she carried sail longer than they could. Outside of the island the sea was very rough; but while the Josephine made good weather of it, the yachts labored, and were finally obliged to take in their light sails aloft. When they had passed the Needles, the vessels went close-hauled against a head sea, till they were off the southern point of the island, when the "Stars and Stripes" were a mile ahead of the "Red Cross" at the peaks of the cutters. Here they tacked; and the sea was even rougher than on the other side of the isle, and the Josephine gained more rapidly than before. Everybody on board, including the ladies, was intensely excited, for the motion and the speed of the schooner were really thrilling.

At eight o'clock the Josephine came into the harbor, and was received with plentiful cheering by the yachts and pleasure boats lying at anchor, which

AROUND THE ISLE OF WIGHT.—Page 304.

were returned with a will by the students on board. Half an hour later they joined in the applause bestowed upon the victorious yacht, which came in fifteen minutes ahead of her rival.

"You did not tell me that McLeish was in the cage again, Captain Kendall," said Grace, reproachfully, when, after the schooner had come to anchor, she ascertained the fact; for she had been too much excited by the race to think of anything else during the passage.

"I did not wish to spoil the pleasure of your excursion," replied Paul, who proceeded to give her the history of her *protégé's* misconduct.

"Will you let me see him again?" she asked.

"Certainly, if you desire it."

McLeish was brought into the cabin by Cleats, while all the rest of the party were on deck watching the yachts.

"I am very sorry you are again a prisoner, Mr. McLeish," said she, after shaking hands with the culprit.

"It's no my fault this time, miss. I've done my bast, but I couldn't betray my friend."

"But if anybody is a thief or a robber, he ought not to be your friend, or any good man's friend," replied Grace.

"My friend is not a thief, nor a robber. He came honestly by the money, or I would tal all about it."

"How do you know he did?"

"I know very well. He only broke through one of the regulations, and that's no very bad. Even the principal says we are not to give voluntary testimony against our shipmates for breaking the rules," protested McLeish.

"But the safe has been robbed, and the officers believe you are the guilty one."

"I am not, miss; and as long as I am innocent, they may just think what they please."

"This is wrong; you are helping to conceal the guilty person."

"You don't understand it, Miss Arbuckle. Will you promise not to speak to any one about it, if I tal you the whole story?"

"I will not promise," replied Grace, promptly.

"I would like to tal you, for I don't wish to have you think I am guilty."

"I can't help believing so while you behave in this extraordinary manner," added she, warmly.

"I am not guilty, and my friend is not guilty."

"If you can prove to me that your friend is not guilty, I will not mention his name," she continued, after a little reflection.

McLeish was satisfied, and told the whole story of his relations with Wilton, after sending Cleats out of the cabin. He gave her the name of the bankers, from whom Wilton, in his desire to make his explanation plausible, declared he had obtained the money.

"If he obtained the notes of T. Wiggin & Co., as he says, I shall believe you are innocent. I will go there myself when we reach London, and ascertain," said Grace.

"If you find Wilton did not get the money as he told me, you may just tal the captain what I say as soon as you please," replied McLeish. "If my friend cheated me, I don't care what becomes of him."

"I will keep your secret, but I am sorry you will have to stay in the brig several days more."

"As long as I am innocent, I just don't care," laughed McLeish. "I have labored hard to be good. I think you are an angel, and you —"

"Thank you!" interposed Grace. "I hope, O, I do hope, you will be proved innocent."

"I shall."

Grace knocked at the door of Captain Kendall's state-room, and Paul joined her. The prisoner was sent back to the brig, and the fair reformer acknowledged that she had not been able to change his purpose.

The crew of the Young America returned to the ship, the passengers were landed, and the day of excitement was finished.

CHAPTER XIX.

UP THE THAMES.

THE afternoon of the next day was devoted to the visit on shore. The Knights of the Red Cross waited with feverish impatience for the arrangements to be completed. They were confident they should be kept on board, and an opportunity thus afforded them to carry out their daring plan in regard to the Josephine. They were punished still further, and obliged to remain on board, as they had anticipated, and a boat was left on the davits for their especial use, apparently.

The shore party landed at West Cowes, and by invitation paid a visit to the Old Castle, now converted into the Royal Yacht Squadron Club-house. It was a circular fort built by Henry VIII. for the defence of the coast. It is now a regular club-house, having a dining-room, library, reading-room, and other apartments. The harbor was full of yachts belonging to the club, for Cowes is its headquarters from May to November of each year.

The Royal Yacht Club is a great institution. It is composed of about one hundred and fifty members — noblemen and gentlemen who are owners of yachts of from forty to four hundred and fifty tons. The tonnage of the yachts belonging to the squadron exceeds ten thousand tons, and gives employment to fourteen hundred seamen. The association is generously encouraged by the government, for it fosters and keeps alive a taste for nautical affairs, and is a nursery for the navy. Three days in August of each year are devoted to regattas, when the yachts sail for the plate presented by the queen, valued at one hundred guineas.

Cowes is composed of two parts, one on each side of Medina river, which at its mouth is about a mile wide. The two points of land were formerly called the "East Cow," and "West Cow," from which its present name is derived. The party crossed the ferry, and obtained a partial view of Norris Castle and Osborne House, the latter being the sea-shore residence of her majesty, and the former was occasionally used by the Duchess of Kent, the mother of the queen. The Osborne mansion is an Italian villa on a large scale, with a flag tower one hundred and twelve feet high, and a clock tower ninety feet high. Prince Albert, it is said, assisted in making the designs for the house.

The park extends down to the sea-shore, where there are bathing-houses for the use of the royal household. Half a mile from the house is a romantic Swiss cottage, where the brood of young princesses used to amuse themselves in doing kitchen and dairy work. Adjoining this cottage are the gardens wherein these young ladies used to cultivate vegetables with their own hands; and it is said that "Her Royal Highness, Victoria Adelaide Mary Louisa, Princess

Royal of England and of Prussia," has vegetables sent to her from this garden up to the present time. She was a good girl, but probably she could not make her living by raising potatoes and cabbages.

The Osborne estate contains two thousand acres, most of it, of course, being used for mere pleasure or ornamental purposes. Her majesty can ride eight miles without leaving her own grounds. Yet the queen occupies this residence only a few weeks of each year. Royalty is an expensive luxury, for the sovereign keeps and occupies four palaces — Buckingham, Windsor, Balmoral, and Osborne. Her majesty's "privy purse" amounts to one million seven hundred and twenty-five thousand dollars. This is the annual allowance paid to her by the government, in addition to which she has an immense private fortune. The Prince of Wales has two hundred thousand dollars a year, besides his private revenues, and his wife fifty thousand dollars. Other members of the royal family are paid from fifteen to seventy-five thousand dollars out of the nation's pocket. Prince Alfred has three times the salary of the President of the United States.

At six o'clock the excursionists reached the landing-place at East Cowes, where the boats were waiting for them in charge of the adult forward officers. The Josephine still lay at her moorings — a fact which may not be credible to the reader, after being informed of the well-laid plans of Wilton, Perth, and other members of the valiant order of Red Cross Knights. Everything had been left on board of the ship and her consort, apparently as the prophets had predicted.

The cooks and under stewards were the only persons left in the vessels, so far as the conspirators knew.

"All ready!" said Perth, as soon as the boats had left the ship. "Now is our time!"

"Don't be in a hurry, Tom," interposed Wilton. "We musn't let the shore party see us."

"What if they do see us? We can get the Josephine under way before they can reach her."

"Perhaps we can; but—"

"We can slip the cable!" said Perth, impatiently.

"And go to sea without any anchor, or with only the heavy spare one! You are too fast, Perth. Just wait till Lowington crosses over to the other side of the river, where he won't see what we are about. There isn't more than a six-knot breeze blowing."

"What odds does that make?"

"They will chase us. Lowington would get a steamer, and be after us. We must have two or three hours' start of him, or it's no use," said Wilton, decidedly.

Perth considered this good logic, and was content to wait. In less than an hour the boats of the squadron crossed the river, and disappeared within a basin. There was no longer any reason for delay, and the conspirators brought up their pea-jackets. The cooks and stewards were at work below, getting supper and preparing the tables. No one was to be seen on the deck of the Josephine, and everything seemed to be remarkably favorable for the execution of the scheme.

"Man the falls!" shouted Perth, when all were ready.

"Where are you going?" asked Murdock, when he was satisfied something unusual was in progress.

"What's that to you, Greeny?" replied Wilton, in the most unamiable of tones.

"If you are going on shore, I want to go with you," answered Murdock.

"You can't go with us. We don't believe in you."

"Let me go with you — that's a good fellow."

"No, sir!" replied Wilton, decidedly. "I won't have anything to do with you any how."

"Why not?"

"Why not, you humbug! Didn't you lie to Lowington, and tell him I had some money of yours?"

"No, I didn't. I sold you. I haven't said a word to the principal about the money, and don't mean to do so."

"You can't humbug me. I know you did."

"Upon my word I did not! You know he hasn't said a word to you."

"What did you tell me you did for?"

"Only to tease you, just as you teased me. Let me go with you — that's a good fellow."

But it did not suit Wilton's purpose to have Murdock go, even if all grounds of prejudice against the applicant had been removed.

"Bear a hand, and be lively, fellows," said Wilton to his companions.

"I'll give you something if you'll let me go," persisted Murdock.

"What will you give me?" asked Wilton, hardly heeding him.

"I'll give you five pounds," added the applicant, determined to overcome all obstacles by a liberal offer.

"No," replied Wilton, who was fearful that the new hand would defeat his plan if permitted to join the party.

"I'm a Red Cross Knight, you know."

"Who gave you the sign?" demanded Wilton.

"I heard you telling it to Monroe, in the steerage. I pretended to be asleep afterwards," laughed the new hand. "I will give you ten pounds."

"No, you eavesdropper!" growled Wilton.

"I'll give you twenty."

"Where's your money?"

"Down below. I'll go for it."

"Where did you get twenty pounds?" asked Wilton, interested in spite of himself.

"My father sent it to me in a letter."

"Come, Wilton! What are you about!" interposed Perth. "We are all ready to lower the boat."

"Lower away then!"

"What does all this mean?" demanded Mr. Fluxion, who had just come up the companion-way, and at this moment stepped into the midst of the boys.

The conspirators were stunned and appalled by his presence. The professor of mathematics had been troubled with a severe sick headache, and instead of going on shore, had lain down in his state-room, directly under the part of the deck where the students stood.

"So you are going ashore — are you?" continued he, sharply.

The boys who had hold of the fall ropes belayed them again. Mr. Fluxion was a decided person, and the idea of running away before his eyes did not occur to them. They retreated from the spot, and looked as sheepish as though they had been caught in the act of stealing chickens. He ordered one of the conspirators to throw the coats out of the boat, and drove them all below.

"Our game is up!" said Wilton, when they reached the steerage.

"I had no idea Fluxion was on board," replied Perth.

"No matter; our time will come," added Wilton. "I won't give it up yet."

"Nor I. Fluxion has no idea what we were going to do."

"What were you going to do?" asked Murdock, who had mingled with the conspirators.

"We were going on shore to ask the town-pump where you got twenty pounds," answered Wilton.

"I haven't got any twenty pounds. I was fooling you," said Murdock, fearful that he might have injured himself by his generous offer.

The conspirators kept their own counsel better than conspirators usually do, and Murdock was none the wiser for anything he had heard. When Mr. Lowington came on board with the ship's company, the irregular proceedings of the twenty-six students undergoing punishment were reported to him, and they were at once summoned to the tribunal at the main-mast for discipline. Murdock hung back, for he did not regard himself as one of the guilty party; but

Mr. Fluxion ordered him to toe the mark with the others.

"I was not going in the boat," pleaded he.

"You were standing by, talking to Wilton, when I came on deck," said Mr. Fluxion.

"But I wasn't going in the boat, and I didn't know anything about it till I saw them together."

"Was Murdock going with you, Wilton?" asked Mr. Lowington.

"No, sir."

"That will do, Murdock; you may go," added the principal.

"He offered me twenty pounds to let him go with us," added Wilton, maliciously.

"Twenty pounds!" exclaimed Mr. Lowington, a large gleam of light flashing into his mind.

"I was only funning, sir; I have no twenty pounds," interposed the new hand, aghast at this revelation.

It was not necessary to settle the matter then, but Murdock's offer of twenty pounds was the most important part of the whole transaction, for it was the key to much that had not yet been explained. The attempt of Wilton and his party to go on shore without permission was simply an act of disobedience, which could be easily atoned for, and which was to be expected from such boys as they were. It suggested that so many of the students should not be left on board without some one to take charge of them, and Mr. Fluxion's sick headache proved to be a fortunate event. The six and twenty culprits were duly lectured for their misconduct, and sentenced to be deprived of three days' liberty on shore, under the impression of the principal that they only meant to visit the town in the boat, and return at night. Of course no one outside of the order of the Knights had the remotest suspicion that they intended to capture the Josephine, and run away to sea in her.

As soon as supper had been disposed of, the pilots came on board of the vessels, and they sailed for London. That evening the principal had another long talk with Murdock, who still denied that he was in earnest when he offered twenty pounds for a passage to the shore; and the young rascal felt that it would have been better for him to give fifty pounds than remain on board any longer. He was so artful and so persistent in his denial that Mr. Lowington was unable to satisfy himself in regard to the guilt of the suspected student; but his impression was stronger than before that he was the robber of the safe.

Thus far the plan to run away with the Josephine was a failure; but the conspirators were fully prepared to carry out their purpose as soon as the circumstances would permit. On the passage to the Thames, the Red Cross Knights were cautioned to be extremely careful, and never to speak of the affairs of the order, and especially of the grand scheme, where there was the slightest possibility of being overheard. Nothing was to be said in the steerage or on deck; only when aloft, or out on the bowsprit, were the Knights allowed to allude to the business of the association. This intense secrecy rendered the affair all the more exciting and fascinating.

Wilton's trials were not over when the principal had dismissed him, for the chaplain, fearful of the safety of his young lamb, lectured him for half an hour on the folly and wickedness of disobedience in general, and of his own disobedience in particular. If the conspirator had had even an apology for a heart, he would have been touched by the earnest and faithful efforts of the simple-minded but thoroughly good and pious man. He was no match for the cunning of an unprincipled student, but he was so gentle, tender, and loving, so truly earnest and Christian in his desire to promote the moral and spiritual welfare of the students, that, with few exceptions, they honored and respected him, while they smiled at his simplicity.

The wind was light from the south-west all night, and the squadron was off Beachy Head at seven bells in the morning; but it breezed up fresh in the forenoon, and in the afternoon the vessels passed within a few miles of Folkestone and Dover. These places are the points from which the steamers start for France, in the two principal lines between London and Paris. The time by either of these routes is about ten hours. The sea passage from Folkestone to Boulogne is only two hours; from Dover to Calais, one hour and a half. The steamers of the latter line leave at uniform hours through the season, while those of the former leave only at high tide.

As the vessels sailed up the Straits, one of the steamers of the Folkestone line came out of the harbor, headed for Boulogne. She was a small, "one-horse" affair for such an important route, and the students could not help comparing her with the palatial steamers which ply on Long Island Sound. They are stanch, strong, and weatherly vessels; but American enterprise would not tolerate such insignificant boats on such a great thoroughfare.

The vessels continued on their way through the Straits, and as the day was clear, the students obtained a distant view of the French coast. Ramsgate and Margate, popular with the Londoners as watering-places, were passed, and about dark the vessels reached the Nore Light Ship, which is moored at the mouth of the Thames. Twenty miles farther up is Gravesend, where the squadron was taken in tow by a couple of tugs, and at midnight came to anchor off Greenwich Hospital. The principal had decided to lie at this point, rather than in the crowded river above, where it would be more difficult to control the students. Greenwich is about five miles below London Bridge, with which there is frequent communication by railway or steamer.

In the morning the rigging of both vessels was crowded with students eager to view the surroundings. They gazed with wonder and admiration at the lofty piles of buildings composing the Hospital, and watched the strange craft which went up and down the river. In the forenoon, while the students were attending to their lessons, the head steward of the ship was sent up to London to procure the mail for the squadron.

Among his letters, Paul found one from Grace. She had been with her father to T. Wiggin & Co., and ascertained that no money had been paid to C. Wilton, but there was a credit for twenty pounds in his favor, and another for the same amount for I. Monroe. Grace, in accordance with her instructions, then informed Paul that McLeish had received the twenty pounds from Wilton, who falsely alleged that he had drawn this sum at the bankers' in London.

As soon as the recitations were finished, Paul hastened on board of the ship with his letter.

Peaks was ordered to commit Wilton to the brig, and Captain Kendall returned to the Josephine to release McLeish. The prisoner was brought into the cabin to receive the explanation of this order.

"I told you I was innocent," said he, triumphantly.

"But you were not innocent so long as you concealed the person who gave you the bills," replied the captain. "Your confinement in the brig for a week was perfectly just, and you may thank your own folly for it. Wilton lied to you."

"It is not possible he robbed the safe, for he was no in the Josephine while at Holyhead."

"That may be, but the principal has the means of tracing the money."

"Wilton cheated me, or I would not have betrayed him, even to the young lady," added McLeish.

"So far you have done well. This evening, after the students return from the shore, you will go on board the ship, and the whole affair will be investigated," said Paul, as he dismissed the prisoner.

The boats were all ready, and immediately pulled for the landing stage at Greenwich. The principal object of interest in the town is the Hospital for Infirm Seamen. It contains accommodations for twenty-seven hundred and ten persons, all of whom must be seamen or royal marines; and here some of the veterans of England's great naval battles may be seen.

The buildings composing the Hospital are arranged so as to enclose a square. The site was formerly occupied by a royal palace, in which Henry VIII. and Queen Elizabeth were born; but in the reign of William and Mary it was given by the queen as a hospital, after the naval battle of La Hogue, when no suitable place for the wounded could be found.

The students visited the Painted Hall, the Chapel, and the Dormitory; in the first of which there is a large collection of portraits of naval heroes, and pictures of naval victories. In this hall the body of Nelson lay in state for three days. In another part of the building the coat and waistcoat worn by him at Trafalgar, and the coat in which he fought the battle of the Nile, are exhibited in a glass case. The pensioners wear blue frock-coats with brass buttons, and soft hats. They are entirely provided for by the institution. The Greenwich Observatory, in which the Nautical Almanacs are calculated, is also located here. On one of its towers there is a " time ball," five feet in diameter, stuffed with cork, which is let fall every day at one o'clock, to enable ships to regulate their chronometers.

The town of Woolwich, three miles distant, was also visited. It contains a dockyard, which is claimed as the oldest in England, and the Royal Arsenal, occupying one hundred acres of land, and containing not less than twenty-four thousand pieces of ordnance, and immense quantities of small arms.

"Paul, do you know what Greenwich is celebrated for, besides the Hospital, Park, and Observatory?" asked the doctor, when they returned to the landing-place.

"I don't know; but I see something in the guide-books about white bait, but I haven't the least idea what white bait is."

"It is a celebrated dish, and no one visits Greenwich without dining on white bait. We will try it."

They entered one of the eating-houses near the landing stage, and the doctor called for the popular dish. Presently it appeared, and the host enjoyed the astonishment of Paul.

"Why, it's nothing but little fishes!" exclaimed Captain Kendall, as the waiter placed about a quart of them before the Americans.

"True, but they are a dish for a London alderman."

The little fish were white, and had been fried in flour. They averaged about an inch in length, and lay upon the dish with their eyes wide open, staring at the diners. They are eaten whole, with the heads on, entrails and fins all in the natural state. A little lemon juice was dropped upon them, and Dr. Winstock declared they were elegant. Paul was not fascinated. The open eyes and the distended stomachs were objectionable; but, rather to please the surgeon than himself, he tasted of them. Certainly the flavor was very delicate, and with a little more practice he would probably relish them.

After the experience at Cowes, the conspirators were not allowed to remain on board without some one competent to take charge of them, and Mr. Fluxion was left to keep them from running away. The professor was a shrewd man. It was hard work for boys to get ahead of him. Without seeming to watch them, he kept one eye on them all the time. It was plain to him that those left in his charge were plotting mischief. Their earnest conversation in the tops was not without a purpose, but he could not hear anything, and the secrets of the Red Cross were not opened to him. But he noticed that Murdock was not with them.

The new hand was continually dreading an explosion. The plot seemed to be thickening around him all the time. Wilton had just been committed to the brig, and he heard that McLeish had been released. It was hardly safe for him to remain in the ship another day. The river was full of boats, which frequently came alongside. After dark he might drop down on the bobstay and hail one of them, and the boatman for a consideration would set him ashore. He determined to take his chance that very evening.

He must be ready to leave at any moment, and it was necessary once more to procure his stolen treasure in the hold. This was an easy matter, for the steerage was empty, and he went below for this purpose. About this time Mr. Fluxion missed him, and went down through the cabin to ascertain what he was doing. As he opened the door between the cabin and the steerage, he saw the scuttle leading to the forward store-rooms, in the hold, opened by some one underneath. He stepped into one of the mess-rooms, and waited for further developments. When Murdock came up with the money in his pocket, the professor seized him by the collar, and dragged him into the cabin without the slightest ceremony.

Murdock protested against this treatment, but he was searched on the spot. The eighty pounds was found in his pocket, and he was tumbled into the brig with Wilton.

CHAPTER XX.

LONDON. — FAREWELL TO ENGLAND.

WHEN the principal came on board, Mr. Fluxion made his report, and delivered up the eighty pounds he had taken from the thief. Murdock and Wilton had made an effort to understand each other during the few hours they had spent together in the brig; but the enmity ran so high between them that neither of them obtained any satisfaction.

After supper, Captain Kendall, with McLeish, came on board, and Wilton was conducted to the cabin to be put "upon the harrow," as he expressed it. According to his usual custom, he denied everything.

"I wouldn't say a word, sir, if he hadn't cheated me," said McLeish, when called upon to tell his story. "He gave me the twenty pounds to keep for him, and then wished me to exchange the bills for gold."

"I didn't give him the bills, Mr. Lowington. He is putting it on me to get his own head out of the halter," protested Wilton.

"You did not give him the bills?" said the principal.

"No, sir; I did not; and he knows I didn't."

"Did Wilton tell you, McLeish, where he obtained

the twenty pounds in bank bills?" asked Mr. Lowington.

"He did, sir. He said his father sent him a bill for twenty pounds, and he drew the money of T. Wiggin & Co."

"I never told him so; he is making it all up, sir."

"Do you think he made up the name of T. Wiggin & Co., well-known bankers?" asked Mr. Lowington.

"We all know that firm. My father told me, before I left home, if I wanted any more money, he would send it to me through T. Wiggin & Co., and I suppose I have mentioned the name twenty times."

"You have funds there now," added the principal.

"I didn't know it, sir."

"Probably there is a letter for you at the bankers'," added the principal, who comprehended that the student's father must have sent a bill of exchange to him.

Mr. Lowington had his theory. He was satisfied that McLeish had told the truth, and that Wilton was lying. Mr. Fluxion had handed him the bills taken from Murdock, without specifying the amount, and he concluded that the twenty pounds which Wilton had passed to McLeish was part of the funds from the safe. Therefore he sent for Murdock.

"It is plain enough now that you are the person who robbed the safe," continued the principal, when Murdock was brought before him.

It was plain enough to the culprit also, and he saw that it would be worse than folly for him to deny it; so he said nothing.

"Did you give any of the money to Wilton?" asked the principal.

"No, sir; none from the safe," replied the new hand.

"I gave you eighty pounds, Mr. Lowington," interposed Mr. Fluxion.

"Then of course the twenty pounds was no part of the money from the safe."

"I haven't used a penny of it," added Murdock; "I only took it for fun, and didn't mean to keep it."

"We don't appreciate that description of amusement," said the principal, dryly. "If I keep you in the brig a month for fun, you will see that there is as much fun in the one as the other. You said you did not give Wilton any money from the safe. Did you give him any money at all?"

"Yes, sir; I gave him twenty pounds which I had when I joined the ship," replied Murdock.

Wilton opened his eyes and puckered his lips with an expression of astonishment which would have staggered persons less experienced than the principal and the professor of mathematics.

"That's an awful lie, sir. I had some disagreement with Murdock, and he is down upon me," said he.

"We had no disagreement except about this matter of taking my money and not giving it back to me," added the new hand, who then described the interview between himself and Wilton, when he had given the money to him.

"I suppose I may as well give it up, if Murdock and McLeish both intend to lie me down," growled Wilton. "I have tried to reform, and do my duty; but it's no use if the worst fellows are to be believed against me."

"Won't you please to read that letter, sir?" said Murdock, handing the principal one he had received, by the last mail, from his father.

The new hand had actually written to his father for the numbers of the Bank of England notes paid to him for his last monthly allowance, as he told Wilton he had done; but he did not write till after he had told him. He had taken this step in hope of scaring the keeper of his funds into giving them up.

"These are the numbers of the notes your father paid you in July — are they?" asked Mr. Lowington.

"Yes, sir."

"Thirty-three thousand eight hundred and one to four," added the principal, reading from the letter.

"Those are the numbers Pelham took in Bristol," said Paul, taking from his pocket-book the paper the second master had given him.

"Wilton, both the statements of Murdock and McLeish are proved," said the principal, after some reflection. "No better evidence could be asked."

"That letter of Murdock's was got up for the occasion," said Wilton, cast down, but not quite destroyed.

"No boy wrote this letter, which is post-marked Manchester. Wilton, you are a hypocrite as well as a knave," continued Mr. Lowington, sternly. "It is proved that you robbed one of your shipmates."

"If he hadn't done it, I shouldn't have touched the safe," added Murdock.

"I thought you did it for fun."

"So I did, sir. I went into the Josephine's cabin, and then into the captain's state-room. I saw the safe with the key in it, and I couldn't help opening it."

"You found the key in the safe!" exclaimed Paul.

"I did."

"How came it in my coat pocket?"

"I put it there, and put the coat on the cabin table, so as to make you think you left it there yourself. I only did it for the fun of the thing."

"Do you think there would be any fun in being sent back to Holyhead, where the crime was committed, and being tried by the court and sent to prison for six months or a year?" demanded the principal.

"I don't think there would," replied Murdock, alarmed at such an array of terrors.

Both of the culprits were sent back to the brig. Mr. Lowington wrote immediately to Murdock's father, informing him of the crime his son had committed, and that he was confined in the brig. The next day was Sunday, and the chaplain spent two hours in the brig with the prisoners. Wilton professed to be penitent, and acknowledged his error when it was no longer possible for him to deny it; but he persisted that he had changed the bills for gold with the intention of giving the money to the poor, as he had agreed with Murdock. He wanted to get out so as to execute the grand purpose of the Red Cross Knights.

Although McLeish had no claim to sympathy on account of his confinement in the brig, he obtained no little credit among the students for refusing to divulge the name of Wilton; and when it was proved that he was not guilty of the robbery, he rose highly in the estimation of the officers. He was treated with much consideration by the captain, who wished to encourage him to do well. In spite of the drawbacks which had disturbed him, he continued to persevere in his efforts to do well. Of course he succeeded just in proportion to his endeavors. The help he needed was never wanting. Grace Arbuckle visited the Josephine while she lay at Greenwich, and her influence was more powerful than that of all others combined.

During the succeeding week the ship's company who were entitled to liberty on shore visited London every afternoon, and saw the principal objects of interest, though a month is little time enough to become familiar with the city. A full description, even of what the students saw, would require a volume, and only a few extracts from a letter of Paul Kendall to his mother can be given. It was finished the day the Josephine sailed for Hull.

"My dear Mother: We are in London at last, and I have seen just enough of the metropolis of the world to make me wish to see more; and some time I mean to spend a month in the city. On Monday morning we went up to the city, for the first time, in a little steamer. There are hundreds of them running up and down the muddy Thames. They are very smart boats, and they handle them with great skill. Instead of having bells to direct the engineer, there is a small boy on the main deck, who communicates the orders from the captain on one of the paddle-boxes. The steersman stands on a raised platform at the stern. The captain moves his hands as signals for the boy, who interprets them for the engineer, in the funniest language I ever heard. 'Ayse air,' he sings, which means, ease her; 'sto' pair' (stop her); 'back hair' (back her); 'star' tair' (start her).

"We landed at a floating stage, just above London Bridge — famous London Bridge! It is wide enough for four vehicles to go abreast, and it is always so crowded that there are two continuous lines of them going each way. In one line the horses trot, and in the other they walk. Policemen stand in the roadway to make the drivers move along and take the right line, as they wish to walk or trot. We went up King William Street, passed the Monument built to commemorate the great fire, which is two hundred and two feet high, and two hundred and two feet from the place in Pudding Lane where the fire broke out. We went into the Bank of England, which is a low-looking building, though it covers a large area; into the Exchange, the General Post-office in St. Martin's-le-Grand, and then to St. Paul's Cathedral. This is a big church, and very grand in its proportions, but it is as black as charcoal. Dr. Winstock and I went all over the building, even to the ball, three hundred and sixty feet high, and into the crypt, where Nelson and the Duke of Wellington are buried. The funeral car of the Iron Duke is kept in this place, and is a very showy and costly affair. The main floor and the vaults are full of tablets and sculptures in honor of great men. I bought the pamphlet guide to the Cathedral, which contains a full account of the building, with pictures of the more important monuments. It costs three and two-pence to go all over the building; and the idea of making a show of a church don't seem to be just the thing.

"From St. Paul's we went to the Tower of London, which is very interesting indeed. We paid sixpence for admission; and as soon as a party of a dozen had gathered, one of the heralds (who are old soldiers, dressed in antique costume) conducted us through the various towers and apartments. The Tower is the greatest thing I have yet seen; it is full of ancient armor, old cannon, and specimens of weapons. On the walls and ceilings of some of the rooms the most fantastic designs are wrought of guns, pistols, swords, daggers, or parts of them. A couple of serpents are made in this way, so that they look quite natural. We saw the dungeons where kings, queens, princes, and other persons had been confined, and the block on which some of them had been executed. In a small, dingy room, the crown jewels, worth three millions of pounds, including the crown of the queen, of the Prince of Wales, and a lot of sceptres.

"We finished the first day in London by visiting the Thames Tunnel, which is a gigantic failure, without a doubt, though it shows what man can do. It cost an immense sum of money, but it can only be used for foot passengers. You have to go down a lot of stairs to get to it. There are two roadways, but one of them was closed up. The other was lighted with gas, and there were plenty of stands in the niches for the sale of all sorts of trinkets and fancy goods. The toll is two-pence.

"On Tuesday we went out to Windsor Castle, where Queen Victoria resides most of the time. We first went into St. George's Chapel, which contains the stalls of the Knights of the Garter, who are installed in this building, and the royal vaults, in which many of the kings and queens, including Henry VIII., Charles I., George III., George IV., William IV., Jane Seymour, Queen Charlotte, and Queen Adelaide are buried. We went through the state apartments, which are magnificent, adorned with paintings and sculpture. As the queen had gone to Germany to visit her country cousins, we obtained a special order from the lord chamberlain to see the private apartments of her majesty, where she eats, drinks, and sleeps, and has the headache, as common people do. Everything was as splendid as it could be; but, mother, I don't see the use of it all. Of course the poor people have to pay the fiddler when the queen dances. She is a very good woman, but it seems to me it costs too much money to support her.

"On Wednesday we went to the British Museum, which is such an immense establishment we could only walk through without stopping to look long at anything.

"On Thursday we took a stroll through Hyde Park, Green Park, and St. James's Park, with outside views of Buckingham and St. James's Palaces. We also went to Kensington Museum, which contains a vast collection of articles connected with the useful and the ornamental. There were paintings by Landseer, Rosa Bonheur, and others. There were some splendid models of men-of-war, steamers, and boats. In one of the patent rooms I saw the first locomotive ever built, the Rocket, constructed by Stevenson.

"On Friday we went out to Sydenham, to which the Crystal Palace, used for the World's Fair in London, was removed. At each end of it there is a tower two hundred and eighty-two feet high. I don't like to overdo anything, mother, but I haven't the least hesitation in saying, in my sober senses, that a visit to the Crystal Palace at Sydenham is worth the trouble of crossing the Atlantic, even if the person is very seasick. We walked for hours through its floors and galleries, without examining a tenth part of what it contains. We passed through courts got up in imitation of Grecian, Roman, Assyrian, Pompeian, and Egyptian houses, which were adorned with statues and other sculptures. There are copies here of many of the most celebrated works of art. In one part there are tropical gardens, with plants and even tall trees growing; in another, models of ships, bridges, machinery, and specimens of the animal, vegetable, and mineral productions of all countries. The gardens in front of the palace are magnificent, with statues, grottos, fountains, and flower-gardens in great profusion.

"On Saturday we went to the Palace of Westminster, which is the Parliament House. It is open to visitors only on Saturdays, and even then one cannot get into the House of Lords without a ticket from the grand chamberlain. I suppose you will think we had to call upon some duke or lord, and humbly beg permission to see the palace; but we didn't, for there was a score of loafers around the building who had handfuls of these tickets, which they sell for sixpence apiece, though on them is printed, "It is particularly requested that no payment be made to any person on account of this ticket." We entered at the Victoria Tower, where her majesty goes in, passed through the House of Lords, which is a splendid room; but it is only ninety feet long and forty-five feet wide. The House of Commons is smaller than this, and a much plainer apartment. We left by St. Stephen's Hall, which is adorned with statues of eminent British statesmen — Hampden, Pitt, Burke, Fox, and others.

"We walked through Westminster Abbey, entering at the Poets' Corner, where there are busts, tablets, and sculptures in honor of all the most noted poets of England. The nave, transepts, choir, and several chapels are filled with monuments to great men, kings, queens, princes, and nobles. The Abbey is very old, and contains the tombs of kings who reigned nearly a thousand years ago. I almost held my breath when I stood by these monuments crumbling with age. The sovereigns of England are **crowned here, and I sat down in the chair which twenty-two** of them had occupied when **the crown was placed** upon their heads — but I speak to common people as usual!

"That **evening I** went with Dr. Winstock to see Madame Tussaud's collection of wax figures of distinguished characters. I never thought much of 'wax figgers' before; but, as the school girls say, this was perfectly splendid, and as natural as life itself. I sat down by the side of an old gentleman, as I thought. He kept very still, and did not pick my pocket, so that I did not discover **till I got up that he was a** 'figger.' **I was just going to beg** pardon of an old lady for brushing against her, when I saw a label informing me that it was a very correct likeness of Madame Tussaud herself. **Some** extraordinary curiosities are **exhibited here, and are vouched for by letters in the** catalogue as genuine, **such as** Napoleon's Waterloo carriage; the camp **bedstead** used by the emperor at St. Helena; the cradle of his son, the King of Rome; **the carriage in which Napoleon made the campaign of Russia;** the one he used at St. Helena; various swords, a watch, tooth-brush, handkerchief, and other things used by him; **the** coronation robes of George IV.; the original **knife** from the guillotine by which twenty-two thousand persons were executed in the French Revolution, including Marie Antoinette, the

Duke of Orleans, and Robespierre, 'bought by the Messrs. Tussaud of the grandson of the original executioner.' The Chamber of Horrors contains figures of all the principal criminals. If you ever visit London, mother, do not neglect to see Madame Tussaud's exhibition.

"On Sunday I went with Professor Stoute to Surrey Chapel to hear Mr. Spurgeon preach. His church holds about six thousand people, and is always full. The congregation do the singing, and the effect of so many voices was grand. Mr. Spurgeon is a stout man, plain spoken, and his discourse was so simple that a small child could understand him. I liked him very much indeed.

"On Monday and Tuesday we did up a lot of odd places, like Lincoln's Inn, Smithfield, the Mint, and Cremorne Gardens. I have been up and down the Thames as far as Chelsea half a dozen times. Mr. Lowington thinks we may come to London again. I hope so, for I want to see more of it.

"Give my love to everybody, and believe me ever
"Your affectionate son,
"PAUL KENDALL."

After Murdock had been in the brig three days, his father, in a flurry of excitement, appeared on board of the ship. He insisted on seeing Spenser at once, and was conducted to the steerage by the principal.

"Poor boy!" exclaimed he, when he saw the new hand through the pales. "This is an outrage upon the boy," he added, turning wrathfully to Mr. Lowington.

"Perhaps you do not regard it as an outrage for a student to steal; but we think it a greater outrage than the punishment," answered the principal, with dignity.

"But, my dear sir, you must know that it was merely a boyish freak. Boys will be wild, and I dare say he did it for the fun and excitement of the thing," said Mr. Murdock, impatiently.

"When students, we punish them severely."

"How long has the poor boy been in this cage?"

"Since Saturday night."

"Mercy on us! Three whole days!" ejaculated the indulgent father. "Pray, let him out immediately."

Peaks appeared, and the prisoner was released.

Mr. Murdock protested against such "barbarity" for a "petty offence," and the conference was ended by the discharge, at his father's request, of the student. They went off together, after Spenser's twenty pounds had been given to him, the weak parent condoling with his son for the "bad treatment" inflicted upon him. That boy's future is easily predicted, for one with his tendencies could not stand such stupid indulgence.

After a passage of thirty hours the squadron anchored at Hull, from which the students made an excursion to York, and explored its old cathedral. The ship and her consort sailed for Antwerp.

On board of the Josephine everything worked well; the discipline was perfect, and even McLeish persevered in carrying out his good intentions. Paul's last letter, written at Hull, to Grace Arbuckle, was very warm in its commendation of her penitent. He appeared to be reformed; and the only thing which vexed the young commander was the fact that McLeish wrote an occasional letter to the young lady, though it is difficult to see why he should be vexed at such a trifle.

Wilton was now the only occupant of the brig. When the Young America sailed from Hull, he called an officer and requested to see the principal. The prisoner promised so fairly, and the tender-hearted chaplain pleaded so warmly for him, that he was set at liberty. Mr. Lowington knew that he was a hypocrite, and had but little hope of his reformation. He directed all the professors and officers to watch him closely, whatever pretensions he made to goodness and fidelity.

The Knights of the Red Cross were not defunct, and their stupendous secret had not yet leaked out. On the very night of Wilton's release, he discussed the whole matter of the intended capture of the Josephine with Perth, while they were together in the main top. They rearranged their plans, for the embryo captain of the consort had invented a new scheme by which the grand purpose was to be effected; and we may add that their talk was not wholly in vain, for the Josephine was actually taken afterwards, and the conspirators went to sea in her.

The next day at noon, the low shores of Belgium were seen from the decks of the squadron, and the students were filled with lively anticipations in regard to the new country before them. England did not seem like a foreign land to them, it was so much like their own country. On the continent they expected to find strange sights and sounds, for there everything was different; their mother tongue was not the language of the people, and their manners and customs were not those of England or the United States. They were not disappointed in their expectations; but what they saw and did, what incidents occurred, and what adventures they had, shall be told in DIKES AND DITCHES, OR YOUNG AMERICA IN HOLLAND AND BELGIUM.

www.ingramcontent.com/pod-product-compliance
Lightning Source LLC
Chambersburg PA
CBHW030326240426
43673CB00040B/1290